Shards of Love

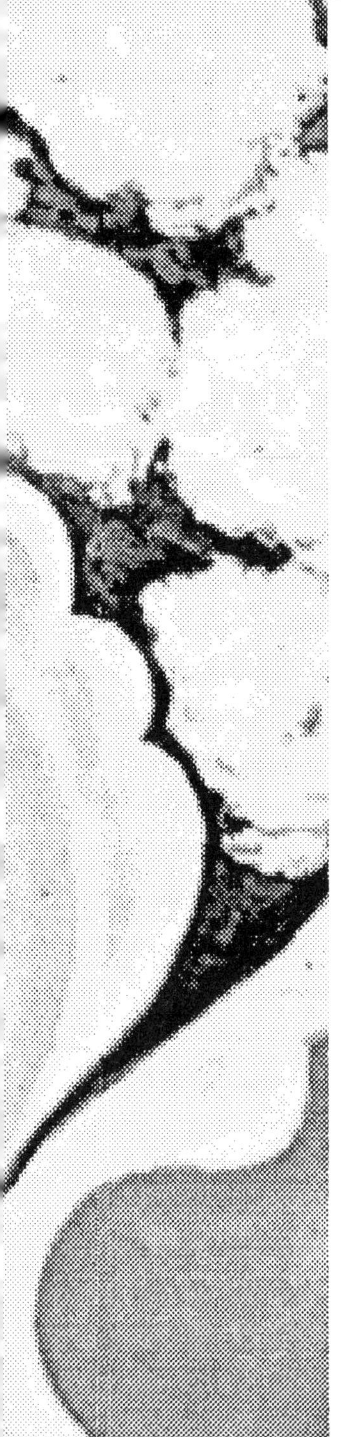

SHARDS OF LOVE

Exile and the Origins of the Lyric

María Rosa Menocal

Duke University Press Durham & London

1994

Printed in the United States of America
on acid-free paper ∞
Designed by Cherie Holma Westmoreland
Typeset in Palatino and Benguiat display
by Keystone Typesetting, Inc.
Library of Congress Cataloging-in-Publication
Data appear on the last printed page of
this book.

Cover and frontispiece art based on *Layla and Other Assorted Love Songs*, Derek and the Dominos, courtesy of Eric Clapton.

FOR TOTTY DELMÁS MENOCAL

Contents

Prelude

> Lucky me, to be born in Havana
> And then I became a singer of songs. . . .
>
> **Celia Cruz**

Lucky me, to be able to acknowledge my many debts.

I am indebted to José Piedra for the invitation to speak at the Renaissance Society of America meeting at Duke University in the spring of 1991, the seed of this book. He asked me to dwell, as a medievalist, on the notorious epistemological problem of the division between Renaissance and Middle Ages, and I wrote about ten pages called "The Horse Latitudes" that eventually became the far longer introductory section of this book. My interest in that general historiographical question seemed to coincide felicitously with the range of 1492 commemorations and questions, which, in fact, began in 1991. I am grateful to a number of institutions and individuals for invitations to speak that allowed me to either invent or rehearse other portions of the book. Among these, I must single out a few of special importance.

Dimitri Gutas, my colleague in Arabic at Yale University, and then-president of the Oriental Club of New Haven, invited me to speak at that venerable institution toward the end of the winter of 1991, and it was then that I first worked out other parts of "The Horse Latitudes": crucially, the problem of the synchronicity of 1492 events. I am especially grateful to Dimitri for his always sparkling friendship in New Haven and for the fact that he thinks less of me only for being a fuzzy-wuzzy literature type and not, as he might well, for being a failed Arabist. That failure is also charitably overlooked, now outside of Yale, by the eclectic group of Persianists, Arabists, and Hebraists who meet annually as the Middle East Literary Seminar. Since 1989 they have graciously welcomed me into their midst, and their discussions of my work have been consistently enriching. It was for the 1991 meeting, in Princeton, that I wrote the original version of the chapter now entitled "Chasing the Wind." Without the warm reception for that first performance of my "Layla" from this collection of superb scholars, who actually know all the original Layla texts, I might never have played it in public again. I am especially glad to be able to thank the warm and brilliant Walter Andrews, premier Ottomanist, for all sorts of inspiration. Meanwhile, Manuel Durán, the most gracious of colleagues, invited me to write an article for a special issue of *Catalan Review* on Ramon Llull. The result was an earlier, far more rudimentary, version of "Love and Mercy." I thank Manolo for this and countless other acts of generosity since we first met, appropriately, at a celebration of the life and work of Américo Castro. Finally, in the early spring of 1992, when the manuscript was ostensibly finished, I read a version of the "Inventions of Philology" chapter for the Department of Comparative Literature at Stanford and was treated to a full day of *romanische Philologie* incarnate. To Sepp Gumbrecht go my warmest thanks for an unforgettable day of real intellectual riches, for the suggestions that ended up making me invent the epilogue, "Desire"—Sepp's title, I believe—for his sympathetic reading of this manuscript, and mostly for being the embodiment of that most vigorous model of what I have tried to evoke in the philology chapter.

Although the manuscript of this book was originally completed in the fall of 1991, and although Reynolds Smith, my editor at Duke University Press, and I had originally imagined it would come out in 1992, thus partaking of the 1492 commemorations into which the book is in some measure inscribed, events reeking of Kabbalah subtracted that crucial year from the life of the book itself and have made it appear a year later. Because my life was so radically redefined—questioned, taken away, then given back—during that year about which I had so arrogantly presumed, ahead of time, to write a book, I have written the final draft from the always surprising perspectives of a new life and a new place. The book thus has inscribed within it, often indistinguishably, perspectives that lie, nevertheless, on either side of 1992, on either side of a liminal personal experience which seems, in ways, to mock and mimic my first, pre-1992 attempts to grasp the liminalities of 1492 as that crossroads of lyric and narrative, of life and death, of home and exile. My first thanks, from this threshold between old and new, my last book and this one, which is very much its sequel, go to Reynolds himself, cool and loyal editor, probably the only active rocker who also acquires manuscripts for a university press these days, and thus probably the only one who could really love my "Layla." Two other accomplices should have been thanked, along with Reynolds, for formative readings of *Dante's Cult of Truth* that have conspicuously spilled over into the making of this book. I offer an only partly belated acknowledgment to Elizabethann Beaudin, who has been kabbalistically a part of old life and new life, several times around now—and I of hers—and who has lovingly read page proofs and prepared the index of both that book and this one, and has done a first copyediting of this book, to boot. The generosity of the Griswold Fund at Yale University helped make these projects possible. Plus, she seems to always be around to try and answer my riddles, to cock an eyebrow at my crazy schemes, to tell me when I need to play "Layla." Albert Ascoli read the manuscript of the Dante book with astonishing care and made me write its Prologue, and then he reread it as a finished book, with undiminished passion, and asked many of the questions that this book tries to answer. No doubt he remains unsatisfied, but I am thankful he did not make me write an introduction for this one.

Lucky me, I have had translators to open up very special worlds for me. I thank Robert Myers for his translation of the bit of poem that is the epigraph to the chapter on philology, and for sharing with me his superb knowledge of Brazilian poetry and songs that so uninhibitedly embrace so many medieval songs as their brothers in arms. Michael Sells is an astonishing translator of Arabic, a language that defines itself, scandalously, as untranslatable, the real voice of God. It is with real gratitude that I have used Michael's defiantly powerful translation of the key poem of Ibn ʿArabī's around which the chapter "Love and Mercy" is structured, as well as his renditions of the pre-Islamic odes. The brilliant renderings of Adonis' poetry by Michael Beard and Adnan Haydar have been with me for years now, and I thank Michael and Adnan for the many ways in which they have made Arabic literature a part of my life. Ray Scheindlin has made me the wonderful gift of Judah Halevi's sea songs; thanks to both his work and his infinite personal generosity, I have, after many years of standing just outside, finally been allowed into the lovely garden of Sefarad. Lowry Nelson has showered me with many special gifts since I first met him, shortly after I arrived at Yale: his memories of Cuba, his recollections of Auerbach, his lovely translations of so many of the poets of exile, his books, on rainy New Haven afternoons, his loyal love. The translation of the most famous poem of Jaufré Rudel is just one more in the long list of presents for which I can never really thank him.

My considerable ignorance of music is matched by the great luck I have in good friends who have generously shared their expertise and sensibilities. I thank Jeffrey St. John and Lee Calhoun for their time and the passion with which they have helped me to listen to *Layla and Other Assorted Love Songs* and to describe its musical structures, especially those of "Layla." Without other friends who are writers in the music business, namely Anthony DeCurtis and Daisann McLean, I would not have been able to find the wonderful Bill Levenson, who secured for me, with the help of Roger Forrester, Eric Clapton's permission to use the famous cover of the album for this book's cover. I express my warmest gratitude to Eric Clapton for this generosity, and for the enduring pleasures of his extraordinary poetry and music.

It is astonishing to me that over two decades after I first sat in a classroom with him, I can still rely on Sam Armistead for instruction of every sort. He is probably astonished that, going on fifteen years after he marked up every page of my dissertation, my manuscripts still need so much from him. I am grateful, in fact, for his meticulous reading of this manuscript and for his endless bibliographical suggestions on every subject it treats—and some it doesn't and should have. Most of all, I hope this book reflects what I take to be his most significant teaching: that medieval literature is alive and well, especially when it has lived in exile. Indeed, although I used to think I wasn't really a very good student of his because I never followed many of the paths he has opened up—ballads, the romancero, the beloved Sephardim—in writing this book I realized that I am clearly the student of a man who would punctuate graduate seminars in medieval literature with songs he sang himself. In any case, I am lucky to have such ties to this man who has dedicated his life to the salvation of a whole song tradition, that of the Sephardic Jews, which would otherwise be gone with the wind.

If this is a book about exile, and I believe in many ways it is, then it has been written and rewritten in the fragmented but powerful company of people who have taught me that in exile a spectacular home can be—must be—crafted out of the love of scattered but kindred souls. My sister, Joan deJean, teaches me constantly about strength and courage, about rice and beans. From my other sister, Sylvia Peck, a cloak sister, I am trying to learn about the magic of birthdays, about love and mercy. Francis Howland was there, and will always be there, *nel mezzo del cammin*. More than anyone, Francie, who is like a rainbow and does come in colors everywhere, knows about fragments and shards, and knows how to love them, how to hold them in one embrace without diminishing the loveliness of any single piece. For a number of years now, and especially during the first half of 1992, I incurred truly awesome debts with J. Douglas Smith, whose extraordinary house in New Haven was always the proverbial, sonorous, safe haven. Indeed, it was always the place to go to shower off the sweat of a hard game of squash, or the dust from a long drive from Boston, the place to get the coldest beer and the finest meal in New England—all with the invariably loving and loyal companionship of Ginny Jewiss, who brings so much beauty and laughter to my life. But then, in June 1992, Doug, my very own nephrologist, abandoned that ship to go out to do his years in the desert, in New Mexico, thus setting us all up for the dramatic events of the summer, at the end of which I had lost a kidney, and then some. So, now he is in deep hock to me. A kidney is a lot for a nephrologist to owe. Finally, most of all, among this very bad company, Harold Bloom lavishes on me his faith, kabbalistic and otherwise, his incomparable insights on the inseparability of life and literature and criticism, and, best of all, an affection which sometimes makes me want to weep. From him I hope I have learned, at least a little bit, how not to put myself aside in my writing, and when to weep.

Now we come to the cliché of book acknowledgments, the one

about the individuals without whom this book would not have been written. That role is played by the two people who have most made Yale for me, Roberto González Echevarría and Giuseppe Mazzotta. Without Roberto, I would know precious little, if anything, about the texts of my own exile, about the other side, this side, of 1492. Without Giuseppe, I could not have imagined the shape of this book, I would probably never have had the vision to see that it is—what else?—that elusive philology that I have been trying to rewrite, all these years, and that links *The Arabic Role in Medieval Literary History* to *Writing in Dante's Cult of Truth,* and then makes this book necessary. It is a lot to owe: texts and vision. It is thus fitting, perfectly synchronistic, that this book, in losing its planned attachment to 1492, which would inevitably have suggested a tie to an essentially impersonal history, instead comes out in the fall of 1993, alongside kindred books by Roberto and Giuseppe, thus reflecting the far greater power of personal history, even—perhaps especially—in scholarship.

Finally, George Calhoun has read it all, always passionately, sometimes unflinchingly, sometimes in horror. He has asked the toughest question about the chapter that lies at the center: how does a man like Dante come to know the shape of Hell, and come to know it with such certainty and clarity and passion that it carries with it, centuries and cultures and languages removed, the certainty of Truth? How does he come to know that Hell is shaped in concentric circles that spiral downward, ever tighter, until you reach Betrayal?

As Celia Cruz sings, lucky me, to be born in Havana. . . . I am lucky, indeed, to be able to dedicate this book to my mother, who gave me life, the first time, in Havana, and then, in Philadelphia, in 1992, gave it a second time. At a moment of real bleakness, she made it possible for me to live, with her ferocious courage, her indefatigable nursing, and, most of all, by being mother to my own children, when they had no other. For life given twice, this small book is but a paltry gift, but it is given with much love.

New York June 1993

Note on Sources

This book contains extensive bibliographical essays in lieu of discursive footnotes. These essays, one corresponding to each chapter in Sections I through III, can be found in Section IV, Readings and Sources. The reader is urged to consult this critical apparatus in conjunction with reading the principal chapters.

I THE HORSE LATITUDES

It is in fact the conquest of America that heralds and establishes our present identity; even if every date that permits us to separate any two periods is arbitrary, none is more suitable, in order to mark the beginning of the modern era, than the year 1492, the year Columbus crosses the Atlantic Ocean. We are all direct descendants of Columbus, it is with him that our genealogy begins, insofar as the word beginning has a meaning. . . .

Tzvetan Todorov
The Conquest of America

1

When the still sea conspires an armor
And her sullen and aborted
Currents breed tiny monsters,
True sailing is dead.

Awkward instant
And the first animal is jettisoned,
Legs furiously pumping
Their stiff green gallop,
And their heads bob up
Poise
Delicate
Pause
Consent
In mute nostril agony
Carefully refined
And sealed over

James Douglas Morrison
"The Horse Latitudes"

These are the first days of August 1492. If we go down to the docks in the great Spanish port of Cádiz we are overwhelmed, barely able to find a square inch on which to stand, scarcely able to glimpse the ships amassed in the harbor. The throngs of people are unbearable, particularly in the damp summer heat, and worst of all are the tears, the wailing, the ritual prayers, all those noises and smells and sights of departures. This is the day, the hour, the place, of a leave-taking more grievous and painful than that of death itself, an exodus inscribed in all the sacred texts, anticipated and repeated. For the Jews of Sefarad, what Christian nomenclature calls Spain, this is the last day in that most beloved of homelands, the one that had almost made them forget that it, too, was but a place of exile, a temporary home in a diaspora.

But the second diaspora did come, and the second day of August had been set, months before, in March, as its permanent marker. Indeed, the doubly poignant story, revealing the profound sense of redoubled history of the Jews on the eve of this diaspora, is that while the original Edict of Expulsion called for the final day in Spain to be exactly three months later—which would have meant the 31st of July—the visionary rabbis who had access to Ferdinand and Isabella pleaded for a slight but crucial change of date. It was thus that Isaac Abravanel (whose son Judah, eminent Neoplatonist author of the *Dialoghi d'Amore,* would live out his exile in Italy, known as Leone Ebreo), playing his final cards as influential courtier with the Christian monarchs, had the date reset to the 2nd of August. In the liturgical calendar this was the 9th of Ab, the anniversary of the Destruction of the Temple. With kabbalistic precision, then, the diaspora of 1492 would mimic the first Diaspora, and the tears for Sefarad would be indistinguishable from those for the first Temple. Exile on Diaspora. And, during that summer, all roads led to the sea, to ports such as Cádiz, to the desperately overbooked ships, and they were filled with the sounds of exile, that mingling of the vernacular sorrow of the women and the children with the liturgical chanting of the men.

But only one among the thousands of trips launched that summer, all begun on that same 2nd of August, would be remembered as that perfect marker of a rip in the fabric of world history, the one we commemorated at school every year, as children, the one whose centrality our own children now continue to commemorate, even as they question its "value." For, to lay yet a third anniversary onto the commingled exile and diaspora, it was on the same day—but from the inferior port of Palos because Cádiz, the natural first choice, was far too overcrowded with the "Jew-bearing ships"—that Columbus sailed the ocean blue. The scandalous suggestion has been made that Columbus himself was the most conspicuous of the exiles that day, one of the *conversos*, those converted Jews usually readily identified by their excessive devotions, their fanatical and public enactments, of the banal and ritualized pieties of Christianity. But what matters, for the recounting of that exodus, is not as much Columbus's profoundly enigmatic personal history—and whether he "really" was or not—as it is our ability to understand the intimate ties that do, in fact, bind the narration of the two seemingly opposite kinds of voyages to each other. What is conspicuous in the standard narrations, even those of 1992 that indulged in all manner of supposed soul-searching, is that the two are divorced to such an extent that it is only the suggestion that Columbus might have been one of the Jews himself that calls our attention to what we then call the "coincidence": the voyages of exile and the voyage of discovery begin at the same hour, in the same place. In all other versions it is no more than a coincidence, an odd coincidence, and it is not the role of our histories, literary or otherwise, to account for coincidence. The word itself, for which we can sometimes substitute something like synchronicity, suggests exactly that it lies outside our purview: an intersection that would be highly meaningful—if only it were not so fantastic and obviously meaningless, impervious to rational exegesis.

At the heart of our repression of this synchronism, of this meaningful layering of histories, of this knowledge that it is the very day, the precise day, that Columbus leaves Spain that is the beginning of the second diaspora—itself the most mournful of commemorations of the first Diaspora—is the simple fact that "Columbus" himself is the first to look away and ignore. In that most enduringly canonical of biographies of Columbus, Samuel Eliot Morison notes with clear and considerable puzzlement in his tone that Columbus completely ignores the remarkable scene of the expulsion of the Jews that was not only the event of the season, and all around him, but which obviously complicated and even directly compromised his own obsessive mission. But Morison, and most other tellers of the story, are mesmerized by Columbus's gaze—and we have all looked away with him; we pretend not to see the others on the docks that day, although out of the corner of one eye, the scene is explosive and central and shapes everything Columbus does, beginning with the long-sought approval of the trip, granted only, conspicuously, in the aftermath of both the expulsion decree and the taking of Granada, that last outpost of Muslim Spain. (Indeed, into the first fistful of coincidences we must now begin to stuff others. It is at the beginning of that fateful year, on January 2 of that same 1492, that the closure of al-Andalus, of a certain kind of medieval Spain, is finally consummated, and from that will follow, as if written, the forced conversions and then expulsions of the Muslims; and with an irony few have noticed, the first grammar of Castilian is published, while the exact date of the expulsion is being bravely renegotiated. But that subject leads down other paths, so let us not yet walk away from the first and the sharpest of the overlaps.) If the very possibility of Columbus's voyage cannot be imagined, at its origins, without the expulsion of the Jews, no less telling and compromised are most of the small, at times dirty and painful, details, and least of all the biggest of the details. In the rerouting from Cádiz to Palos, Columbus lost not only the better port as such but the far better market for experienced seamen. Most sailors that August were already engaged for the hundreds, perhaps thousands, of trips into exile by the Jews during those months between March and August.

Morison the historian is thus right to be baffled by Columbus's stark avoidance of the subject since even—perhaps especially—the profoundly obsessed Columbus could not have failed to be deeply affected. But Morison ends up following in Columbus's path precisely because the extant memory of the famous trip, the one we take for Columbus's own, is in fact the one famously rewritten by Fray Bartolomé de las Casas. Indeed, if there is a marked rip in the fabric of history in 1492—as Todorov, mimicking Foucault, claims in the passage at the outset—it is certainly visible in this erasure and rewriting, this palimpsest. In stark and simple terms, Columbus's irregular vernacular, the rough-edged language of a man of many tongues, is smoothed over and cleaned up. Months after the publication of the first grammar of a European vernacular (this also a clear marker of that shift, of "modernity" and "genealogy," as Todorov might have it),

Bartolomé de las Casas, whose own history of the Conquest (*Historia de las Indias*) would play a crucial role, to this day, in shaping our perceptions of those stunning events—simply rewrote Columbus's narration of that first trip. If the fabric is torn, Las Casas is speaking the new language, this new language of a Nation—and what he has overwritten—corrected—is the language that came before. In miniature and exemplary form the transformation of Columbus embodied in that rewritten story—and let us not forget the essential and irreducible fact that it is *the* story of *the* voyage—is a perfect example of the sort of palimpsest a medievalist is likely to face when she contemplates the diminishment and regularization of the medieval world that took place in what we have come to call the "Renaissance." This crucial fact of historiography affects all branches of history, no doubt, and it certainly affects literary history, that point so effectively signaled by the events of 1492 of turning the page from premodern to modern. The turning of the page to where the narration is grammatical. The turning of the page to where the Kabbalah of the 9th of Ab is written out and seems preposterous, and where Columbus can no longer see the Jews, wailing, on the docks.

It is one of those clichés with immense power behind it that the whole idea of the Renaissance, beginning with the very name, acquires meaning, first of all, through contradistinction to a medieval past whose various deaths require various rebirths. As Thomas Greene has so lucidly put it: "The ubiquitous imagery of disinterment, resurrection, and renascence needed a death and burial to justify itself; without the myth of medieval entombment, its imagery, which is to say its self-understanding, had no force. The creation of this myth was not a superficial occurrence. It expressed a belief in change and loss, change from the immediate past and loss of a remote, prestigious past that might nonetheless be resuscitated."[1] If there is one simple thing that can be said about both popular and scholarly views on this period without fear of contradiction, it is that the medieval period is always something not modern, never a part of modernity. And that is perceived as being true regardless of the specific point of comparison. The easiest and thus most deeply ingrained emblems of "modernity" make the point readily: "1492," Petrarch (who serves with uncommon regularity, at least in some of his various personae, as "first modern man"), and even the classical cultures that diachronically precede the medieval period. Todorov's statement might provoke a request for some fine point of clarification but hardly a direct contradiction. In the inventory we easily perceive what Petrarch himself was at pains to show throughout his long career; the unpardonable sin of the long period that precedes him is that it separates him from the wonderful story of the development of culture in Greece and its trip to Rome. We scarcely add much to his version of the story since, as is the case with Las Casas and the grammar of the recounting of what Spain was like in August 1492, he has given us the very language with which we tell the story.

What becomes the "modern," almost without further explanation, is thus some version of the unbroken story line, the grammatical text, the totalizing, comprehensive, and comprehensible narrative. This accounts for how the period before the Middle Ages is a part of the modernity that will pick up again with the second age of modern man. Petrarch—as he himself tells us—is the first explorer, and after 1492 all civilized men are heirs to the superb act of memory he performed to set the stage, to clear the rubble. Again, Greene's work on "Imitation and Discovery" sheds telling light when he reminds us how deeply and dangerously the humanist enterprise was rooted in the "effort to exchange one recent past for another, distant one."[2] In the end, of course, the success of the enterprise was astonishing, and our own most powerful narrative of history is very much an heir of the Renaissance. And, in one of the most extraordinary acts of rhetorical legerdemain, it is a form of both perceiving and telling history that so brilliantly insists on its own absolute value and veracity that we forget that it too is a product of its own history—and of historical contingencies that required it to uphold absolute and transcendent truth.

The enormous power inherent in this kind of claim to truth is (obviously) that it arrogates universality and makes contingency, even certain notions of history itself, seem without value. We can see its strong pull in the irony that the most fundamental and successful revisions of our view of the medieval period have been those which have fully embraced that Renaissance concept of the smooth narration; this is the sort of thing a scholar like Charles Homer Haskins wanted to show—rightly, from one perspective—that the "rebirth" actually takes place much earlier (thus the famous "Renaissance of the Twelfth Century"), that Aristotle was brilliantly commented on in the eleventh century, and so forth. Obviously, this sort of work, which is how medievalists—myself among them—have generally tried to rehabilitate the period to which they tie themselves, is deeply compromised in that same narration; we are bringing to bear the same rules of grammar to texts that the grammarians had said were ungrammatical. In the area of literary studies, at least, what is remarkable about scholarship is the degree to which it is still—ever increasingly, I think—responding to Petrarch's accusations of estrangement from the master narrative by simply saying it ain't so: we *are* part of that master narrative, we *did* know the classics (and thus medievalists, notoriously, are the only group of scholars outside classical studies required to know Latin), our values were *not* so different, and so on. The ironic poignancy, in Albert Ascoli's felicitous articulation, is that "the values and practices of the dominant contemporary medievalist scholarship are directly descended from an early modern humanist movement which arose in polemical opposition to what its advocates already took to be the ahistorical procedures of their medieval predescessors. . . ."

Few have ever asked what fundamental (and thus unspoken) values were at stake in that great Petrarchan horror at the medieval past (and its extension in the master narrative that has followed) and whether we wish to share, and thus perpetuate, those values. When we accept the definitions of all sorts of value (from grammaticality, say, to how much of the classics we ought to know) as defined by the "Renaissance," then the medieval period, above all, is found lacking. And in this acceptance of the transcendent value of the paradigm that the Renaissance takes on as its own paradigmatic mantle—although it should be understood as a paradigm rather than as a "reality" or the "real" Renaissance—the modernist (the postmedievalist) and the medievalist are like two sides of the same narrative coin, one unthinkingly accepting the grimness of the Middle Ages, the other saying it really wasn't grim, both of them equally accepting the largely unspoken standards for what constitutes darkness. Everyone, after all, wants to be part of the Master Narrative.

In this context the Las Casas rewriting of the original Columbine text must be viewed as an exemplary act. What is wanted is a coherent narration in a language with a codified grammar, a smooth trip across the Atlantic; what is thrown overboard in this kind of narration—the success of which is everywhere visible—is still believed by many people to have been darkness, ignorance, superstition, and chanting. But let us ask instead what the voices are that go unheard; let us talk instead of the sailor's accents and songs, of all they shared with the other ships that left on the 2nd of August. Indeed, let us tell the story from an aesthetic posture that is not horrified by cacophony (as Petrarch was, and as Bembo would be, and as medievalists will be). Let us instead take pleasure from fragments and the riotous pluralities and often-chaotic poetics that made much of the medieval world so resistant to that smooth narrative. In fact (and this too carries almost unbearable poignancy), Petrarch himself is, famously, the most divided of men; his fear of the violence and the ruptures of different kinds of chaos lives in querulous intimacy with his fascination with that same apocalyptic threat. And then he writes those wonderful love songs in a vernacular. He is Columbus and Las Casas, but we have let the Las Casas tell us how to read the Columbus.

But Columbus's voyage was far from seamless. Partway out, things slowed down, inevitably. We have the starkest and loveliest of terms for the doldrums—and it is an expression that is said to come from Columbus's times—"The Horse Latitudes": "either of two belts or regions in the neighborhood of 30 degrees North and 30 degrees South latitude characterized by high pressure, calm and light baffling winds." The etymology, which smacks of delicious apocryphalness, is that they were so named when sailors—the captains, of course—trying to make it across the Atlantic, desperately stuck in these sailing ruts, began throwing everything overboard to lighten the ship and restore movement. Even the precious horses—horses that you imagine you may need desperately when you finally get there—even those horses had to be thrown overboard. This is the superstitious sacrifice that takes place on the high seas; we jettison those powerful and scary beasts to get the winds blowing again. And we propitiate those who are superstitious about the story of the trip in the same way: we pretend the Jews were not sailing that same day; we throw out the mongrel vernaculars that were overwritten in standard grammars; we anguish over Petrarch's claim, which we know to be both ironically and poignantly untrue, that he gave up writing love poetry when he was no longer a young man.

But for the medievalist who has dwelled on the fragments and the ruins without feeling Petrarchan despair and Humanist pathos—not because there was no fragmentation, let us pretend, but because we might want to value that fragmentation, and ruins as well, because we might not be horrified by chaos or, like Gabriel García Márquez, in *Love in the Time of Cholera,* not think love or its poetry ought to be unchanging—Columbus is poignantly medieval in a world ever less understanding of his unruliness, a stranger in a strange land. What we have left of his language, in that first diary, that very first document from the brave New World, the other side of the tear, is a copy of a copy of his sailor's log. And it has been turned into good Castilian by Fray Bartolomé de las Casas. Columbus, the professional peripatetic and seasoned world traveler long before he sailed across the Atlantic, was one of those men who spoke a language at every port, but he did eventually find it advantageous to learn (although it is unclear to what degree of grammaticality) the two codified languages that appeared to have some control over his destiny, Castilian and Latin. And he knew what the lingua franca of the civilized world was and provided himself with a speaker of classical Arabic to serve as translator when he reached the Indies.

Indeed—and this bit of great and fitting lyricism is also left out of most of our narrations—the first official diplomatic conversation in the New World took place between Luis de Torres, a Jew of recent conversion, speaking in the lovely Romance-accented Arabic that was the language of both high culture and stunning nostalgia—and a Taíno chief in the hinterlands of Cuba, in the Cubanacán that Columbus took to mean "el gran can." This stunning story is all too much like the one about the unseemly concatenations of the 2nd of August; it is known, it was there, but it has never made it into the story, it is an absurd embarrassment, it is "bizarre."[3] And it is thus that the bizarre—or the kabbalistic—details are jettisoned from our reasonable and "modern" narrations, and it is even true, as is the case with Columbus, that some of the narrations that are perhaps most strangely lyrical seem to disappear altogether and resurface only in more grammatical terms; the other primordial text describing the New World in the earliest years after Columbus's voyage was that written by Fray Ramón Pané, whom Columbus left in Hispaniola in 1494. Pané, a Catalan who spoke Castilian imperfectly, was to write a report on the indigenous peoples, and so he duly went and lived among the ill-fated Taínos. By 1498 he had produced the seminal *Relación acerca de las antiguedades de los Indios*, but the original of this manuscript, too, in an odd twist of fate, was lost. The oddest twists, though, follow when Columbus's son "preserves" the text by copying it into a biography he writes of his father, but this also is eventually lost. What survives, again, is a translation of a translation, the Italian version of the Columbus biography.

What is really lost is not so much the original in any Platonic sense, but the senses of both cacophony—the chaos of dialects and songs sung differently every day—and of all those things we now find bizarre or inexplicable, the resetting of clocks so that exile fits into diaspora, the speaking of Arabic in the New World when in the Old it is being outlawed. Good and smooth paper is made from the pulp of the illiterate and undisciplined. Order is made from chaos, and we call it History. And on this paper is written a smooth trip, over placid seas, all according to the new rules of the new universe, all following the rules of Nebrija's grammar of Castilian—that perhaps being the best example of the first text of the Renaissance, "our" modern period, in Spain. At least in the codification of its language, Spain, forever embarrassed about the inadequacy of its modernity (a problem notoriously attributed to its mongrel past), was the first among the moderns in Europe.

The tension and the problem here is that histories *are* written and rewritten in the languages of the great grammars, and philology can describe only the dialects of Romance in the tongue and the rhetoric of the grammarians. In this, as in so many other things, Dante—in this instance as the author of the *De vulgari eloquentia*—is our most immediate professional ancestor, he, not the Germans of the nineteenth century, the inventor of Romance philology. What is difficult or even repugnant about the parts of the story not told—the parts that made Petrarch and his many successors, including ourselves, resentful—is that it seems to be tellable only in the near incoherence of the lyric. What is missing from the Las Casas version of Columbus are not only the Jews and the Moriscos—that is crucial and obvious—but the accents, the bad grammar, the songs in all the dialects that must have helped pass the time as the time out on the sea took longer and longer. But for Las Casas, heir to the narrative lines of Petrarch, that kind of irregularity would constitute a severe failure in narrativity. (And the brilliance and the "medievalness" of Dante's *De vulgari* is that it so explicitly sets out the folie à deux that is the dialogue between the love lyrics and the Latin descriptions, that "dialogue" between father and parricide.) Like the hermetic lyric, the bumps in the story, the radical pluralisms, the horses we are afraid are keeping us from moving forward, all these have resisted the smoothing effect of institutional exegesis and the successful historical narrative we have inherited, as a standard, from the Renaissance—or at least from a very powerful ideology that has called itself "Renaissance." The result of such successful resistance—of getting thrown overboard, in effect—is that we scarcely know them, have almost never heard the songs or seen the horses. The alternative has been what medieval scholarship (what we even sometimes call philology) has been doing: telling us that the accents were not so bad, and that we are moving purposefully—struggling inexorably—toward pristine Castilian, or pure Italian, or perfect French.

The story told without smoothing over all of its many bumps could perhaps only end up—to steal a title and phrase from the great Cuban novelist Alejo Carpentier—as a baroque concerto. Without Carpentier, there is none of the magic realism (how wonderful a medieval expression that is; isn't that what the 2nd of August is?) that rewrites and rocks the world of fiction today. Carpentier understood this change, just as he understood and set out in his last major work that Columbus's authentic relics are everywhere in the New World and that all the claimed burial sites are authentic. Like all Cubans, the mongrel Carpentier, son of French immigrants, is in every way a descendant of that conversation that took place in the fall of 1492 in a magical place called Cubanacán between the Jew who spoke Arabic with a strong Andalusian accent and the Taino who spoke a language that never had the chance to resonate for us. There, once again, is the rub, for the Taíno is gone from history because he did not have Nebrija to fix his language and write its grammar and make its singers sing on key. It did not have Las Casas to rewrite it and edit it, to turn the pulp into good paper. That is the dilemma, because with few exceptions what survives is the palimpsest, the accentless narration. And the explorer who makes it is the one who can make his men forget the difficulties, can invent the smooth sea and even sailing, and he is the one who is willing to throw the horses overboard in the painful and too-long days of the horse latitudes. Future readers of Carpentier will miss the greatest joke of all, because in his texts his Spanish will be read in some sort of classical accent. But Carpentier had a strong French accent, which only made his native Cuban Spanish more mongrel, more lyrical. More medieval and Columbuslike. The question is whether that grammatical narration, that rewriting, which we willingly call "Renaissance" because it so fears the chaos of its closest past that it calls it death itself, is what we have to accept because it is the price that must always be paid to make it into the future at all. The challenge for the writing of history—literary history in particular, but no doubt all kinds—comes in finding a solution to this curious dilemma, in finding a way to reconcile baroque poetry with classical lines, a way for the Renaissance to talk to us about its mongrel and accented ancestry, about the texture of that interruption that seems to separate it from the desired past.

2

> An aged man is but a paltry thing,
> A tattered coat upon a stick, unless
> Soul clap its hands and sing, and louder sing
> For every tatter in its mortal dress,

Nor is there singing school but studying
Monuments of its own magnificence;
And therefore I have sailed the seas and come
To the holy city of Byzantium. . . .

William Butler Yeats
"Sailing to Byzantium"

Memory and History. How do we figure one without the other? Did the medievals have only one—Memory—without the other? Can *we* write one—History—without the other? Can these questions even be clearly distinguished?

There is a distinctive and enduring view of the medieval period, in its basic form usually attributed to Erwin Panofsky, that the medievals lacked what we usually call historical perspective. But listen to the transparent evaluation implicit in that apparently simple and descriptive formulation. Clearly, we "believe" in "historical perspective"; implicitly, it is part of what separates moderns from not-moderns, civilized from uncivilized. In any case, we have got historical perspective because here we are writing it, contemplating it, valorizing it with our very narration of the shift from its absence to its acquisition. A relatively rare medievalist—Lee Patterson is the most eloquent at the moment—will argue that this cliché about the "lack of historical consciousness and perspective" is another unfounded prejudice against the medieval period. But even this argument implicitly valorizes the notion of "historical perspective." At the heart of the matter is the perspective of value, and virtually everything that follows from that perspective. Do we really need to think "historical consciousness" or even "objectivity"—both defined in highly Renaissance-paradigmatic ways—are what we want or need to believe in? Are they really, as that paradigm claims, transcendent values? And what if we momentarily put aside our desire for the pleasures of the Grand Narrative, of that smooth flow of History?

It is actually easy to argue, particularly in the light of fine work by scholars from Frances Yates to Mary Carruthers and Anthony Kemp, that the medieval concept of History provides the only viable model of a modality of History and Memory that does not—did not—need to play by the rules of the great totalizing narrative that has had a stranglehold on Western culture for the last five centuries. That medieval modality is squarely at the heart of what we now call the postmodern condition, the search for a way out of the totalizing History that begins—now, I think, tellingly—with a rejection of the medieval. The medieval is a modality that, to put it simply, is memorialistic, which means it does not seek to "objectivize"—which means distance—the past but quite the contrary. The past is intimately involved with ourselves, it is one of the functions of Memory, it is most to be valued when it has meaning in our own contingencies. The gesture of aligning the 2nd of August so that it is the 9th of Ab is incomprehensible otherwise: irrational and not narratable. Not History but Memory (or worse, Construct).

What we sometimes know but usually forget, especially if we are medievalists, is that the very notion of narrativity, and the commensurate values of development, objectivity, orderliness, and so forth, is a *value* that lies at the heart of the great narrative. But we need accept that value no more than others from that "great tradition." Or, if we want to embrace it, we ought to want to. Or, yet again, that there might be other mistresses we would want to embrace. Thus, the real question is whether we ought to talk about the "History" of the medieval period in the radically different language of "History" of the Renaissance and later. Within the discipline of History the epistemological revolution began decades ago, and the *Annales* school and its many distinguished historians have acted, fundamentally, out of a sense of rejection of the strong narrative and in an embrace of different historical values—a different notion of what might even be called History. But in literary studies the revolution, with great irony, has basically stopped at the palace gates; behind those gates, medievalists, who know full well, by and large, that "their" authors believed there was a conflation of History and Memory and of personal and universal histories, are the staunchest defenders and most rigorous practitioners of the paradigms of historiography that are the legacy of the Renaissance. If we suggest that, instead, we follow Hugh Kenner's advice (and example) that the critic should mimic the language of his poet, the voice of that Renaissance paradigm answers sharply that this is not real History. The real and difficult question which follows is that of contingency—not, as the standard formulation has it, whether we *can* escape it or not, but rather, to put the question in terms of value, whether we *should* escape it, whether we *want* what comes from those acts of distancing and objectification.

At the end of the complex introduction to one of the most influential books on literary historiography—particularly, but not exclusively, that of the Renaissance—Thomas Greene notes, with palpable poignancy: "Reading imitations makes even larger claims on the historical imagination than most reading and underscores even more cruelly our cultural solitude. It asks us not only to intuit an alien sensibility from a remote *mundus significans,* but also that sensibility's intuitions of a third. Nothing perhaps is more calculated to impress on us our temporal estrangement. Yet nothing perhaps immerses us so forcibly in the flow of literary history. . . ."[4] To which one might answer, far less eloquently, that all of this is true *only* when one has rejected intimacy with the past, only within that paradigm that has, curiously enough, established a chasm between the different parts of the self, its history, its poetry, and its consciousness, and that has defined literary history precisely as something that is *not* an intimate part of us or our personal histories, something that is the direct counterpart of the scientific discourse, a "discipline" rather than an affair. When we distance ourselves—our own contingencies and how we might imagine our histories interact with the texts we read—then, indeed, there is poignant estrangement.

How to do otherwise? How do we mimic, if that is what we choose, a historical mode rooted in something alien to what we believe we ought to be as historians of literature: a synchronic (and thus sometimes synchronistic) view of time and events that intimately molds the relationship between self and text, self and history. At a minimum, this entails two epistemological adaptations: first, that we reconceive our own relationship to earlier texts and culture as part of our fundamental personal and present histories, now part of the memory traces which profoundly inform our present selves, our everyday readings, our work; second, and clearly by extension, that our "study" of medieval literature in particular restore, for others as well as for ourselves, the radical presentness of the medieval past just beneath our consciousness. If we can fight back the incredible strength of the paradigm of diachrony, we might see in medieval texts strong likenesses to ourselves for reasons that fall far outside the time line, that have little to do with those texts prefiguring us. The principal way in which we are—or should be—like Dante, or other medieval authors, is in embracing our own history and time and songs. We have to reorder the past inside the structures of our memory—eliminating first of all the most arbitrary and meaningless of ordering principles, diachrony—so that we can remember and recite just the right text at the right time, not as an exercise in erudition but as the reflex of intercourse, and so that we can begin to hear, again, that polyglot and lyrical Columbus beneath Las Casas's classicized version—deeply buried memory, almost forgotten. No doubt there is a reader who at this point says, "Gone, they are so forgotten that they are gone." But, like many deeply buried memories, the right prompting cue in the present can perhaps make it come back.

Like almost everyone else, I started out with the normative schoolchild's vision of 1492 that is sketched out in ditties and filled in during secondary schools and college—and ratified by the many pronouncements, like Todorov's, from which it seemed difficult to escape in 1992: it is the beginning of the modern world, as we know it. The standard narrative of 1492, in fact, serves as the perfect example of many of the paradigms I have been discussing. We begin with the discovery of the New World, which, in turn, is crucial to this perceived birth of modern man, not only because the discovery per se made available a whole other continent, with the spaces for growth and expansion that modern civilization would require, but, no less, because the symbolic importance of the act of exploration and discovery itself created a will to action dimly perceived as modern. (Even in the revisionary and penitential mode so prevalent during the year of the quincentenary, modern was still modern—even when it was evil. But the medieval is always backward, usually evil.) Part of the Columbus story crucial to this vision of 1492 is the strong resistance to his trip put up by all manner of authorities; there, we see the first modern man, adventurous, with science and gumption on his side, struggling against the last gasps of a superstitious past. The old orders walk about in dark robes at the court of Isabella, whispering in her ear that modernity is blasphemous. But even in the Old World, in Europe, the end of the long age of darkness is at hand, and the Renaissance and modern man are at the door. The Discovery of the New World thus has a neat and meaningful parallel in the Rediscovery of our true heritage—that culture of the ancient Greeks and Romans that makes us modern and civilized, again, after the Darkness.

This amazing cartoon is worth redrawing because it *is* of astonishing durability and enduring primacy, even if the versions we have absorbed and which we parrot more or less indirectly are articulated in a far more glossy fashion. I did not begin to glimpse the fundamental structural limitations of this paradigm until I began to study medieval Spain and was surprised by the dazzling world originally refashioned by Américo Castro. During late winter afternoons in Philadelphia, all sorts of people would sit in utter stillness and absorb, with Samuel Armistead, this at first unimaginable medieval Spain; it was part of a Europe far removed from the pious world that "medieval" meant elsewhere. In contrast, this universe teemed with the productive chaos of people of all sorts of languages, and accents, and faiths and no faiths. It was a universe that sang; and often the songs were either vulgar or had a great beat—or both. To go from there into other medieval courses, other constructs, was to be stunned by the stillness of tradition and the faith that hung heavily in the air. For me, then, that first vision was replaced with a second and largely parallel vision within which 1492 is not a beginning but an end, and a lamentable closure. For those who in medieval Europe saw an eclectic, polymorphic, and highly productive culture in great measure shaped and fueled by the Islamic colonization begun in 711, for those of us, in other words, who came to realize how thoroughly "Oriental" is the heartland of the Western tradition, the expulsions symbolized by 1492 can be read as nothing short of tragic. As John Boswell says, there is real and heartrending horror in that radical inversion of universes of racial and cultural syncretism and of religious pluralism and tolerance that is aptly signaled by 1492. We move into the "modern" world, the Renaissance, and the culture of humanism through an act of violent expulsion of a culture of highly productive hybridity.

But the real end had begun long before, and the last of the Muslims would not be officially expelled for a while yet. I will argue later, in fact, what others have suggested: that for all intents and purposes the severe and shaping discontinuity lies, roughly, between the culture of the tenth through thirteenth centuries, on the one hand, and that which follows it, which is quite visible, again roughly, by the fourteenth. (That is why Petrarch may be seen as the foundational figure of an aesthetics and a historical ethos that does not reach its full and unambiguous political manifestation until 1492.) Yet 1492 has great value; it is an uncannily precise rip in the fabric of history because it does conflate life and death, beginning and end. The implications of that conflation—the newly established modern period's writing the Muslims and the Jews out of the Western tradition (and the commensurate "discovery" of Plato and Aristotle)—are hard to contemplate without embarrassment. So, we do not dwell on it often.

We love being modern, and we love being the present-day descendants of the Greeks, but since it is harder to publicly and professionally delight in the other side of that particular coin, it is elided and ignored. After 1492 we forget that in 1225 or 1230 to sit at Frederick II's dinner table in Palermo it was de rigeur to have intimate knowledge of Plato and Aristotle, of Maimonides and Ibn Rushd, as well as to be able to tap one's feet to the rhythm of the latest *muwashshaḥa* brought from al-Andalus. Instead, we remember, and claim as our ancestor, poor Petrarch, first Renaissance man, heroic for living much of his life with a barely literate Calabrian Greek, in the apparently vain effort to learn a smattering of the new holy language of the newly "discovered" ancestors. Except among the intellectual descendants of Don Américo, whose work it has been to restore those particular memories, these odd juxtapositions are largely set aside. Within this minoritarian construct, this other version of 1492 is a memorialistic one, an act of recuperation, but also one of profoundly sad, melancholic closure, perhaps uncannily like Petrarch's when he thought of what he had lost as he sat contemplating the ruins of Rome.

But the day came when I discovered—and I use that verb with a full sense of its irony and fatuousness when we talk about the New World—a whole canon of literary texts which in my own studies, within the configurations of the disciplines of philology and medieval literary studies, lay very far away: those of Latin America. It is true that few literate people in this day and age are likely to admit in public that they have not read *One Hundred Years of Solitude.* (In fact, García Márquez publishes so frequently in the *New Yorker* that he can scarcely be avoided by such people.) Neither are they likely to be unaware that Octavio Paz has written poetry (if nothing else, his long-awaited Nobel Prize guaranteed that recognition). If these cultured people are modernists of any variety—which here literally means someone who works on texts written after 1492—then García Márquez's novel and Paz's poetry might well be read as part of the continuum of their work. But for medievalists, such texts are viewed as alien to our texts, as distant and hard to grasp as the Greeks and the Romans once were to those who stood on the frontier of the Dark Age. And we almost never take the next step and attempt to imagine that these New World texts might fit into the memorial structures of our literary universe. Done overtly, such imagining would constitute "anachronism" (a fine irony). Far more powerfully and unconsciously, we are constrained by the epistemological divide marked by 1492—the same one, of course, that prevents Latin Americanists (like any other self-respecting modernists) from reading much medieval literature, in the end not really literature at all, in all the modern senses, except as a curiosity or when it is required, probably some vestige of the old philological structures of literature departments. The handful of conspicuous exceptions—Dante's *Commedia* at the head of this smallish group—proves the rule. As Lee Patterson notes: "Most literary scholars and critics consider medieval texts to be utterly extraneous to their own interests, as at best irrelevant, at worst inconsequential. . . ."[5]

At this point, any Latin Americanist would note with some bemusement that the canonical status of Latin American literature itself—despite Nobel prizes and frequent appearances in the *New Yorker*—has been both hard-won and relatively recent, and in certain ways it still has a long way to go. The case was made strikingly by

Roberto González Echevarría at the Modern Language Association's convention in 1985: "in 1968 Spanish was a discipline controlled . . . by the literature of Spain. There were many specialists in Medieval and Golden Age Spanish literature, which was to be expected, but what was more questionable was the horde of specialists in eighteenth-century, nineteenth-century and modern Spanish literature. . . . Latin American literature, in most Spanish departments, had at most one representative who took care of the tradition from Columbus to Cortázar, while Spanish was carved in ever thinner slices."[6] In 1985 the canonical situation was the same at many important institutions. At the University of Pennsylvania, where I had studied and where I was teaching, it was exactly as described. A place like Yale, in fact, was clearly exceptional; although, even there, even now, the liminality of Latin American literature even in these exceptional cases can be glimpsed in subtler but perhaps stronger forms: the curricula and faculty of departments of comparative literature and the range of texts exploited by major theoreticians.

To put it most simply, then, my first critical awareness of Latin American literature cast it into exactly the same boat as much of the literature I worked on, since even within the medieval literature canon the writings of al-Andalus are invariably at the margins (the minority within a minority, to appropriate the phrase that both Salman Rushdie and Edward Said have used about themselves). So, when I moved from Pennsylvania to Yale, I ended up in a place where I could not avoid hearing the many sounds of a literature barely overheard elsewhere. Thus, when I began reading Latin American texts, I thought of them explicitly as kindred souls to the abandoned Hispano-Arabic or Judeo-Hispanic texts I (like many others in that field) read with the tender passion and personal affection one saves for children too little loved by their families. At the same time, the parallelisms made me more acutely aware of the damage done to the literary history of Europe by the textual banishments that corresponded to the diasporas of 1492 and 1612—1612 being the far less famous date of the final expulsion of the Moriscos from Spain. There could scarcely be a better or more poignant case of the present mediating the past (or a better argument for reversing the process). The still intractable problem in reading and writing the literary history of medieval Spain is the stark one that the established lines of institutional medieval scholarship correspond to the post-1492 universe. Where a massive rip indisputably exists in the fabric of history, we act as if patching it were an acceptable mode of historical vision. The literature and culture of the Jews and the Muslims, which in many ways dominated the cultural landscape of medieval Europe in its happiest and most productive years, are fully exiled from the narrative of "European literary history." That Arabic, for example, is not one of the languages of European literature in the eighteenth century is one thing, but that it is not so for the twelfth is a glaring omission. The linguistic divisions that have come to be treated as sacrosanct and objectively valuable divisions of knowledge impose on the past—on medieval Europe—an epistemological and linguistic system explicitly rooted in an attempt to *forget* that medieval period or, at best, to make it more like the Renaissance present. Clearly, our institutions, departments, fields are key narrators in the tradition of Las Casas and Petrarch.

The textual losses in this adaptation of our memories are grievous. However, the most painful aspect of forcing the medieval world to dance to the very different rhythms of the modern age is less frequently identified—that is, by making the smooth narratives and the grammatically regular languages of 1492 and its aftermath the rules by which medieval texts must play, we are ratifying the diasporas, the violent exiles. Don't we embrace the expulsions when we say, for example, that medieval Spain is to be studied in "Spanish"—by which we mean the Castilian codified in 1492 and so intimately tied to the other events of that year? The Castilian that first overwrites the first text of Columbus and the New World is not merely anachronistic (now using the term in its strong value so privileged by our narrative): the ex post facto privileging of the dialect that was, in this period, one among many and certainly not the prestige norm. No less, far more, exactly this sort of erasure and cleaning up of the multilingual (and multiracial past) is what the Christian monarchs had in mind when they so infamously and cruelly abrogated the accords under which Granada had capitulated.

Within this sad capitulation in which medievalists have played roles at least as significant as modernists, there is no better present example of the havoc wreaked on our communal memory than that of the polymorphous *muwashshaḥa*—the new and lyric form par excellence in eleventh-century Europe—a subject to which I will return at various times. But here, in mapping out some of the implications of 1492, a few rudimentary explanations are in order. Perhaps we can begin by saying that in the realm of literature the *muwashshaḥa* was the sort of achievement that is an appropriate emblem of the creativity and subsequent influence of that synthetic and polymorphous Andalusian culture. In some ways it is like Ibn Rushd's commentaries on Aristotle that revolutionized (and radicalized) philosophical thought in the rest of Europe in the thirteenth century. In other ways it appears to evoke the image of those wonderful black and white stripes of marble that define the Christian monument that is Pisa's cathedral and tie it indelibly, even though we mostly choose not to see, to the mosque at Córdoba. What do we make of the griffin that stood guard at Pisa, adorning its eastern gable from late in the eleventh century until 1828, a griffin clearly Arab and Muslim, superb artifact of the Taifas—those same city-states that were inventing the songs with the difficult name of *muwashshaḥa?* Like the presence of the griffin in the Campo at Pisa, the resonance of these songs has to be conceived as part of what we should perhaps call the "mudejarism" of so much of medieval Europe: that ability to dress in the fashions of the Arabs while the institutions of authority claimed that Islam was an enemy. Such "paradoxical" intimacy—miscegenation, even—is a hallmark of much of the modern world, and we would be reluctant to deny ourselves the possibility of this sort of cultural complexity. But it is no less visible—and, perhaps even audible—in a medieval Europe no less sophisticated. And the *muwashshaḥāt*, if we listen to them, help us hear and see a medieval Europe crafted out of that most intimate of dances with the other—an other who lives very much within our house.

The *muwashshaḥāt* invent new Romance and Arabic and Hebrew poetics in one swoop, all in the same poem: strophes both defined and differentiated by rhyme schemes; in contrast, in the classical languages—Arabic, Hebrew, Latin alike—this was unheard of. Within these poems, which in fact are songs and are best referred to in that way—this is a crucial issue to which I will return repeatedly—we hear a calliope of languages and voices, including, most heretically and most foundationally, something called the *kharja.* The *kharja* is the refrain of the song and, as such, almost invariably appears as the last of the strophes. But this description inadequately conveys the centrality and pervasiveness of this refrain that establishes both meter and rhyme scheme and is almost certainly repeated after each stanza, as are refrains in almost all popular song types, past and present. This refrain is composed—and here is both heresy and creation—in a vernacular that contrasts sharply and poignantly with the rest of the poem. But (simplifying a highly complex argument) these lyrics are far more than "just" bilingual; they are poems that embody and literalize in song many of the most telling features of their medium, of their world.

In the lovers' dialogue within the poem, carried out in languages previously segregated as incompatible—the vernacular and the classical, is but one of the shocking pairings—we have a stunning playing out, first, of the paradoxes of love. As almost all great love poetry has portrayed it, the love that can be sung in poetry is oxymoronic; it needs suffering in order to have happiness, it craves distance in order to see and feel close, it takes joy from anguish itself. This is far more than "mere" love poetry (if there is such a thing). This is no less explicitly a poetry of and about the creation of a new language for poetry, of a new literature. In that emphasis it strikingly resembles its nearby and equally radical Provençal cousins. In the end, this is the newly coined, literally invented poetry of a society of marked pluralisms, for which the classical poetic forms, with their linguistic and stylistic orthodoxies and unities, were transparently insufficient. Thus, a new generation of poets wreaks havoc with classical traditions, rooted in singularity and the immutable written language, by making them sing to and with the Other—the vernacular, the explicitly vulgar, the fluid and oral, the female voice. And in such a union, unheard of on all sides, each of the original and separate traditions is transformed. Not only is the classical voice made, literally, to dance to the beat of the street singer, but she, in turn, becomes respectable enough to play at court.

Here, I interrupt the story of the poems "themselves" to interpolate the story of their discovery. And, once again, the word is fraught with ironies. Because our scholarly approaches mimic the modes and assumptions of the classical traditions (since those are what we believe it takes to make us modern and objective and thus good scholars) we were completely unable to figure out—to discover and classify—what the *muwashshaḥāt* were until about forty years ago. In a couple of the small corners of Arabic and of Romance studies one can hear tell the story of the great discovery of the *kharjas* by Samuel Stern in 1948. But this was not a discovery in the ordinary sense of the word, since the Andalusian *muwashshaḥāt* had been amply known before then. They had existed in printed editions for decades, and the widely read Ibn Khaldūn (along with other medieval critics, less-known) talked about them and their uniqueness, their Andalusianness. Their medievalness.

The problem was, and to a remarkable extent continues to be, that the mode of being medievalists is dictated not by those paradigmatic modes of medievalism, but by the modalities of Renaissance historiography, of those constructs so aptly recalled by enumerating the key events of 1492. Thus, the poetry's polymorphism was—still is—unintelligible to scholarly modes neatly divided among Hebraists, Arabists, Romanists. Arabists had been handling *muwashshaḥāt* for decades and had edited them and printed them, all without any notion of what the gibberish was at the end of the poems; moreover, they had little interest in figuring any of it out, since the rest of the poem, in classical Arabic, was characterized by such nonclassical (perhaps best to say anticlassical) idiosyncrasies as strophic forms and rhyme schemes. (This view has scarcely been vitiated in recent years; the greater visibility of the *muwashshaḥāt* is even publicly lamented on occasion. At one of 1992's innumerable quincentenary conferences, this one about the expulsions, an Arabist decried the elevation of the form, saying that everyone knew, of course, this stuff wasn't *really* Arabic poetry at all, certainly not good Arabic poetry.)

Hispanists failed to get even that far. They were oblivious to the existence of such poems, since the belief has always been that even if there were cultural phenomena in medieval Spain that were not in Castilian (or, stretching the point, in some other Romance form), they would belong to the other traditions, for our tradition is defined by our derivation from Latin. (This is a view rooted in that notion of diachrony and narrative so dominant in literary historiography, the view that defines History as a narrative progression. Thus, in this case it is as if the vernaculars had always been struggling inexorably to improve themselves and eventually achieve grammaticality with that great triumph of the Grammar of 1492, a triumph that necessarily entails both Conquest and Expulsions.) In this way, in the end, the honor of "discovery" went to a Hebraist, Stern, although not because that tradition was any more liberal than the Hispanist or Arabist in its defined object of study. (Work now in progress by Lourdes Alvarez will explore the ways in which Stern's discovery is conditioned by the concatenation of events and ideologies of another remarkable year, 1948.) At the most banal and telling level, however, it should be said that Stern was able to discover these poems because he did happen to know Spanish (having been, as I understand it, an undergraduate Spanish major). Crucially—and here lies the mapping of territory without which no discovery is possible—it occurred to him in looking at these songs which history has handed down in Hebrew script that it might be more logical for the refrains to be in some form of transliterated Romance, the vernacular of al-Andalus that we call Mozarabic, than in gibberish.

In the small and at times petty kingdom of Hispano-Arabic studies, some might interpret observations such as these as belittling Samuel Stern and his achievement. Instead, it seems to me an elevation of the achievement of Stern (who has become a distinctly Columbus-like figure in the mythology) to point out that what he did was to read some poems from eleventh-century Spain as if eleventh-century Spain had been a multicultural, multilingual society whose cultural artifacts might reflect such bastardy—and not as if they were the products of one of the three great pure and grammatical traditions. Most other critics had been following the traditional lines that, rather than drawing one hybrid culture, circumscribe those three separate and separable ones which in a moment of historical freakishness just happened to share a peninsula for a while. And it must be emphasized that the very insight—that cultural mapping—which is the basis for the discovery of these songs is still forcefully resisted and denied by powerful bodies of scholarship. As I have said in the past and as others have said more recently, the tragic irony is that we really have not progressed much since then; we have not risen to the level of Stern's insight. As Ross Brann so aptly puts it: "Yet the literary form which seems to capture vividly the richness of cultural interaction between confessional communities on the western frontier of Islam and medieval Europe is often treated as evidence of the cultural hegemony of one Iberian community over another rather than as testimony to their cultural convergence."[7] The notion that culture—just like standardized languages—must be staunchly grammatical, hegemonic, is the memory of 1492 to which we cede center-stage in our modes of constructing history.

But there are different memories of Columbus to be drawn from the literature of Latin America, which is enamored of him as a founder, the first narrator, the creator who discovers a New World, and Others, precisely because he knows there are Others there in the first place. And this Columbus, and certainly this Stern, know that those Others are the necessary new voice, the *kharja,* without which the rhymes and rhythms of the classical world make little sense. When we resituate ourselves squarely in the New World, a world whose essential definition is inseparable from the many complexities of exile from the Old World, it turns out that the *muwashshaḥa* is not such a strange bird, after all. But let me not get ahead of this next story of discovery, which, once again, begins with the foundational work in Latin American literature done by González Echevarría. One day he handed me a copy of an article of his on the Cuban poet Nicolás Guillén, for Cubans second only to the virtually sainted José Martí. The gesture, during my first few months at Yale, was in great measure that standard marker of collegiality, but in some small measure it also was conditioned by our shared exile, by the assumption that I might actually read it; I might know nothing about Latin American literature, as I had confessed, but I was still a Cuban and had spent my earliest childhood in Cuba. Such is the stature of Guillén as tribal poet, and this too is shared with Martí, that I did, in fact, read it because I had a distinctly Joycean singsong memory of some fragments of his verses, sung to me, no doubt, in my age of babble.

But if I read the article in the first place because I expected it to provoke Memory, what it provoked far more powerfully was History. This seminal study of Guillén immediately confounded my perfectly normal sense of the strict division between medieval and Latin American literatures. Its opening pages rehearsed an argument the foundations of which I had myself rehearsed endlessly: why and how the classical norms of both poetry and its scholarship account poorly for the literature of the New World. Instead—and now I will stay on this side of 1492 and the Atlantic for a while—it is a literature that models itself explicitly on the Spanish baroque "considered an anathema by neo-Classicists in and out of Spain and Spanish America," a distinctly different poetics that "broke away from mainstream European aesthetics." What was stunning to me in González Echevarría's description of the aesthetics of the Baroque (which he calls "the first literary movement to bear an original Spanish seal") was how precise a description it might be of the aesthetics of hybrid Andalusian literary culture of the eleventh and twelfth centuries. Speaking about Góngora, the ultimate Baroque poet, González Echevarría notes that an adequate reading

> does not attempt to make the Cordobesan into a poet of light but to celebrate the difficulty of his language, his hermeticism, his eccentricity, his difference . . . his poetics worked at the margins of the Western tradition, at the point where the tradition subverts itself by nurturing forces that negate its mainstream ideology. . . . Góngora's poetry is inclusive rather than exclusive, willing to create and incorporate the new, literally in the form of neologisms. . . . Góngora was the first to write poems imitating the speech of blacks or, better yet, in the speech of blacks. . . . Góngora's style is not always "high" nor does he attempt to purge reality of base or heterogeneous elements. . . . Everything can be a part of beauty, even that which is not altogether comprehensible. . . .[8]

In these and other passages I read analyses and insights that would have constituted the most articulate reading of the culture of the *muwashshaḥāt*—if anyone had got so far along, but no one had. Disturbingly, kabbalistically, these readings existed with absolutely no awareness that the same issues, the same phenomena, permeated and defined the poets of that same Córdoba which Góngora would later haunt, no doubt communing with the ghosts of four or five hundred years before. At this point, the most transcendent of my readers is saying: Well now, so, after all, those ungrammatical voices were never fully silenced, the mongrel culture of the Middle Ages was never erased.

The greatest surprise was yet to come, the most stunning reversal of the present mediating the past. In the New World, most fully on the other side of 1492, Góngora and the Baroque had become the most cherished of ancestral figures, remembered at an almost unimaginable distance from the memory of a staunchly classicizing Europe in which Góngora is a sort of hyper-Latinate archconservative, an improbable and excessive and often unbearable conceit. The ancestral portrait is painted in ever-richer colors: "The Baroque allowed for a break with the Graeco-Latin tradition by allowing the fringes, the frills, as it were, to proliferate, upsetting the balance of symmetry, displacing the balance of Renaissance aesthetics . . . through its capaciousness and proliferation the Baroque inscribed the American. . . . This aesthetics of difference is another way of saying that the Baroque incorporates the Other; it plays at being the Other. . . ."[9] And the Other, as it turns out, is to be seen as a forgotten memory trace in a crucial poem from the canon of Nicolás Guillén, a poem very poorly understood he tells us because its second part, a strophe that clearly mimics a refrain, has always been assumed to be gibberish: a "sonorous refrain," one critic called it; "purely sonorous facts," said another. "But why empty this second part of the poem of meaning?" asks González Echevarría. " 'Sóngoro cosongo' is a poem in two parts written in different languages. It is a diglossic poem. The first part is written in Spanish, the second in . . . what?" To a medievalist deeply immersed in the polemics of the *muwashshaḥāt*, thus to reread, in scarcely different words, the drama of Stern's discovery, can scarcely have been a more uncanny text. Whereas the deeply encoded puzzle for Stern had been (already halfway decoded):

> B'n sydy b'n 'lrqrd' sh tntb'n
> Dsht 'lzm'n bn flyw dbn 'ldy'n
>
> [Ven sidi veni el querido esh tan tabeni
> De este al-zameni ven filyo de Ben al-Dayyeni][10]

the scratches on this stone were (far more legibly):

> Sóngoro cosongo
> songo be; sóngoro cosongo
> de mamey; sóngoro la negra
> baila bien;
> sóngoro de uno
> sóngoro de tre.
> Aé
> bengan a be;
> aé,
> bamo pa be;
> bengan, sóngoro cosongo,
> sóngoro cosongo de mamey![11]

The analysis of Guillén's poem after this dramatic question resonates as eerily as all the rest. The "nonsense" or "pure sound" is, in fact, the written version of the oral Congo culture so central—yet so ignored—in Cuban culture, much as the Mozarabic verses were explicitly cast as the songs of indigenous women; these Congo verses are explicitly a song—a chant or ritual song—and, as is no less explicit in the *kharja,* it is in this fusion with the "classical" tradition, Spanish in one case, Arabic in the other, that the oral is introduced into the "high" culture of the written word. This analysis concludes with crucial observations about what happens when these disparate elements do come together, and, in delightful contrast to most work done on the *muwashshaḥāt,* the author understands the poetic point of this unholy matrimony. The *kharjas*—in Congo or in Mozarabic—were not there as anthropological or philological specimens, provided by these cultural historians *avant la lettre,* as one preeminent Hispano-Arabist has put it. Instead, these bastard forms both lay bare the pluralisms in our cultures and play out the fundamental facts of intimacy: when the different strands come together, they work together, reshape each other, create a new poetics different from all older ones. Poetic "unity," like History, can in fact be defined in ways that violate all the basic rules of our classical definitions. For poets like Guillén or the Cordoban ancestors of Góngora—those ghosts that are essential ancestors to the New World, even as they have been erased in the Old—the hope and desire is, transparently, that the hybrid child will be more beautiful and vigorous than either parent. But we have forgotten that we are those children, their children. It began to occur to me that this was what 1492 might mean, and that the crucial bit of lost memory was that it was this lyricism and this resistance to the powerful narration of classical cultures that had left Europe, from Palos, that fateful year.

3

I know this super highway
This bright familiar sun
I guess that I'm the lucky one
Who wrote that tired sea song
Set on this peaceful shore
You think you've heard this one before

Well the danger on the rocks is surely past
Still I remain tied to the mast
Could it be that I have found my home at last
Home at last. . . .

Walter Becker and Donald Fagen
"Home at Last"

Postmodernism is one of those words that is everywhere. Nowadays, one can hardly open the pages of any journal or magazine or newspaper that has any intellectual aspirations—whether it is the *TLS* or *Time* magazine—without bumping into a discussion, in many cases heated and overwrought, of what modernity and postmodernism have done to Western culture. In the past decade the particular focus of the issue has skittishly jumped about (depending on the latest scandal from the academy or the latest book decrying cultural illiteracy). But whether it is the ferment about the Great Books course at Stanford, or the vigorously renewed attacks on deconstruction after de Man's wartime writings were brought to light, or the increasingly intemperate discussions about political correctness or the purported "death" of literature, the underlying issues in almost all cases are bits and pieces of the fundamental questions raised by the state of fracturedness called postmodernism and its effects on a (supposedly) once-unified culture. "Tired of postmodernism?" is the opening sentence of a review of a number of key philosophical texts. And the second sentence now seems an almost comic underestimate of what was to come: "There seems to be little sign of relief from this complex and vexed phenomenon or from our current, at times almost obsessive, concern with it."[12] It is worth noting that although Richard Shusterman was dealing with books by theorists (Habermas, Jameson, Rorty), who some might classify as philosophers rather than literary scholars, all three are major figures in literary studies, a pointed reminder that one of the many supposed (and, to many, supposedly dire) consequences of postmodernism has been to turn literary scholars away from literature "itself" and toward heuristic and hermeneutic problems that once were outside their concern. This, too, is part of the fragmentation that has crumpled the old classical lines and made so many cry out in horror at the cultural apocalypse already engulfing us. It is even true that the phrase "Dark Ages" surfaces now and then.

This controversy's bearing on an attempt to reconceive the medieval period is obscured, intractably, by the fact that even in its most palatable guises the picture we carry of that moment is of a dark cleric or—at best—a pious copier of lovely manuscripts. It seems all too obvious that those are the types seen walking around the Cloisters in

New York City or as the human component of invariably solemn medieval collections at other museums. A glance at the *International Thesaurus* (to steal from and then add a page to Patterson) reveals in the starkest possible terms what we intuit or know more diffusely. There we see "medieval" as part of the listing headed by *antiquated,* which also includes as principal entries *superannuated, antique,* and *archaic.* This entry is one of twenty-six subentries under the broad category "oldness" (which follows "newness"). And those twenty-six subcategories—the first cousins of "medieval"—run the gamut from *tradition* and *ancient* to *primitive, stale, obsolete, old-fashioned,* and *out-of-date.* (It is particularly difficult not to laugh when one sees the last three categories, each with taxonomic listings: *Stone Age Cultures, prehistoric men and manlike primates,* and *prehistoric animals* (*including types of dinosaurs*). We know what we will find if we go to "newness." There, we have innovation and creation and freshness and originality and, of course, modernity and modern and modernism (but not postmodern, yet). It is enough to make one wonder if Ezra Pound was mad as a young man as well, when, original and brash, he preached making it new, vigorously helped generate modernism, and did it all in open and reverent and productive communion with a bunch of medieval poets. They aren't new, they're dinosaurs.

We have retained little articulate memory of what horrified Petrarch so greatly as he looked at the things that separated him from the classical world. The parts we do remember and have woven into our own version of the story are largely spurious: "darkness" (by which is mostly meant the range of "superstitions" and their draconian punishments); extreme religiosity and orthodoxy; and general cultural conservatism. And a literature—often as not a preliterature—to correspond. Since we tend to believe that we are digging out truth and then narrating it, we rarely look closely at the values that are the indispensable basis of these discriminations. Moreover, in setting up a "Petrarchan" paradigm—in the person of a certain version of Petrarch himself—as the first "modern" man, or the period after 1492 as the "modern" era, we bypass the fact that there are *two* openly contradictory ways in which to be "modern."

The first, the widely used meaning of "modern" can be seen in the opening epigraph from Todorov: "even if every date that permits us to separate any two periods is arbitrary, none is more suitable, in order to mark the beginning of the *modern* era, than the year 1492, the year Columbus crosses the Atlantic Ocean."[13] In the discussions above, I have used the word "modern," reproduced it and variants of it, to convey that same imprecise but strongly connotative import as Todorov's, and I have suggested that "modern" is used to mean the positive and valuable condition of being "civilized." This, in turn, is closely tied to the intertwined twin virtues of elevating "reason" as the dominant ethos and of being a part of the strong and essentially continuous narrative of Western culture. That is why, for example, the Greeks are allowed a major role as either near-modern or proto-modern, and why non-Western societies, particularly those not colonized by the West and thus neither woven into our narrative nor convinced that "Rationality" is a god with which they want to replace their own, are characteristically considered "not modern." In the middle ground of striving toward this kind of modernness are those parts of the world imperfectly assimilated to the paradigms. (Latin America, so often tarred as "feudal," is a telling example.) To repeat what I have been saying in different ways, the medieval period stands as the starkest example of how and when the West was, clearly, not modern.

It is perhaps not despite but even because of the extreme generality of this taxonomy, and this sense of modernity, that it is so exceptionally powerful and can be seen to hold across a wide range of otherwise disparate ideological postures. Thus, the (perceived) role of women in modern versus nonmodern cultures would make bedfellows of feminists and conservative cultural critics like Alvin Kernan, who otherwise are in very different and antagonistic camps. In the modern culture narrative, women have been moving toward the limited degree of social equality that they now have achieved in the most civilized societies, in great measure thanks to the sway of Reason and the diminished importance of other gods. Conversely, the position of women is most lamentable the further one strays from the modern world: struggling, but with possibilities, in places like Latin America; hopeless in Iran, which in every other way has turned its back on these paradigms. The Khomeini revolution and regime was insistently referred to as "medieval" by the media, and what they meant was precisely the return to a world that cannot be narrated in the line from Greeks, to Renaissance, to us, and which once again has embraced unreasonable gods.

Thus, in discussions and reassessments of the university curriculum in particular and of our culture in general, this hierarchy of values corresponds neatly with the fundamental evaluations of those struggling to restore "Western culture's" preeminence. So we perceive that in this most general, and most generally compelling, meaning of modern, there is a second, widely used meaning that fits uncomfortably but surely into the paradigm of "progress." Strictly speaking, this other modern is in most uses really postmodern, but for the moment I will leave that precision aside in order to evoke the crucial context of ideology and value. This meaning of modern explicitly differentiates the values of feminists from those of cultural conservatives. This modern seems to lie at the end of the narrative line, and, depending on one's ideology, it is either the lamentable end of the values of Western civilization or the long-overdue transformation and implementation of those same values into the reshaping of a more egalitarian and enlightened society and culture. Modern here, therefore, is the highly valorized term that differentiates (1) those who, for example, see "the end of literature" as the lamentable loss of the values that made possible that great narrative continuum of civilization from (2) those who describe the same phenomenon as the marvelous inscription into that same narrative of those whose voices (accented, dialectal) have been excluded until now simply because the narrative demanded the relative uniformity of the single, highly grammatical language of the traditional ruling elites.

In his seminal "On the Margin: Postmodernism, Ironic History, and Medieval Studies," Lee Patterson suggests that postmodernism, whose virtue is to inscribe difference as a positive feature of History and thus bypass the sort of effacements and palimpsests that have so brutally disfigured the medieval period, will give medievalists (if they are willing to seize the moment) the theoretical and discursive means to alter in positive ways the place of medieval literature in our canons. I believe that Patterson is suggesting that the medieval period should now be the beneficiary of the qualities of postmodernism, as a historical construct, that have been used in what we call the modern period to break the back of the *grands récits* and to see difference where the Renaissance paradigm sees binarism and evolution. In other words, to hold in abeyance the values of the Renaissance paradigm. The first revelation that this nonevolutionary view virtually pushes onto center-stage is that the horror of the medieval period is what we would in any other context unhesitatingly label as postmodernism itself. In his role as arbiter of high cultural standards, Petrarch—who, alone in his own room in the dead of night is very much the lover of vulgarity and scatteredness—and the tradition that follows him all the way into our classrooms is horrified by all the same things that horrify others today: the reveling in pluralities; the refusals to cultivate the great tradition; the writing of literature in the crass dialects instead of in the great literary language; the embrace of the popular and ungrammatical into the exclusive clubs only the learned could once join; an ethnic and religious variety that would be unequaled in Europe thereafter; the secret and unholy alliances with the heterodox "cults," and so forth. In contrast, the reactive posture is that of longing for a golden past when real men were really educated, of lamenting the barbarous society all around us now that the noises of the rabble have been let in as real literature. I am convinced one could translate any one of Petrarch's passages on these subjects and pass it off as a letter to the editor of either *Time* or the *TLS*.

To be able to claim that medieval culture is postmodern—and from this point on I will use that term consistently—at the outset involves rejecting that notion of History that places the highest value on narrativity, causality, evolution, and diachrony. Progress. And, in turn, accepting that these are *not*, except within the master narrative that has so effectively erased the difference of the medieval period, the requirements of History itself. Thus, the criticism, which will doubtless be leveled in any case, that this is an anachronistic association (a favorite accusation when one is anywhere near medievalism) is itself located very much in the heart of the Renaissance narrative, which, let us not forget, both loathed the postmodernist values of much of the medieval period and, concomitantly, sought to obscure the strong readings of the literature produced under those conditions. The anachronism, then, is to allow the powerful contingencies of the paradigms that sought to unwrite the medieval period in order to continue to write it. Beyond this criticism, I must now introduce a number of specific caveats, demurrers, brackets, and restrictions that I hope will clarify the strongly historical specificity of medieval literatures and the cultures that produced them, and that will let us see how starkly lyrical and ungrammatical and revolutionary, at least from time to time, this world could be.

Clearly, the issue is "from time to time," and not all the time—no more than any other culture or any moment of culture can be uniformly anything. (What better case than the Renaissance itself, what better incarnation of the "from time to time" nature of paradigmatic characteristics than Petrarch himself?) In this case, the limitations are particularly crucial, and they are of a temporal and geographic nature, but first and foremost their nature is dialogic. It would be foolish to utterly deny the foundations of the stereotypes of the medieval vision we have inherited, to say there were no superstitious monks or pious copyists. Those are the features that have allowed us to talk about the Middle Ages in a way that both makes it fit into the Western continuum but diminishes its value vis-à-vis that which comes before and after. I am suggesting that we see there *was* a strong counterculture in a precarious agon with the strong institutional cultures of the time. While medievalist scholarship has hardly failed to identify and study the key aspects of the insubordinate character in the little drama—in this book I will deal with the vernacular lyric, which I think is very much the young and bad rebel—this insubordination is all too often read and set out in ways that make it respectable again. This occurs because of the instinct of medieval scholarship to see everything as "medieval": traditional, religious, respectful. No less, it occurs because of the effects of some of the distortions of time and history constructed as a narrative and as development: that is, because the troubadours succeeded so well in their radical project, they not only were assimilated into the mainstream narrative, but they were made part of the line of venerable ancestors.

But the caveat is that the disobedient child exists when there is a parent and rules to follow. And the story of the Middle Ages has been written as if in that period there were only old people, and whatever children were around were either perfectly obedient or never amounted to much. I am far more interested in the very bad children who amounted to a great deal, but whose voices have been heard far less strongly—and then only in scholarship that is itself at the margins of the project of writing large the history of Western literature.

The other two principal limitations in my argument coincide to some extent with more traditional subdivisions, as well as with much thinking on refining the contours of that vast periodization of "The Middle Ages." First, as to time. The use of the unadorned "medieval" will mean, with rough edges, the tenth through the thirteenth centuries. The rough edges correspond to all those obvious variations that have made periodization such a tricky business and so doomed it to failure if the highly frontierlike nature of the temporal map is not fully appreciated. In this case, the shifting frontiers are also geographical, and I have drawn a map of what I think of as the heartland of the lyric: from al-Andalus in the southwest through Provence at the center to Sicily and Tuscany in the east. This map, all too clearly shaped by the contours of the Mediterranean, runs along its rocky shores, and it was, until he reached the frontier of Italy, the sort of map of *languedoc* that Dante conjures up in the *De vulgari eloquentia.* The map I have drawn leaves northern France out of this study, as well as what are now England and Germany in most of their contours, but it is not a grievous limitation since this map is precisely the one that hangs in most high-culture classrooms in which we find "The Middle Ages."

But there is a far more complex problem in the temporal limits I have suggested, since we are left with the vexing difficulty of what to call (and do with) that roughly two-century period, the fourteenth and fifteenth centuries, that is almost invariably lumped with the Middle Ages but which is in all its textures so different from the preceding period. If we were able to resolve the temporal problem more satisfactorily, the mapping of space and sounds I have suggested would be all the easier to see, since the two have some striking correspondences.

So what do we call this other "middle age"? From all sorts of perspectives it is clear why no one wants it in their camp—and why the Renaissance people, who have been setting most of the rules, have made sure they did not get stuck with it, even though this period does come after Petrarch, who is so foundational a figure. In part, this reluctance stems from the superb loveliness of 1492 itself, which would make having the Renaissance or the modern age start at any other moment not nearly as memorable. There it is, the perfect year in which to start a new universe: just enough years off the exact turn of the century to be precise but still poetic, and then that remarkable syzygy of transparently monumental events, the diaspora, the discovery, Lorenzo's death in Florence. But there is also the fact that those two centuries, the fourteenth and the fifteenth, are the most "medieval" in some of the worst senses of the stereotype. It is the time of the catastrophic effects of the Black Death, which reigned over much of Europe during those centuries and created palpable darkness and a host of cruel repressions where there once had been tolerance. And precisely because this period constitutes *at least* as severe a break from the ethos of the previous centuries as it does from the later ones I specifically exclude it from my own axiomatic definitions of "medieval" in this study. For the picture I wish to paint, it is critical to understand that when Petrarch mutters about the horror of it, it is *not* the repressions and devastations of the fourteenth and fifteenth centuries he is looking at. It is regrettable, for many reasons, that the problem has remained unresolved terminologically, despite widespread recognition of the remarkably severe ruptures and radical differences in aesthetic and moral values. On one side of the divide, we have the time that was the Golden Age of the Jews, to pluck out one example from many, as well as a moment of astonishing, "surprising" tolerance for homosexuality. On the other side, there are the severe persecutions of both those groups. If there are rips in the fabric of history, then surely the one here is among the most glaring.

Where, then, does this leave poor old Columbus? Will we be reduced to calling him a "fourteenth-fifteenth century" man? Names sometimes are everything. And the figure of Columbus has always fascinated, within the traditional narrative, not only because of his undisputed foundational status but precisely because while he makes a gift to us of his discovery of the modern era, like Moses or Dante's

Virgil he is not himself, for reasons that always seem hard to fully accept, really a part of that brave New World. Or, as Todorov puts it, much as others have: "Columbus himself is not a modern man, and this fact is pertinent to the course of the discovery, as though the man who was to give birth to a new world could not yet belong to it."[14] And there is, indeed, a small but telling strain of Columbus and New World studies that has focused on what, at first glance, might appear to be something much like the subject of this book: the "medievalness" of Columbus himself, of the project that led to his discovery of the Americas, and of the first stages of Hispanic culture in Latin America.

But the principal difference between what these studies do and what I believe I am doing lies precisely in the root definition of "medieval." The "medievalism" that is ascribed to Columbus, or to the plans for his trip, or to the features of life in New Spain in its first several hundred years, is that "medievalism" drawn largely from the landscapes and portraits of the fourteenth and fifteenth centuries. It is distinctly, even pitiably, pre- or unmodern (as the Todorov quotation makes clear), and it is Columbus's astonishing (and obviously unmodern) piety, and most of all that crusading spirit formed in the Reconquest—these and other comparable qualities help shape the trip and, in the aftermath, the new land. The *Reconquista* is that construct of Spanish historiography so starkly like the Petrarchan one: the horror at the immediate past, the desire to imitate and restore the distant and prelapsarian (before the barbarians invaded) past, purer and more "really" Spanish. In the Spanish context, however, a new and powerful twist is added. A small and brave band realized from the very start that the corruptions had to be resisted, and they began the fight to expel the Moors, to "reconquer" the real Spain, before the initial fighting of the Conquest was even over.

The sonorous connection between Conquest and Reconquest has suggested other connections, but this link is based, evidently enough, on the more than dubious notion that the Reconquista *was* the medieval ethos in Iberia and was thus the most fundamental condition of the Spanish *mentalité.* This is a widely accepted construct (whose major advocate has been the Spanish historian Claudio Sánchez Albornoz), and it has endured, at least in part, because it so neatly dovetails with the rest of the paradigm of what the Middle Ages are supposed to have been like. In Spain, we see the staunchest of Catholics in pitched and endless battles against the infidels, ever since 712. In one of the classic works of scholarship setting out the basic features of this transfer of the "medieval" from the Old World to the New (and it is worth noting that it comes from a lecture given to the Medieval Academy of America), Luis Weckmann minces no words in his descriptions: "some of the old medieval trends, perhaps nowhere stronger than in Spain, the land of perennial crusading, greatly influenced the early course of Latin American life. That should not surprise anyone. Forced to remain long in the background of European evolution, due to her almost constant state of warfare . . . [and so forth]."[15]

But the very foundations of this notion of what constitutes the salient shared feature of medieval Spain and the New Spain abroad, the supposedly central and shaping value of the drive to rid the peninsula of Muslims, is among the most distorted—and distorting—images of the medieval world, both within the very fluid boundaries of what would come to be called Spain, and in the rest of Europe. Because I have argued this case extensively elsewhere, and because it has been argued well by others, beginning with Américo Castro, of course, I will not rehearse here again the substantial evidence against the view of the *Reconquista* as the axiological heartland of medieval Spain. But one crucial observation does need to be reiterated. As a meticulous and fully detailed 1977 study by Charles Gibson points out, in the course of repudiating the entire Conquista-Reconquista link, the existence of any kind of contemporary notion of a "Reconquista" does not come into existence until well into the thirteenth century. And even then, the evidence for it as a "psychological sense" is both tenuous and scattered. Even texts, like the *Cantar de mio Cid,* blithely described by most as part of the "crusades" or Reconquista, serve instead as unambiguous evidence that while there was all sorts of fighting against all sorts of enemies, the Reconquista construct is nowhere in sight: "mientre que sea el pueblo de moros / e de la yente cristiana . . ." (v. 901). Even to the extent to which one would be convinced that it existed strongly and uniformly in the fourteenth and fifteenth centuries, and that aspects of it do shape and define the Conquest of the New World, the "medieval" I am working with is the medieval that the Reconquista was battling. The Reconquista, as the ideological construct that pits itself against al-Andalus, is not only *not* medieval, it is as *anti*-medieval as they come.

Several simple examples reveal pointedly how the same textual details can be read in dramatically different ways. First, take Columbus himself and his own languages and ethnicity, as I have sketched it out in the first pages of this book. The conventional narrative has suppressed, in different ways, the disruptive details. Columbus's being a man of a thousand dialects is effectively hidden beneath a text of orthodox grammaticality; the strong external indications that at least his mother's family was Jewish are ignored altogether as either silly arguments made by those with a cause (that is, Jews) or "irrelevant"; and the internal textual indications of his being a *converso,* elegantly detailed by the distinguished historian Juan Gil, are taken as indications of his overbearingly "medieval" Christian piety. The point in reviewing these aspects of the person of Columbus himself is that even in reading the smallest details of the story we have obeyed the rules of the Renaissance paradigms: we are conditioned to see most vividly those features that are the links to the earliest golden years of achievement and clarity, and we are inclined to erase the messy and cacophonous and painfully disruptive medieval world. So, again, my suggestion here is that we remember with that different kind of Memory that was so medieval: let us listen to the echoes, in some cases quite remote now because the projects of purification were so effective, of the dialects and of the half-Jews, and let us esteem them *in the same measure* they were privileged in the medieval period, from the tenth through the twelfth centuries, rather than despise them in the mode that begins afterward. Let us not continue to be the narrators of the Reconquista.

Two other small details in the reading of 1492 and its immediate aftermath are worth rehearsing here. The first I have already revealed: the fact that the party Columbus assembled included an Arabic translator (a *converso,* undisputedly). This detail is almost universally left out of the standard narrations, or at best thrown in as an aside, a little note (although it can have something of an ironic and comic ring to it, particularly in the remarkable attempted conversation with the Taíno chieftain). The reasons why it is so unknown, so excluded, should by now need no belaboring, but let me point out that a medieval reading of the detail (rather than the incongruous fourteenth- and fifteenth-century reading) reveals with limpid clarity that Arabic was accepted with matter-of-factness for what it was, the lingua franca of the civilized world—since Columbus, of course, expected to find precisely that at the other end of the ocean. What is most telling is that this real and symbolic commonplace of the twelfth century (although that too is far from fully absorbed into the standard narrative of the medieval period—again, for obvious reasons) is acted out with candor and fullness in the flush of the last victory of the "Reconquista," the taking of Granada early in 1492. The routine and unremarkable inclusion of the translator is an act that is read with difficulty as part of a trip severely conditioned by an expansive Reconquest. How much easier, instead, to read it as an act that is, in effect, indulging in the perhaps unconscious and nostalgic pretense that the world was not changing in all the ways it really was changing—a sad end effected not by any *medieval* religious oppression but by the forces whose most powerful markers lie on the other side of the transition, on the other side of the historical tear.

The other detail is one that, quite unlike the story of the translator, has been widely cited as a prime example of the "Reconquista" mentality of the "Conquista." Cortés, in his *Relación* to Charles V, compares the province of Tlaxcala, Mexico, with Granada and, crucially, refers to Mexican Indian temples as *mezquitas* (mosques). To see these analogies as representing the mind-set of a *Reconquista* we must, first of all, put aside the fact that in its natural features much of Mexico does look stunningly like much of Andalucía; we also must set aside the fact that there is a simple descriptive need here that can be satisfied only by analogy to the visual universe known by the Spanish monarch (who had no way of imagining the topography or architecture of an extremely remote universe). We are left to assume, then, that the detail of the "mosque" itself, to describe the place of worship of a group of people who are not Christians, is so extraordinary and unusual that it can only mean that the Aztecs are seen as if they were Arabs and the conquest as reconquest.

But this reading betrays only how foreign and unusual *we*, the heirs of the "Reconquista" narrative, see the mosque as being. For Cortés, as well as for the king and others for whom the *relación* is intended, it is clear that the mosque is a commonplace and readily visualized feature of the skyline—the perfectly predictable analogy for a Spaniard to use when describing a building used by non-Christians as a temple of worship. The irony is that it sounds so peculiar because *we* are not used to seeing mosques and thus hear great significance in the analogy. Indeed, one peculiar feature of the very un-monolithic stages of the struggles in the medieval period is that mosques were from time to time merely reconsecrated as temples of Christian worship—hence, the famous Cathedral of Córdoba, the adopted mosque. *Mesquitas* were, often enough, Christian temples as well, adding to the utter ordinariness of the thing. Beyond that there is the *for us* extraordinary *mudejarism* of so much of the grand architecture of Christian Spain: churches built that look like mosques where there never were any mosques because that was the style of high culture. The use of the mosque as a guide to his monarch to how he might envision what Mexico looked like is, if anything, an indication of the *opposite* of what it has been taken to mean; it is palpable evidence of how late it was before the "Reconquista"—which is not a medieval phenomenon at all—became so total and obliterating of the still visible diversity of the architectural landscape, of the last remaining memory traces of the world of tolerable diversity in the imagination and lexicon of a man like Cortés.

It turns out, then, that, in crucial ways, the medieval world I see resonating in 1492 and its children in the New World is a virtual opposite of what our thesauruses suggest, of what the grand récit has needed. Here, mosques are around every corner, and the Other lives next door, and all manner of unwritten languages are heard in the marketplace in the early morning. Here, literature struggles and dances around with all manner of cultural alternatives, sometimes, in difficult conflict. To know that the first major writer of Latin America, the Inca Garcilaso, is a half-breed—Inca mother, Spanish father—who writes in the paternal tongue in order to save the mother's history—until then oral—is to know and hear again hundreds of details of the universe of the *muwashshaḥāt,* where the scattered and vulgar songs of Christian girls are saved, made into written texts, because they marry the Poets, that male classical Arabic tradition that has written History. This, however, is a History that has carved Memory itself, that lover's love song, into its heart. This is the kind of History that embraces Memory even when it is made up of heartbreak—love songs are never anything else, nor are family romances—that is as medieval as Dante writing the *De vulgari eloquentia;* this the defense of the songs of the *lingue materne,* written in the formidable paternal *grammatica.*

And while the view until now has been that it is the crusade against Otherness that is the medieval heritage in the New World, a far stronger case can be made that it is a literary culture that is rooted in the multiplicity of Others all around. And whereas the impulse has been to see in the move across the sea the extension of the victory march of those who rendered Spain pure and unilingual, I see the poignant and revealing tie as that of the exiles. Somewhere, deep in his heart and in his memory, we must imagine the Inca Garcilaso taking solace, sharing both cultural ambivalence and the exile that seems to go with that, with all manner of spiritually or culturally or ethnically half-breed Europeans before him: the converts to Islam who were Ibn Hazm's not-so-remote ancestors and Ibn Hazm himself, heartbroken by the destruction of his beloved Córdoba by other Muslims; Dante, writing the *Commedia* in brutal exile, across a desert from the beloved Florence; the Cid, stranger in a strange land, exiled by Christians, ruler over Muslims; and, in the Inca's own time, which Spanish historiography calls the "Golden Age," in unknowing echo of *the* Golden Age of Sefarad, Sephardic writers like Abraham Cohen de Herrera, writing in Spanish, in Amsterdam; most of all, perhaps, he could still hear the echoes of the songs of Judah Halevi, devout Jew, superb singer of the Andalusian songbook, who exiles himself from Sefarad to go and find Jerusalem. His songs of the sea would have made superb music on Columbus's trips.

4

This wind of yours is a perfumed wind, o West.
with saffron in its wings, and apple scent,
as if it came from the perfumer's chest,
not from the chest of the winds.

The wings of swallows flutter to your breath.
You set them free,
like myrrh-tears, from a bundle poured.
And how we long for you, we who ride a wooden board
on the back of the sea!

Never release your grip from the ship
when the day makes its camp, when the day blows away.
Flatten the deep, rip the heart
of the seas, hit the holy mountains
and there take your rest,
O wind of the west!
Shout down the east wind when it makes
the ocean break and creates
a seething pot in the heart of the sea.

What can a man, God's captive, achieve,
who is sometimes shut in and sometimes let free?
All my desire I entrust to Him,
Who shaped the mountains, Who made the wind,
Who knows man's heart and its mysteries.

Judah Halevi (Translated by Raymond P. Scheindlin)

If he did not sing songs like this one, Columbus sang others that charmed the winds and broke the path through the waves, and he made it to Cuba and beyond. Halevi, who wrote superb love poetry to

Jerusalem, did not make it, and he dies at her doorstep—or so the story goes. The end of the story for Columbus has its own sadnesses. He too yearned to see Jerusalem and, the story goes, on the day before he died talked about his long-desired trip there. After he died, in sad obscurity, humiliated and frustrated, his bones would take up the restless travels, going from a first grave in Valladolid, where he had died, to Seville, and then back to the New World, so the story goes. And here, ever so fittingly, everyone claims to have the real thing, and from Old World to New, the temples to the authentic bones are everywhere. The single and true narrative fractures.

This last story of Columbus and the authenticity of his legacy is the story Alejo Carpentier would place at the heart of his last novel, and there it also tells the history of Latin American fiction, obsessed with the question of origins, because, in the New World, across the sea, up the river, and deep in the jungle, the simple story of following in the footsteps of the Greeks and then reinventing Rome could not be told anymore. But, once again, light is shed on the medieval world that fits that simple narrative with equal discomfort. Just as normative readings have made of Columbus the simple Christian of babbling blind faith, the medieval part of this story would no doubt be construed as that odd, vaguely cannibalistic cult of relics. And so it is, in some ways. But no less, it is a whole series of other things—the bones that are restless and searching and that confound easy tagging and that regret they never made it to Jerusalem—that we are used to assuming are ours, as we lie exhausted, done with the grand narrative of European history, postmodern, at the end of the line. But these bones, these lyric fragments, this fragmentation and exile, are exquisitely medieval. Judah Halevi died at Jerusalem's door because, the story goes, he stayed far too long in Egypt, dazzling his hosts with the rhythms of songs invented in the West, songs that made Hebrew poetry dance seductively to the beats of Hispano-Arabic singers and make passionate love and drink wine. Did that make him love Jerusalem less? Did he really repent, as the pious and happy narrative tells us?

In seeing how strikingly the medieval world is what we call postmodern, we see and hear many other things at once: the horror of

Petrarch as he contemplates its many lacks of exclusive authenticity and, then, to tell a story of identity that elides and glosses over the fragments, his discovery—and imitation—of a past that offers cleaner and cooler lines, a unified culture. The terrible problem for him, for many, for a whole notion of History, is embodied in the story of Luis de Torres trying to chat up the Taíno in his Andalusian Arabic. If we are not clearly and cleanly one thing or another, what are we? And if we do not write, and cannot be written about, in the *grammatica,* the great codified languages, then won't we disappear out of both Literature and History? In great measure the answer is that Petrarch was right, and neither Taíno nor the half-Jews—nor, for that matter, the chaos of their conversations—are part of History or Literature, what we call our heritage. They do fall outside its lines; their fractured lyricism, like that of the mystics in many ways, is highly resistant to being narrated. It is like the lesson everyone who tries to teach poetry learns quickly: retelling a sonnet makes it not a sonnet anymore.

But the other answer is implicit in this one, and it clearly lays out that what we are grappling with here are values. Just as we can find other ways of "teaching" poetry, if we believe that teaching itself need not necessarily mimic and carry on the totalizing narrative, we could choose to define History, and then practice it, in ways that did not either flatten the sonnet or leave it out altogether. It is clear that Petrarch grappled most painfully with this dilemma. Long were the nights he stayed up until dawn, writing superb love sonnets in the vernacular, and then he got up in the morning and lamented the fragmentation of the self that the invention of the sonnet and poetry in the vernaculars had wrought on his culture, his age. And he called his lyrics the *Rerum vulgarium fragmenta,* most telling of titles that reveals the horrors—the common street vernacular, the fragmentation of self, the echoes of other poets who cannot be arranged in order of precedence or chronology anymore but surface as they will, in the poems that call them up—in the language of his narrative and his idealized past, taut and orderly Latin. As I have said elsewhere, it is a pity that we have clung so much to what Petrarch preached (and, indeed, fashioned a whole History from it) and so little to what his poetry tells us about the other History, the one made up of the languages of songs and the rooms full of poets where kinship counts and one's place on the orderly time line is but a shallow banality for those who know nothing about poetry. This is the culture of exile and invention—not of imitation and discovery.

So, if we turn to the basic question once again and ask whether it is possible to tell History in the lyrical mode—or doesn't the Petrarchan example prove that the narrative is indispensable—the answer is that we may choose to value and privilege one or the other, and, moreover, that the postmodern construct of History is not only *not* our invention, but one that once shaped a world of difference and dialects as colorful as our own. Indeed, a postmodern culture that flatters itself on being the first to attempt to construct an authentic self from cultural fragments should look first at the medieval world that has been kept from sight, underneath the Latin and the pious Christianity, and there we would see the accommodation of chaos and its transformation into the *trobar clus;* the disdain of simplistic temporality and the kabbalistic belief in the far more powerful principle of textuality; and the relativism that is bred, long before contempt, by seeing minarets in the skyline, and not finding them odd just because you are a Christian. The oddity and the fear come only when we are the narrators of the Reconquista—or whatever other narrative orthodoxy values uniform standards and true and universal values—and when we become afraid of invention, and everyone around us is the same, so that we cannot even imagine exile.

But we benefit doubly, symbiotically, from the adoption of the historical mode that makes "anachronism" a nonsense term. Although we have largely forgotten how to read the mosaics of the medieval world in the Columbus stories, the New World retells these stories with love and irony, and Carpentier and his readers see in themselves the poignancy and the richness of the wanderings about and the multiple authenticities. The light refracted from reading the texts of the New World is of particular value for medievalists because the reading and the narrating of those New World texts have not yet banished them from our present, from our personal memories. Not enough time and change and imitation of a purer past have gone by—and perhaps in the New World they never will—because we are always surrounded by different colors and accents. Memory has not yet been dissipated or dismissed; in fact, among communities of exiles, which are this New World so much of the time, History is never allowed to be divorced from Memory. We have not yet had time or inclination to forget Carpentier's accents and Guillén's blackness, and since we have not yet imagined the Rock tradition as classicized and fossilized, we can still clearly hear its melding of the multiple voices into the standard beats. The horses have not yet been jettisoned in the Horse Latitudes—although many have wanted to abandon them, and maybe one or two have been sacrificed, but certainly not all of them. True sailing is not yet dead.

With equal clarity, I think, we can see the constant struggle, the insistent demands from others, from within ourselves, that we find a simple way of defining ourselves, of telling a neat story with a satisfying ending, even if that endeavor means the sacrifice of the powerful but wild creatures, those odd beasts that must certainly be weighing down the ship and making the winds die down. And the lesson to be learned from hearing the other side of the Petrarchan program, the great love of the songs that (as Petrarch tells us) were sung at neighborhood joints in vulgar accents, is precisely that the great struggle is there. The problem is that the master narrative copes poorly with all this and talks, instead, about darkness or writes over it—thus, the palimpsest of our "age of darkness." So it is in the revelation of the lyricism that not only is the lyric itself revealed, but also its struggle with orthodoxies and institutions. At the same time, then, we are reconstituting History and Memory so that they are not different from ourselves. The arrangement of our texts and our authors is no longer the arbitrary and distancing one of an impersonal time line, but rather one that the narrative will see as fragments, out of order. It is based on value and love and desire and priorities. Objectivity is revealed to be a hollow pretense, and we cease to yearn for distance and seek intimacy instead. Perhaps it is that exile and the tugs of dispersal make us cling more fiercely to our poetry and to that scattering of kindred souls it brings into our hearts.

There is another Columbus story, close at hand, written yesterday by a man whose life and cultures are distinctly medieval—and postmodern. Salman Rushdie is like a kaleidoscope of medieval life stories; he is the cosmopolitan and secular Muslim, the multilingual European listened to avidly in London or Bologna, the al-Andalus savagely invaded and repressed by Almoravids because of such decadence, the library at Córdoba burned, the escape from the grand narrative and the resurfacing as Scheherazade, with stories told to save his life. And now, in tribute to the lyricism of 1492—a small memory buried far beneath the many grand narratives that 1992 would produce, thrown overboard in the Horse Latitudes—he offers us, as Carpentier did, a fistful of moments stolen out of the smooth history. A story, one day, appears in the *New Yorker:* "Christopher Columbus and Queen Isabella of Spain Consummate Their Relationship, Santa Fé, January 1492." The wrenching opening line gives us a universe in the palm of a hand: "Columbus, a foreigner, follows Queen Isabella for an eternity without entirely giving up hope." And as in *El arpa y la sombra,* Carpentier's novel of Columbus where the explorer is having a mad and lusty affair with the Queen, and as in the poetry of Halevi or his brother, Jaufré Rudel, in Provence, who writes the poetry of *amor de lonh,* and teases us with the Princess across the sea, desire for Isabella herself, and for the ships to sail the ocean blue are all dangerously, hopelessly intertwined. "The search for money and patronage," Columbus says, "is not so different from the quest for love." And later: "The loss of money and patronage," Columbus says, "is as bitter as unrequited love." Isabella is the grand narrative, she is great modern History, "She is Isabella, all-conquering Queen," and Columbus, the supplicant, is a thorn in her side: the insolent foreigner who speaks the language imperfectly, who sings songs outside her window; he is raucous, multicolored, and the two of them are profoundly unalike, sonnet to description: "Columbus at Isabella's court is quickly burdened with the reputation of a crazy man. His clothes are excessively colorful and he drinks, also, to excess. When Isabella wins a military victory she celebrates it with eleven days of psalms and the sonorous severities of priests. Columbus crashes about outside the cathedral waving a wineskin."

He desires her, knows it is in her power to give him what will give meaning to life: "Invisible in hot tropical colors, unrequited, he remains, dogging her footsteps, hoping for the ecstasy of her glance." Isabella cannot imagine that she wants him, and, when Rushdie gives us her stern version of events, we hear only the purposeful, the victorious. Listen to the Queen tell us about herself: "*She is omnipotent. Castles fall at her feet. The Jews have been expelled. The Moors prepare their last surrender. The Queen is at Granada, riding at her army's head. She overwhelms.*" But she is also bored, and, Columbus imagines, her ring finger, where so much power is displayed, was perhaps touched when he dared kiss it: "tentacles of warmth spread backward from her fingers toward her heart." And, crucially, it turns out that her great power, her control over History and her ability to dismiss Columbus are compromised because her dreams are prophecies, and Columbus, who has given up, leaving "the Jews to the ships of their exile, waiting in the harbor of Cadiz," has a dream. "He dreams of Isabella, languidly exploring the Alhambra, the great jewel she has seized from Boabdil, last of the Nasrids," and it turns out the dream is of her dream, where she realizes that she needs him. And although Columbus, in his version of the dream, indulges in playing hard to get, to make her beg, to deliver "Poetic justice," in the end he swallows the bitter refusal and tells her messengers, Yes, I'll come.

Rushdie has blessed us here with a hundred questions, with a rich and sustained lyrical tale, with a coat of as many and as lush colors as that of his Columbus. It is true that this Columbus, like Rushdie himself, we cannot avoid thinking, swallows his pride and his resistance at the end and goes off to her, to be a part of her history, of the great narrative which, he certainly knows, will make him great but ordinary, take the love out of the story. But Rushdie—that same Rushdie who said yes, yes, I'll come and embraced Islam—has shown us that it can be told so that the bits and pieces left out of the story we hear as schoolchildren are put back in. Now we see the glimmers, Isabella's enormous vulnerability, and we know the great passion that will have drenched the consummation; we grasp now that Columbus was an odd foreigner who sang love songs outside her window. Best of all, we see the untellable power of visions and hermetic poetry, which have been banished from the story as told by the great modern narrative. And Rushdie tells us—no, shows us—that the story can be written so that it comes out the same, so that Columbus gets his ships and sails the ocean blue, but so that we also know that at the heart of the story, and History, was the still-hot Memory of Columbus's lips on Isabella's finger, and the dream in the middle of the night, in the courtyard with the stone lions facing outward instead of in.

Notes

1. Greene, *The Light in Troy,* page 3.
2. Greene, *The Light in Troy,* page 34.
3. Wilson, "The Form of Discovery," page 167, note 14.
4. Greene, *The Light in Troy,* page 53.
5. Patterson, "On the Margin," page 87.
6. González Echevarría, "La literatura desde el barrio de Cocosolo."
7. Brann, "The Hebrew Girdle Poem," page 381.
8. González Echevarría, "Guillén as Baroque," pages 304–305.
9. González Echevarría, "Guillén as Baroque," page 305.
10. Stern, *Hispano-Arabic Strophic Poetry,* page 131.
11. González Echevarría, "Guillén as Baroque," pages 311–312.
12. Shusterman, "Postmodernism and the Aesthetic Turn," page 605.
13. Todorov, *The Conquest of America,* page 5.
14. Todorov, *The Conquest of America,* page 12.
15. Weckmann, "The Middle Ages," page 130.

II SCANDAL

If only in the land of dreams and mirrors
I had sea ports,
if only I had a ship
remnants of a city,
if only I had a city
in the land of children
the land of lamentation.

I would have them melted down
into ingots
for the wound
I would have coined a song
like a spear
piercing the trees, the stones, the sky
a song
supple like water
untamable
as bewildered
as conquest

Adonis, ***Mihyar of Damascus, His Songs***
(translated by Michael Beard
and Adnan Haydar)

1. Love and Mercy

(iv)
A man and a woman
Are one.
A man and a woman and a blackbird
Are one.

(viii)
I know noble accents
And lucid, inescapable rhythms;
But I know, too,
That the blackbird is involved
In what I know.

From Wallace Stevens
"Thirteen Ways of Looking at a
Blackbird"

In the beginning, the bird is all things: Zen object of contemplation, singer like the poet himself, solitary like the soul—or is it God?—mourning witness to the lover's blight, innocent, joyful beauty itself—or is that the Lover? They are clan brothers (some say it is a cabal) these poets and birds, survivors from forever, from the age of dinosaurs, but they are still, stark on the horizon. They keep us guessing: is he our soul? is she my lover? is she the singer? Does he clarify? Does he mystify? Will he fly away, just as I thought I finally had him in sight?

The fierce dance between the lyric, always modern and birdlike, sitting alone at the top of the tree, and the narratives of histories, which need to hold the lyric tightly and closely and surely, takes place not just in that larger arena which is the wrestling for place of pride in the longest narration. It is perhaps always true that the lyric is constantly engaged in the onerous but exhilarating struggle with the myriad institutions that surround it, and the grand narrative, written hundreds of years later, is but one of them, the one that is the future and thus perhaps most powerful. But within the immediate historical contingency, the modernism of the lyric is wrested from its struggle with both the past, from which it must invent a new present, and the present itself, whose many powerful and orthodox languages crowd around, trying to interpret, explain, control.

At different times and places we can see these stark modernisms of the lyric fully articulated: the wonderful paradox (in what is perhaps Paul de Man's most powerful reading) that is the creation of History itself, a beginning, by trying to destroy ties with a weaker history, the mere past. While those who are professional "modernists" must understand many, perhaps most, of these terms at some level of metaphor, it is the medievalist whose raw material is most literally—as well as lyrically—foundationalist and modernist: lyric poetry that literally, utterly, refuses the paternal tongue, that literally invents and creates the new languages of literature. Thus, one might even audaciously suggest that in significant ways modernism itself is being created, the supreme moment of destruction of a linguistic past and translucent creation of a new foundation—and the lyric thereafter would be but an echo, a metaphor, and a memory of that moment, the whole bit from Wordsworth to Stevens belated. Heady times, these, on those rocky shores of the Mediterranean. But let us not begin with headiness and the often arrogant glow of triumph that are the first years, the first generations. Instead, let us begin in the whirlwind, in madness—at the moment when the love lyric appears to have become something else. In the thirteenth century in the Iberian peninsula we are drawn to the extraordinarily eloquent example of how, from the whirlwinds of political madness, rare souls will surface to preach seemingly naive messages of love. Between them, Ibn ʿArabī and Ramon Llull lived that century-long period of pivot and closure, from the end of the twelfth to the beginning of the fourteenth centuries.

When Ibn ʿArabī was born in Murcia in 1165, al-Andalus was a substantial and substantially intact kingdom under the Almohads, and he spent thirty years living and studying in a Seville that was still in great measure the glorious Seville of the Taifas. The politically turbulent but culturally explosive period of the Taifas, or city-states, defined the better part of the eleventh century in Spain, and it ended when, following the Castilian occupation of Toledo in 1085, the Almoravids invaded the peninsula and presided over a violent and reactionary period whose many and varied intolerances prefigured the events of coming centuries. The eventual disintegration of Almoravid control led to yet a second invasion from the other side of the straits, an invasion that found its justification in unification of Muslim states and in restoration of the orthodoxies. And the Almohads, with their restoration of the caliphate, give a semblance of Arabic political form to the twelfth century in the peninsula—a form clearly not destined to last.

Ibn ʿArabī is thus born into an al-Andalus where both the ruins and the sweet memories of the past lie side by side. As if in response, he becomes a great traveler, within and without the peninsula. In Murcia, shortly after a last meeting with Ibn Rushd, who the West knows as Averroës, the most influential philosopher in Europe in his lifetime and well beyond (I will return to that meeting), the strongly lyrical Ibn ʿArabī has a dream vision that urges him to abandon his homeland and sends him off to the East, as it would turn out, forever. When he dies in Damascus in 1240, his homeland existed no more. Córdoba had already been in Christian hands for a half-dozen years, and Murcia and Seville, his two Spanish homes, would also be lost as Muslim cities within the decade—Murcia in 1243 and Seville in 1248. Bittersweetness and ironies abound. By the middle of the century the reign of Alfonso X would mean massive projects of both translation and history, and in both of these one might readily see that, while the Alfonsine propagation of Arabic texts to the rest of Europe was to inject incalculable vigor into the Christian/Latin cultures on the rise (and thus provide a final and binding measure of Arab ancestry that is still largely unacknowledged), these are also unambiguous signs of the end of the line for the Spanish Muslims and their culture.

But polymorphic culture is not yet extinguished, and in a different part of the peninsula the second half of the thirteenth century would yield a spirit and a scholar astonishingly like the remarkable Ibn ʿArabī. Five years before Ibn ʿArabī's death, a kindred soul had been born in Mallorca, a Mallorca reconquered only a few years before and still largely populated by both Muslims and Jews. The story of Ramon Llull's long life is as good as any of the convoluted and remarkable romances of which he would write the first, in Catalan—thus establishing an important popular literary fad that would reach its peak in the newly translated and rehabilitated *Tirant lo Blanc.* Llull, who seems never to have passed over the opportunity to write (especially when there was a good story to be told), narrated the first of many versions of his life in an autobiography dated 1311 when he was already old and living for a while among the monks of the charterhouse of Vauvert, near Paris. It is vintage romance: the brilliant young man picked out for special favors and training at the court of James I of Mallorca, and then of his son, James II, to whom the precocious Llull had been tutor; lusty years as a troubadour; a well-made marriage; then the magic and crucial turning point, as described by Manuel Durán. "He was immersed in the writing of a lascivious poem inspired by a lady he was intent on seducing when the clear image of Christ on the cross appeared before his eyes not once but five times. He took it as a warning from Heaven to forsake his frivolous life. . . ."[1] (To the provocation of his conversion, we will return.) Meanwhile, the classic and archetypal retreat from the life he had led follows, but crucial aspects of it are contingently part of the story of medieval Europe. Llull spent the decade after his conversion becoming so proficient in Arabic that when he began to write, when he came out of his ten years of wandering among books to find the answers, he did so in a remarkably fluent Arabic.

He emerges from those ten years of desert, and he sets out preaching an almost completely unintelligible *Ars*—this, his infamous *Ars Magna,* his magical book to end all books—that got him in trouble with authorities everywhere, including (perhaps one should say especially) with the powers that be within a Church often distinctly uncomfortable with his idiosyncratic proselytizing. While the historical record is abundantly comfortable with the figure of Llull as a species of intellectual crusader against Islam, the narratives smoothly omit both his astonishing knowledge of Arabic (to a degree and extent that have conspicuously little to do with any simple or naive missionary effort) and his equally conspicuous heterodoxies, lurking among which, for example, is the ease with which he absorbs and reflects the rudiments of the vibrant heterodoxies of both Islam and Judaism—the Sūfis and the kabbalists—that so distinctively shape the culture of both Provence and al-Andalus in that period. In fact, from the beginning and until several centuries after his death, Llull's work and views were strongly opposed by the Church's watchdogs; the Dominican campaign against him eventually resulted in his papal censure and the banning of scores of his works. None of this is surprising since even a cursory and naive look at the writings (and astonishing, kabbalistic drawings) that Llull believed central to his doctrines reveals strong symbolic and epistemological affinities with the other arcane underworlds in which his doctrines of magic writing and God as Lover would have been well-received. Actually, it is far more surprising, in the end, that modern scholarship has gone as far out of its way as it has to rehabilitate Llull and render him not only orthodox, but an exemplary defender of Christianity.

Even when and where Llull dies is novelistic, ambiguous, and controversial—although these facts, too, have become part of the story that has been cleaned up. The original, compelling story is that he died in 1316 in what is now Tunis, but a competing version maintains that the first story is a myth and that the itinerant was not stoned to death in Bougia but rather "died of natural causes in Majorca at age 84."[2] A different legend, serving different needs. Within either of these versions, however, the world at hand was vastly different from what it had been when Llull had first sung his love songs in *languedoc,* had first learned to read and write with the Arabs, had first traveled the neighborhoods of kabbalists. Nothing but a politically besieged and morally embattled Granada was left to bear odd witness for the next two centuries to the richly polyvalent world of Iberia which had nourished both a Llull and an Ibn ʿArabī. And even that witness was a witness to failure. Granada retreated to its own orthodoxies, both to lick its many wounds and to save its skin, and it became more purely Arabic and Islamic than anything in Spain had been for centuries.

In the historical narrative, these two men, whose scattered reflections are in equal measures encyclopedic and lyrical, are largely overshadowed by the other encyclopedist of the age, Alfonso the Wise, who, in stark contrast to Ibn ʿArabī and Llull, ably wielded both political power and the totalizing historical narrative. Without a doubt, Alfonso's most enduring and significant achievement was the creation of a strong narrative language for the new nation he was carving out; and from the obsessive and massive histories of the world, the universe, the homeland, that he was shaping and creating, Castilian emerged abundantly victorious. Only when he needed a respite from the loneliness of such grand history, when he wanted to sing a love song, did Alfonso momentarily abandon the powerful mistress he had created and turn to the sort of bird language, a delicate and melodious Galician, that his contemporaries, the Murcian and the Mallorcan, would have sung along with. But there were only a handful of songs to be sung, all together, one evening; for the rest, the other two men are allied in ways that set them apart crucially from Alfonso. They were itinerant, no doubt eccentric, wise, politically powerless. And Llull and Ibn ʿArabī, both of them to be remembered as exemplary mystics, have left us superb poetic testimonies of their vision of a unifying Love. Out of a moment of rapidly encroaching intolerance, they created a breath of something—fusions and unions—far more crucial than mere tolerance or liberalism. It is curious, and not accidental, that each of them, the superbly devout Muslim and the Christian, believed that a reconciliation between their religions was possible and, at the same time, wrote poetic works which suggest that sacred and profane love are no less reconcilable with each other. Love, to paraphrase Ibn ʿArabī, was their religion and their text.

The *Llibre d'amic et amat* (*The Book of the Lover and the Beloved*—hereinafter *Llibre*) is properly a part, chapter 99 to be exact, of Llull's *Llibre d'Evast e Blanquerna,* the romance which is probably the most widely read among his vast corpus of works of virtually every type. It probably was written in 1274, and it coincides with the early years of Llull's conversionary fervor, composed at Miramar. At Miramar the study of Arabic and of Llull's *Ars Magna* were the principal subjects of instruction for the Franciscans who ended up there—both to achieve the greater understanding of Islam that Llull believed was necessary for a reconciliation of the faiths and to train as missionaries. No less significantly, this "collection" of 366 brief observations about a Lover and his Beloved, or about Love (a description that fits Petrarch's *Canzoniere* as glove to hand), was written shortly after the completion of Llull's major work, the *Llibre de contemplació en Déu*, a work originally written in Arabic, then translated into Catalan.

Remarkably, then, Catalan as a prose literary language, like Castilian, is born in translation from the Arabic, and Llull, in this way, is Alfonso's counterpart, although the massive encyclopedic work, as well as the translations, were executed by Llull himself, whereas Alfonso had a far more limited role. Nevertheless, and despite all manner of other manifestations, there are the usual denials of or limitations to the degree of Arabic "influence," particularly to the notion that Llull might be a Sūfi in Christian guise. Thus goes the contention in the introduction by Lola Badía to the 1985 Castilian edition of the *Libro de amigo y amado*, where Sūfi thought is not even classed among the "fuentes claramente detectables," "clearly detectable sources"[3]—despite the explicit acknowledgment of Sūfi inspiration by the narrator, Blanquerna, within the work itself.

Although the *Llibre*, a charming but generically somewhat perplexing book, is Llull's most enduringly popular (no doubt because of its apparent simplicity, brevity, and accessibility, since so much else of his writing is far more hermetic or philosophically difficult), serious study of his work has been carried out primarily by those whose interests are not literary. Or, put more precisely, the critical attention paid to the *Llibre* has seen it, *grosso modo*, as a "version," in the linguistic clothing of "courtly" or other secular love, of Llull's "real" interests and convictions, which have to do with divine love and are not literary but doctrinal. The regnant model comes from the simplest interpretation of the conversionary moment as Llull—the old man in Paris, many times over now the repentant, compunctuous poet—described it: in the midst of writing a poem of forbidden love, he sees Christ and turns to religion. From this fundamental and paradigmatic starting point, the exegetical tradition has cemented two key oppositions, that between profane love and love of God, and, in direct correspondence, that between poetry and doctrine. Thus, the most common approach or interpretation, one fully consonant with the broadest critical tradition that deals with "mystical" poetry, is that of metamorphosis. In this tradition, there is what amounts to a simple substitution of divine for profane; the writer has indulged in a sort of secondary metaphor by imposing spiritual meaning, which is clearly of central (and essentially unambiguous) importance, on the language of courtly love poetry, which is, no less evidently, of secondary importance.

This interpretive model, which distinguishes clearly between the realms of mystical love and religious thought on the one hand, and profane (especially "illicit") love and the trickier hermeneutics of such poetry on the other, is not uniquely applied to Llull's work, although it possibly exists here in an unusually clear form. Llull is almost never studied as a poet as such. A great one-sidedness exists in a scholarly tradition that classifies him as strictly postconversionary, as turned away from the kind of poetry on his desk when he saw the light. Indeed, more often than not, the complex and often puzzling relationships between secular and religious love and their respective lyrics have been handled simplistically by critical traditions that apparently are uncomfortable with ambiguities in this realm. Such treatment has left many unresolved and intriguing problems in the study of both "courtly love" and mystical poetry. By and large, our received methods and their epistemological bases have dictated a neat separation of these as two "distinct" kinds of love and, therefore, a separation of the poetry that sings each of them.

Astonishingly, we hew to this divided model even in those cases in which the inseparability of the two would appear to be precisely the issue and when the poet flaunts the fusion of the "different" loves. Within this exegetical mode, these cases of overlap exist because of the superficial similarities in the phenomenology of "love" and because it is assumed inevitable that poetic language itself will bring to bear certain resemblances of expression. Thus, a certain contamination between the two kinds of love may be found in different periods, specific poets, given poems. But these analytical schemes generally provide that this apparent fusion is one of expression rather than of essence, that the allegory can be revealed. The language of love used for a human lover may be superbly expressive of a certain kind of passionate love for God (this mode of analysis often emerging to deal with "mystical" poetry). Conversely, a language of worship in principle drawn from and suited to the adoration of God will reappear, perhaps faintly blasphemously, in the context of a human relationship (the model that has served the analysis of much "courtly love" poetry). In the end, in the concrete terms of a (presumably) real order of things, the lover loves either God or a mortal, the poem is "about" the love of God or of a mortal lover, but, obviously, the two are not the same. The poet may tease both language and the reader with the possibility of parallels and overlaps, but that is all they are, parallels and overlaps.

However, in the very story of the conversion that Llull recounts—a story already strongly colored by his complex historical relationship with that conversion and with his myriad difficulties with Church watchdogs who suspected him of heterodoxy, as well as with a classic compunctuousness—we can still make out the remarkable difficulties swept away in such a scheme of things. How was it that a poem of profane and illicit love could have been the text to provoke such a conversion? In the classical "Augustinian" mode, and as Llull was fully aware, the conversion is strongly conditioned by the nature of the text that is its trigger. Thus, Augustine recounts his picking up Scripture, and, in an emphatic rewriting, Dante has Francesca and her lover reading and imitating the illicit kiss of Guinevere and Lancelot. For the time being, we will leave aside the even more remarkable and undigested events that have to do with texts read and roads thus taken, the odd fact that after this Christian conversion the newly converted Llull spends ten years learning Arabic and its philosophical traditions well enough to himself begin writing within that tradition.

But the puzzle here, in this version of what we call "mystical" poetry and, on the other side, "love" poetry, is that it is not clear how and why the two modes of expression would be able to serve each other's needs and remain inadequate to serve their own. In other words, it may be plausible to maintain that the lover can adequately express his passion only in the tropes of adoration that his linguistic and religious traditions have refined for praise of the Maker. Conversely, it might appear easy to understand and analyze the impulse to appropriate the language of a lover for the expression of a "lover-like" relationship with God—noting, of course, the problematic tautologies in the descriptive forms themselves. But a distinct problem emerges once one has admitted not only that both modes of expression do exist, but that they may cross paths and stand, in a significant number of cases, as interchangeable. What, then, is the basis for their ontological distinction of which we seem so instinctively sure? As a result, our criticism has been notoriously at pains to deal with a series of texts where the referential distinction between love of God and love of a human lover is not only not clear but explicitly confounded. Thus, the status of the Beatrice of the *Vita nuova,* or that of the elusive "Good Love" of the *Libro de buen amor,* to name just two of the most significant major texts, has evolved and remained the focal point and constant conundrum of Dante and Juan Ruiz criticism.

Curiously, crucially, the critical approaches to these and comparable texts rarely involve a truly serious—a straight-faced and believing—consideration of the real fusion suggested by the language and tropes of such texts. In writing about these kinds of texts it seems implausible to take as true a proposition that is not considered to be true within our own cosmological and belief systems, particularly those vulgarly held to be reasonable. We are particularly reluctant to imagine that major figures who have been largely (even if with difficulty) absorbed into the histories and standards of their institutions might have written grossly heterodox poetry (let alone "actually" held such beliefs). Exegesis (and in this literary criticism is often not easily distinguishable from other types) is there to make things "intelligible," to explain to us why Solomon's bride is "really" the Church. The result is that when we encounter a text—and those I will focus on here are exemplary of this type—which appears to suggest that what in other contexts may be separately identified as God and Lover are actually and essentially indistinguishable, the most substantial implications of the radical proposition are fully avoided. Ironically, but not altogether surprisingly, this approach has meant that much of what is called mystical poetry is read and commented on through the prism of the belief system(s) from which such mysticism explicitly sets itself apart.

Thus, texts that might be read as explicit expressions of the essential fusion between a God and a Lover are read, instead, to conform to a hermeneutic system which may permit the use of the language of one to describe the Other, but within which the distinguishability of the two is an essential, implicit dualism that provides the linguistic framework of veils and representations, one for the Other or One for the other. Here, as elsewhere, all the little touches play a part. Capitalization added by modern editors of the work can and does inscribe a primary level of meaning and interpretation, and more often than not the modern editor and/or translator will capitalize the names of the Lover when it is God and render minuscule the names—often the same—when the name might refer to a human creature. Are we to assume that the reader needs this visual help in distinguishing what is presumably clear (rather than an interpretation)? Or is this practice merely a reflexive piety?

The most general issue at hand, within which are embedded the multiple puzzles of how to read "mystical" poetry such as Llull's and Ibn ʿArabī's, is that of the nature of the relationship between what we tellingly call primary texts versus the secondary texts that constitute criticism and exegesis. What I think is revealed by the almost intractable case of mystical poetry (in this, as in other things, closely allied with the highly hermetic lyric that is another of the "developments" of the vernacular love lyric) is an insidious false modesty at play. What has styled itself "secondary"—and strenuously defends the "merely" explicatory function of literary studies—has in fact taken over the "primary" role. Ibn ʿArabī knew exactly how primary such exegesis could become, how tightly it could control reading, and so he wrote his own exegetical readings for his own hermetic poetry. The exegetical mode's primacy has been instrumental in rendering forms such as the lyric (especially the mystical and hermetic lyric) to conform to the institutional paradigms—to notions of Lover and God, for example, that are part of the fundamental codes of our institutions and "rational" historical narratives. Conversely, and ironically, writing that reacts to other texts within a framework that does not facilely distinguish between texts that require explication and those that provide it, and that do not seek to level and "resolve" the paradoxes and ambiguities of poetic language (and it is crucial to realize that examples of this critical mode come from all historical periods and are certainly not the invention of "deconstruction"), are generally perceived as failing to give the primary, poetic text its due primacy. But how do we imagine we privilege the songbird's song when we make it into the prose of those who would clip its wings and lay it bare in the form of smooth and easy doctrine?

Ibn ʿArabī left stories of his several meetings with the other Andalusian Muslim luminary of his epoch, the Aristotelian Averroës; in these much-recounted anecdotes we hear the varieties of faith that characterize Islam—as they do Christianity and Judaism. When the narrator was still a young man and Córdoba still, just barely, the old Córdoba, the first meeting is instigated by the already old and venerated Ibn Rushd, who has heard tell of the prodigious youngster's spiritual enlightenment.

> When I entered, the master arose from his place, received me with signal marks of friendship and consideration, and finally embraced me. Then he said "Yes" and I in turn said: "Yes." His joy was great at noting that I had understood. But then taking cognizance of what had called forth his joy, I added: "No." Immediately Averroes winced, the color went out of his cheeks, he seemed to doubt his own thought. He asked me this question: "What manner of solution have you found through divine illumination and inspiration? Is it identical with that which we obtain from speculative reflection?" I replied: "Yes and no. Between the yes and the no, spirits take their flight from their matter, and heads are separated from their bodies. . . ."

Ibn ʿArabī has a second encounter with Averroës in a vision that is summoned in a moment of spiritual ecstasy. The third and final meeting, which lies halfway between the pure vision of the second and the materiality of the first, is back in Córdoba, in 1198, when Averroës has died in Marrakech and his bones are returned to the remnants of al-Andalus for burial. This meeting, like the others, starkly defines both men.

> I had no further occasion to meet him until his death . . . in Marakesh. His remains were taken to Cordova, where his tomb is. When the coffin containing his ashes was loaded on the flank of a beast of burden, his works were placed on the other side to counterbalance it. I was standing there motionless . . . [After another observer notes that the books serve as counterweight to the body, he continues]: Then I stored up within me [the other's words] as a theme of meditation and recollection . . . and then I said: "On one side the master, on the other his works. Ah! how I wish I knew whether his hopes have been fulfilled."[4]

As the masterful Henry Corbin notes, the three episodes, in their narration by Ibn ʿArabī, tell volumes about both men, but especially we grasp the power and possibility of a lyrical "narration." In Ibn ʿArabī's story we glimpse the young man who bears witness to knowledge acquired without human teaching and the poet who bears witness to the truth of theophanies. And, in his rendering homage to the master philosopher, Ibn Rushd, the Averroës whose commentaries on Aristotle would transform the course of European philosophy and make him both a great hero and, in other quarters, a feared and thus banned writer, we are struck by both the poignancy and the plainness of the image of Averroës and his works balanced on the mule. Ibn ʿArabī seems to believe we can retell the bird singing at the top of the tree with the unflinching gaze of another bird in the branches of the next tree. Let us look at his own song, the most famous and most cited of his poems:

Gentle now,
doves of the thornberry and moringa thicket,
don't add to my heart-ache
your sighs.

Gentle now,
or your sad cooing
will reveal the love I hide
the sorrow I hide away.

I echo back, in the evening,
in the morning, echo,
the longing of a love-sick lover,
the moaning of the lost.

In a grove of tamarisks
spirits wrestled,
bending the limbs down over me,
passing me away.

They brought yearning,
breaking of the heart,
and other new twists of pain,
putting me through it.

Who is there for me in Jámʿ,
and the Stoning-Place at Mína,
who for me at Tamarisk Grove,
or at the way-station of Naʿmán?

Hour by hour
they circle my heart
in rapture, in love-ache,
and touch my pillars with a kiss.

As the best of creation
circled the Kaʿba,
which reason with its proofs
called unworthy,

And kissed the stones there—
and he was the Natiq!
And what is the house of stone
compared to a man or a woman?

They swore, and how often!
they'd never change—piling up vows.
She who dyes herself red with henna
is faithless.

A white-blazed gazelle
is an amazing sight,
red-dye signaling,
eyelids hinting,

Pasture between breastbones
and innards.
Marvel,
a garden among the flames!

My heart can take on
any form:
a meadow for gazelles,
a cloister for monks,

For the idols, sacred ground,
Kaʿba for the circling pilgrim,
the tables of the Torah,
the scrolls of the Qurʾān.

I profess the religion of love;
wherever its caravan turns along the way,
that is the belief,
the faith I keep.

Like Bishr,
Hind and her sister,
love-mad Qays and his lost Láyla,
Máyya and her lover Ghaylán.

(Translated by Michael Sells)

The abundant exegetical tradition certainly has not exempted this poem from that most shaping of ontological principles: it is believed to be inaccessible without numerous layers of commentary that decipher all manner of explicit and arcane allusions, most of them either Quranic, or in any case theological, and bearing on Ibn ʿArabī's highly influential and remarkably difficult mystical thought. With the conspicuous exception of Michael Sells, whose elegant translation lays bare the stark and at times Stevens-like transcendence of so many of the verses, criticism has been rooted in the problematic presumption that mystical poetry can be (and should be) transferred into the explicitly nonmystical language of exegesis. A further problem is that if we reject this procedure (as would any good student of Zen poetry) as one that misses, at least in part, the implications of several cornerstones of mysticism, it is not immediately clear what manner of public reaction might remain. Focusing on this poem and on the general hermeneutics of Ibn ʿArabī, Sells articulates a critical impasse that goes far beyond this case.

> No particular expression or manifestation of the central principles is self-sufficient or transparent. Each new passage reveals something and veils something. There is always an obscurity, an undefined term, a new paradox. On a positive level each passage is the expression of a principle. From the negative perspective it is the expression of an aporia. We are led from passage to passage, from one difficulty to deeper difficulties. It is the moving image rather than any particular frame that is significant. Finally, it is impossible to separate what is being said from how it is said and thus impossible to paraphrase faithfully the text (unless one's paraphrase were so modified and qualified that it ended up repeating the original). The beauty of this mode of discourse is that it reflects dynamically the very principles Ibn ʿArabī wishes to elucidate. *The difficulty is that we are not able to remove the principles from their contexts without betraying them.* And the alternative to such betrayal is a

> plunge into a vast ocean of eclectic thought systems and into the serpentine currents of the grand master's style.[5]

The only wise critical choice might seem to be Borges's—that is, to play Pierre Ménard and simply rewrite it all faithfully. Ibn ʿArabī (like Llull) is certainly exemplary of this apparent impasse. Although largely unknown to Hispanists, among other Muslims he is perhaps the most influential Spanish Muslim, the most powerful of Sūfi thinkers. Like Llull, he is far removed from the mainstream and the orthodoxy of his religion. His incomparable place among the mystics of Islam is evoked in his list of other names by which he was and is known among the faithful: Muhyi'd-Dīn, "Animator of the Religion"; al-Shaikh al-Akbar, "Doctor Maximus"; Ibn Aflatūn, "The Son of Plato" or "The Platonist." And the sentiments evoked by even a cursory reading of his poem strongly suggest the fundamentals of his beliefs, commonly described as Neoplatonic.

But as a Muslim, Ibn ʿArabī was ineradicably tied to the Logos and the Book itself, and his mysticism is rooted in features that give us a substantial framework for dealing with his poetry, particularly for dealing with it as something other than an arcanely encoded scripture. Often it is a stunning revelation to students of European literature to discover that the whole concept of the literalness of the Logos (and particularly that crucial concept of Logos as beginning and foundation, which is enshrined in the oft-repeated John 1:1, "In the beginning was the Word, and the Word was with God, and the Word was God"), is fundamental to Arabic letters and poetics because the Qur'ān is not the "revealed" word of God but the word of God, literally. The Arabic of the sacred text is sacred and the power of language itself magnificently enhanced. Indeed, the absolute power of the language, its unique claim to being revelation, is at the heart of the prohibition against translating the Qur'ān. A Muslim *must* learn Arabic in order to commune with this singularly immutable text. (This attitude offers a stunning and crucial contrast with the vernacular literatures of a Christianity obsessed with translating "the Good News" into every conceivable language and thus, from the perspective of Arabic, devaluing the poetic and revelatory privilege of any given language.) This *is* the singular language of God, and the Scripture is the poetry of God that was recited by the last of his prophets. Indeed, within this almost shockingly logocentric universe, a prophet—and the Prophet—is one who can recite God's poetry, and the opening word of the Qur'ān is God saying "recite." A further crucial feature of this merciless privileging of language itself is that visual images (except those constructed from and into words) are altogether banned; the art of Islam is relentlessly aniconic, and only language can be used to create that range of images used within other cultures to provoke states of closer communion with God, from the mandalas of India to Michaelangelo's *Pietà.*

At the same time, orthodox and majoritarian views of and within Islam are (as again, in Christianity and Judaism) explicitly—and no doubt necessarily—grounded in a belief in the essential transparency of that word of God and the essential lack of ambiguity of the Quranic text. The community of belief is likewise grounded in a common interpretation of the text (or texts), which, to a great extent, must be seen as unimpeachable and equally visible to all. But the stance of those we have come to call mystics is distinctly (and explicitly) more personal and arcane—the solitary bird at the top of the tree. Thus, as Corbin so elegantly expresses it, Ibn ʿArabī elaborates a theophany that is "the manifestation of the unknowable God in the angelic form of the celestial Anthropos. . . ."[6] The question of whether God is "knowable" or not in an Aristotelian (or Averroist) mode is one of the benchmarks, and the unambiguous point of Ibn ʿArabī's story of his encounters with Ibn Rushd. For Ibn ʿArabī, who (not surprisingly) has now and then been considered heretical—a pantheist—within Islamic communities (particularly within Sunni communities, where Islam is structured more as a legal than a prophetic or mystical enterprise) his recurring, universal theophanies are explicitly grounded in the Book—a Book that is the cipher of an eternal Word.

The virtue of this construct—and it is this virtue that sheds considerable light on how one can begin to approach his poetry—is that it is an eternal Word forever capable of producing new creations. Moreover, explicitly verbal images and the poetic imagination are in and of themselves central and critical; they are features to be used to embrace and enhance spirituality. Here, far higher value is granted to the puzzling image, to the hermetic parts of a poem, than to the exegesis and commentary. It is not difficult to see, I think, that Ibn ʿArabī's mystical hermeneutics, which clearly reject "mainstream" Islamic exoterism, have powerful implications for a critical hermeneutics, perforce esoteric, for his poetry. In a universe where the Logos is a critical center, the poetry is itself a theophany, and its images, if properly absorbed, are conduits to spirituality. The poem's essential and magical ambiguities and the power of images to provoke the sort of knowledge of God that lies explicitly outside common "knowledge" are an equally explicit departure from the language of exegesis itself—the language of exegesis being that of institutions which, in turn, are grounded in the need for transparent and communal beliefs—readily communicable "knowledge." The poem is the "yes and no" that makes the Averroist—and all other priests—blanch. Again, it tells us how canny Ibn ʿArabī was in providing his own institutional commentary, his exegesis, for his own poems, *not* to short-circuit the yes-and-no functions of the poem, but to be more powerful as a priest and as a master.

A first reading of the poem, then, would be framed by the Zen yes-and-no, revealing, even in language no longer divine (but which, as if in recompense, is even more mantric in a translation that leaves so many names and objects partly knowable), that the poet is exquisitely, perhaps even playfully, focused on all of the exegetical problems at hand. Thus, we see the ambiguous and perhaps ever-changing relationship between the dove(s) and the poet; the intractable and purposeful blurring of sacred and profane love; the famous and often uncomfortable pantheism, which in this context is also profitably understood as a direct challenge to the possibility of the transparent and sayable truths that govern the major truth-systems (and thus make uncomfortable bedfellows of the religious orthodoxies and the Aristotelians and their descendants, the modern rationalists).

If in rereading the poem we assume not that we will be able to "decipher" or "decode" an articulable, essentially orthodox message—if we want or need articulation we can go to the *other* text that Ibn ʿArabī wrote—but, rather, that we will embrace the purposeful contamination of the languages of such a great rainbow of loves (and gods), all climactically played out in the famous "pantheistic" verses toward the end, we can, with the poet, see the clues which language gives us that there are truths that distinctly confound language itself. Not only, then, is it a foolish conceit to pretend to distinguish the Love of the Christian monks and that of the Qur'ān, but, even more so, as a foundational problem it seems naive to imagine we can know the difference between those loves that institutions have called sacred and those that are called sacred by the maddened lovers of beloveds dyed with henna. In seeing, delighting in, and throwing in the reader's face the great muddle where our teachers had told us was perfect clarity, distinguishability, and ranked value, Ibn ʿArabī is very much a companion not only—most obviously—to the poet of the Song of Songs, but to the foundationalist poets of vernacular and profane love poetry with whom he shared the rocky Mediterranean shores. To them, we will return.

Closest of all of Ibn ʿArabī's kissing cousins is Llull who, among other things, is as disconcertingly prodigious. The affinities between these two men, who might be called compatriots if there were a stable patria to which they might be attached (and if they did not reject such facile alliances and characterizations), were perceived early on by the fathers of Spanish Arabism, Julián Ribera and Miguel Asín Palacios, although, all too predictably, both Llullians and students of the great Sūfi's work have recoiled at the idea of the "borrowing," as it is often conceived (or imagined) in such studies. The first stumbling block is the reductive—weak and essentially theological—"origins" in much of this medievalist criticism. (Indeed, to return to the arguments of my introductory section, this is a principal way in which medieval literature is not dealt with as fully developed.) But the point of comparisons such as this one not only lies elsewhere but serves to undermine the standard "origins" and "borrowings" methods of medievalism that end up atomizing and mutilating texts. I hasten to add, on the other hand, that a very different kind of recoiling at the notion that a Christian "saint" might be "contaminated" by Islam has been at the root of the scholarly rejection of the connection between Llull and his Cordoban ancestor.

For the Llull scholar, however, and for readers of *The Book of the*

Lover and the Beloved, my rudimentary presentation of the challenges presented by Ibn ʿArabī's poetry, as well as the striking and unusual contours of a very distinctive life, should sound remarkably familiar. In many of his roles and personae, Llull, too, is both an exemplary Neoplatonist and, as Ibn ʿArabī was (less actively but no less influentially), strongly anti-Averroist. Most importantly, Llull's key *Ars magna* expresses his belief that all reality—and this would include language and its constructs—is a theophany. Whether or not this belief makes the beatified Llull in reality a "Christian Sūfi," or whether we should not view Ibn ʿArabī as a "Muslim monk," is to fall precisely into the categorical, exoterical trap that both mystics are intently steering us away from. Although here, as elsewhere, there is a powerful ideological reluctance to seeing an "Arabic influence" in the work of Llull, who was a generation younger than Ibn ʿArabī, the issue of "borrowings" in the conventional sense is particularly misleading.

Undeniably, Llull's grounding in Arabic is as strong as a non-Muslim's could be. As I have noted (and as is well-known but mostly ignored, merely mentioned as an "and by the way"), his encyclopedic *Llibre de contemplació* was written in Arabic, so he was far from a schoolboy in his knowledge of the language and, perforce, the philosophical traditions borne by the linguistic tradition. From a number of crucial perspectives, Llull is a writer, and a far from negligible or childish one, within the Arabic tradition. Clearly, he could pick and choose the aspects of the tradition he wished to incorporate into his own, as he could reject others, and the fact that his life's active mission (aside from and as part of spreading the wisdom of the *Ars*) was the reconciliation of Christianity and Islam provides whatever further "proof" might be needed that he can scarcely be understood outside an Arabic and Islamic context, as well as within a Christian and Latin and Catalan one (although this is exactly what is regularly done). As is true of Ibn ʿArabī, Llull's mysticism and his encyclopedism are *not* "paradoxically" allied in one person. Instead—and here the fact that we have both a Llull *and* an Ibn ʿArabī helps us see the lyric coherence of the thing—in both cases these are multiple manifestations of a theophanistic spirituality and intellect. It is certainly not coincidental or incidental that Llull, like the Ibn ʿArabī who so often has made traditional historians squirm, was also regularly suspected of heresy—and of pantheistic tendencies in particular. And even though some of the anti-Llullian strictures for which the Dominicans campaigned were eventually rescinded or softened, he has never been beyond producing real unease; it is clear, too, that he was eventually denied sanctification because of amply justified doubts about his orthodoxy.

The *Llibre,* like "Gentle now, doves," explicitly challenges the analytic categories that would conventionally separate Beloved from beloved and analytic procedures that subvert (consciously or no) the text by rendering it exoteric when it is rooted in esoterism. In the explicit, perhaps outrageous, challenge to one of the most essential ontological distinctions within orthodox Judeo-Christian-Islamic thought (an originary distinction which insistently resurfaces in both heresies and texts, such as the Song of Songs, that have been uneasily assimilated), Llull, too, fundamentally challenges the validity of the exegetical mode itself. With good reason. It is only Averroist (or, in our own times, post-Cartesian) rational commentary that could deny what the text actually said and make the neat distinction between God and lover, and it is only through rational explanatory commentary that the purposeful provocativeness of such literature, that which might lead us to contemplate, can be made "clear"—and thus no longer provocative.

The *Book of the Lover and the Beloved* is explicitly devised as a contemplative guide. The prologue tells us about Blanquerna, hero of the romance, who, acting out the textual abandonment of orthodoxy for hermeticism, has eschewed the papacy and become a hermit. Following the example of the Sūfis, as he tells us, Llull has composed brief and difficult lines that arise from and encourage a spiritual contemplation of God. It is further evident that in the sparse but highly charged language of Lover and Beloved, there resides that urging to shift from intellect to spirit, from reason to passion, that is inherent and necessary for mystical contemplation. Thus, we are given 366 thoughts—an extraordinary number of them uncannily reminiscent of the simple difficulty of the poets of Zen (as well as of the Wallace Stevens whose blackbirds are kin to Llull's *aucell*). We have a poem to dwell on each day of the year, and they invite perplexity in many ways. As with Ibn ʿArabī, the most seductive and entrancing difficulty is that of the ineluctable and innumerable paradoxes and mysteries of Love. Let us listen a bit to Llull's birds as they stare unflinchingly at us:

> (3)
> Ajustaren-se molts amadors a amar un Amat qui els abundava tots d'amors; e cascú havia per cabal son Amat e sos pensaments agradables, per los quals sentien plaents tribulacions.
>
> (Many lovers come together to love One alone, their Beloved, who made them all abound in love. And each one had the Beloved as his precious possession, and his thoughts of him were very pleasant, making him suffer a pain which brought delight.)
>
> (7/8)
> Demanà l'Amat a l'amic:—Has membrança de nulla cosa que t'haja guardonat, per ço cor me vols amar? Repòs:—Hoc, per ço cor enfre los treballs e els plaers que em dónes, no en faç diferéncia.
>
> (The Beloved asked the Lover, "Have you remembered any way in which I have rewarded you for you to love me thus?" "Yes" replied the Lover, "for I make no distinction between the trials which you send and the joys.")
>
> (115/116)
> En un ram cantava un aucell, e deïa que ell daria un novell pensament a amador qui le en donàs dos. Donà l'aucell lo novell pensament a l'amic, e l'amic donà'n dos a l'aucell, per ço que alleujàs sos turments; e l'amic sentí muntiplicades ses dolors.
>
> (A bird was singing on a branch, "I will give a fresh thought to the lover who will give me two." The bird

gave that fresh thought to the Lover, and the Lover gave two to the bird to lighten its afflictions, and the Lover felt his own griefs increased.)

(116/117)
Encontraren-se l'amic e l'Amat, e foren testimonis de llur encontrament saluts, abraçaments, e besars, e llàgremes, e plors. E demanà l'Amat a l'amic de son estament; e l'amic fo enbarbesclat en presència de son Amat.

(The Lover and the Beloved met together, and their greetings, embraces, kisses, weeping, and tears, testified to their meeting. Then the Beloved asked the Lover how he was, and the Lover was speechless before his Beloved.)

(236/237)
Demanaren a l'amic qui era son Amat. Respòs que ço qui el faïa amar, desirar, llanguir, sospirar, plorar, escarnir, morir.

(They asked the Lover, "Who is your Beloved?" He answered, "He who makes me love, desire, faint, sigh, weep, endure reproaches, and die.")

(255/256)
Falses lloadors blasmaven un dia l'amic en presència de son Amat. Havia l'amic paciència, e l'Amat justicía, saviea, poder. E l'amic amà més ésser blasmat e reprès, que ésser negú dels falses balsmadors.

(False flatterers were speaking ill of the Lover one day in the presence of his Beloved. The Lover was patient, and the Beloved showed his justice, wisdom, and power. And the Lover preferred to be blamed and reproved than to be like one of those who falsely accused him.)

(364/365)
Amor escalfava e aflamava l'amic en membrança de son Amat. E l'Amat lo refredava ab llàgremes e plors, e ab oblidament dels delits d'aquest món, e ab renunciament dels vans honraments. E creixien les amors con l'amic membrava per qui sostenia llangors, tribulacions, ni los hòmens mundans per qui sostenien treballs, persecucions.

(Love heated and inflamed the Lover with remembrance of his Beloved, and the Beloved cooled his ardour, with weeping, tears, and forgetfulness of the delights of this world and the renunciation of vain honours. So his love grew when he remembered for whom he suffered griefs and afflictions, and for whom the men of the world bore trials and persecutions.)

Two hundred years after the invention of what the philologists would irremediably name "courtly" love—and well after Llull himself, the poet of courtly love, has presumably converted and turned away from its self-pitying conceits—we are struck here by the immutability and the endurance for both tradition and poet of the mannerisms with all their irrational and ultimately rationally unresolvable paradoxes and contradictions: the pain that brings delight, the marriage of trials and joys; the interchangeability of kisses and tears, joy and weeping; the precious lover coveted by all, and the false witnesses and flatterers all about, conspiring against the union of the lovers; the desperate and sickening fear that one is alone and not loved by the Lover, and the cruelty and coldness that is that constant threat and fear. And there he is, perched in the tree—or sometimes flying away or flying back—the wonderful bird that sooner or later is each of the facets of the calliope of Love: poet and lover, God and beloved, witness and soul, poem and singer.

Once again, as in the structurally different but evocatively comparable poem by Ibn ʿArabī, the dual solutions presented by conventional exegesis beg the questions presented by the bird himself: how and why is he my love one moment, my soul the next? Sells's contemplation on the poem emphasizes the explicit fusion of the powerful and unambiguously marked *nasīb* tradition—this, the motif of the memory of the beloved from the classical Arabic *qasida*—with equally unambiguous spiritual themes—the Sūfi state of *fana*ʿ, or annihilation of the self, and the circumambulation of the Kaʿba, climactic station of the Muslim pilgrimage. The melding of the erotic and the spiritual could scarcely be more emphatic. Eros—and the erotic structures of the *qasida* itself, the ode of love—binds the poem, begins it, ends it—although, in fact, tradition has subverted this structuring by essentially discarding the last verse. Remarkably, the penultimate verses of Ibn ʿArabī's poem—those so frequently cited—have become famous for their disputed pantheism; the verse that closes that meditation, and closes the poem itself, is almost never cited. The powerful connotation—the essentially inescapable reading imposed—is that the spiritual or mystical dimension is the climax of both the mystical experience and the poem. What we read, in other words, is:

> My heart can take on
> any form:
> a meadow for gazelles,
> a cloister for monks,
>
> For the idols, sacred ground
> Kaʿba for the circling pilgrim,
> the tables of a Torah,
> the scrolls of the Qurʾān.
>
> I profess the religion of love;
> wherever its caravan turns along the way,
> that is the belief,
> the faith I keep.

Whereas, what the poet wrote is:

> My heart can take on
> any form:

a meadow for gazelles,
a cloister for monks,

For the idols, sacred ground
Kaʿba for the circling pilgrim,
the tables of a Torah,
the scrolls of the Qur'ān.

I profess the religion of love;
wherever its caravan turns along the way,
that is the belief,
the faith I keep.

Like Bishr,
Hind and her sister,
love-mad Qays and the lost Láyla,
Máyya and her lover Ghaylán.

Little else, it seems to me, could more dramatically illustrate the distinct discomfort created by the sharpness of the suggestions that the two are not meant to be distinguished. Indeed, the annotation provided by another able translator, James Monroe, makes explicit (and unusually clear) the reading that in almost all other cases implicitly justifies so outrageous a truncation: " 'We have an example in them,' because God only afflicted them with love for human beings like themselves in order that he might show, by means of them, the falseness of those who pretend to love Him and yet feel no such transport and rapture in loving Him. . . ."[7] In other words, Ibn ʿArabī has shifted from the subject of the pantheism that can be the mystic's love for God to the courtly love he had begun with—all to show the secondariness (and inferiority) of one to the other.

I would argue the contrary. As in Llull's contemplative verses, the poet is suggesting that the varieties of experience of Love are *not* different from each other and that the confusion of love languages is far from the easy and relatively banal metaphor we assume it to be. Ibn ʿArabī makes the point with conspicuous clarity in the midst of a discussion of how rational arguments, philosophy, and "positive" religion are inimical to understanding what it is to love God. "It is He who in every beloved being is manifested to the gaze of each lover . . . , and none other than He is adored, for it is impossible to adore a being without conceiving the Godhead in that being. . . . So it is with love: a being does not truly love anyone other than his Creator."[8] What we face, as readers, is *not* (as most readings would have us believe) an unambiguous metaphorical transfer of the tropes of one kind of love to serve for those of another; instead, we are shuffled back and forth (first it seems to be one and then the other) with an unrelenting insistence on the possible fusion of the languages of love and of the loves themselves. To leave out the final verse, then—or to interpret it as the place at the beginning of the poet's spiritual journey, now transcended—is to avert our eyes from the poem's radical posture. But the bird at the top of the tree is suggesting, with that beady eye, that we think again about the biggest distinctions we make with such great sureness and ease.

It bears repeating that the greatest difficulty here lies in the fundamental parameters of interpretation itself. The resistance to the bird's cocky suggestions is rooted in the strong epistemological urge we have to "make sense" of a text. For poetry, this has meant a double-edged flattening: the conventions of that exegetical making-sense reduce its "irrationalities" (what used to be called the lies of poetry and its language) to something that can be narrated, rationally retold. Thus, to take the most conspicuous of examples (far from fully outmoded in practice), the exegesis of "courtly love" poetry has been shaped, overwhelmingly, by introducing rational explanations for the lack of fulfillment of the love of the Poet/Lover: everything from the Lady's "real" coldness and insensitivity (more likely than not because of her being of a higher social class) to her married state or her isolation on a far Mediterranean shore. These older versions of the need to believe in what is called sincerity and to be able to narrate what the poem means are being replaced by others—women troubadours were singing about their femaleness, and so forth. But, as other readers have insisted, this explanatory mode flies in the face of the text's most conspicuous assertions of purposeful unhappiness, of perhaps "irrational" or delusory fears, of the hundred obstacles that are contemplated by the blackbird. In providing the rational or logical underpinnings (the prose version of the lyric), we are, among other things, painting the blackbird white and making it something that no longer makes us dwell on the conundrums of our existence or on the frightening mystery of what—who—it is that we love.

The case of Llull's and Ibn ʿArabī's stark verses presents a further, unswallowable irrationality in the clearly purposeful confusion of the identity and persona of the Beloved. This confusion is no less blithely "resolved" in an exegesis that, again, explicitly denies what the text no less explicitly has put forth. In both cases, ironically, this assertion of the metaphorical principle is made in a peculiar vacuum, for Ibn ʿArabī as a Muslim, and Llull as a superb Arabist, were steeped in the astonishingly powerful Quranic cult of Language and the Word, part of a tradition at least as Logocentric as the equally unorthodox (and Languedoquian-Andalusian) Kabbalah. In both cases it would seem far more appropriate to see these critical fusions, first, as partly the difficult (because antiempirical) images of a theophany—images *meant to confound* and thus provoke contemplation and ecstasy. As in another great mystical tradition, that of Zen Buddhism (which has produced a distinctive and uncannily similar poetry), it is precisely understood that revelation follows from images and propositions that are confounding, and, conversely, that understanding is completely blocked by the application of traditional, rational, and intellectual exegesis.

One of the greatest ironies of the exegetical tradition of such texts, in fact, is that when it is openly recognized that these poets clearly fall outside the orthodox mainstream and in a difficult mystical corner of their respective religious traditions, then the hermeticism is depicted as the refuge of such poets. Thus, typically, the perplexities of Ibn ʿArabī's poetry will be ascribed, at least in part, to his need to mask unorthodox and suspect thought. (And this is the local version of the argument vis-à-vis courtly love poetry which says that the poet confuses and occludes the identity of the beloved because she is married and he does not want to reveal her real identity.) Yet, if we say that Ibn ʿArabī is seeking shelter from the paradigms of orthodox thought, how can we go on to "decipher" the poetry in fairly standard and articulable theological terms? Isn't this falsifying the presumed principles at hand and denying the poet's assertions of the primary basis and fundamental need for difficulty? In the end, aren't we just trying to find out who the Lady *really* was?

The primary exegetical question is thus raised with considerable force: can there be an exegesis or criticism truly appropriate to this kind of hermetic poetry, poetry that would appear to be constructed precisely as counterpoint to the rational paradigm that we believe *is* the exegetical mode? If we take this poetry at face value, in other words, if we follow both Blanquerna and the elusive spirit contemplating and being the doves perched on the thornberry and moringa, and if we embrace (as they urge us to) their enormous reveling in hermetic poetic language and its expressions of "logically" impossible contradictions, what form of exegesis does remain open to us? What enlightening and articulable meaning is left in the imagistic and theophanic language that has shut the door, as hard as it can, to exegesis—precisely because exegetical language, the language of the mainstream and legalistic traditions of both Christianity and Islam, is radically inimical to the essential iconoclasm of such mystical poetry and can only dim its spiritual magic?

The first and most straightforward answer I have been urging is that we indulge the poets and their texts and that we believe—at least as long as we are reading the poem—in the impossibilities they are urging on us. But sympathy is not so easily generated, and the enormous and fundamental question of contingency is left begging. Indeed, it is precisely in an attempt to confront these more fundamental premises of the exegetical question that I have chosen to look at Llull and Ibn ʿArabī together. The contingency that binds them is not that of the traditional, atomizing, philological dependence of one being the "source" of the other, but a kinship that is far more unsettling. As I tried to suggest at the outset, they are both children of the same storm, both shaped by a whirlwind as strong as the one that buffets Dante's pathetic lovebirds. For, perhaps paradoxically, I would argue that the best reading we can do of this poetry, that which does least violence to the hermeneutic distance it wishes to create with all readers except the True Believers (who scarcely need our critical comments), is one that reunites it with its peculiar and highly complex historical circumstances. Sometimes, memory is contingency.

And the salient, relevant features of the century that is framed by the Muslim mystic at its outset and the Christian mystic at its end are appropriately paradoxical. This is, first, the era of that now almost unimaginable flourishing of intellectual communion among the three cultures (and the vernacular as well as the classical languages), the age of translations represented by Llull's, who writes his philosophical masterpiece in Arabic—and then translates it into Catalan, giving that language its principal model for a prose style for centuries to come. But (in what one might call a contradiction if we subjected the discourse of history to the same post-Cartesian analysis that we impose on so much literature) this is also unmistakably the edge of the madness of civil hatreds that would be used to carve out the modern states and their exclusive languages, their strong "ethnic" narratives. One might see that the almost hysterical interest in, and proliferation of, translations from the Arabic was far more than the calm before the storm; the storm, after all, had already begun and was close to being in full force, and the translations were merely a treacherous stowing away of supplies. As intolerance bred intolerance, inevitably, the ugliness of the Almohads and the Almoravids, each in turn potentially only a dark lapse, became permanent. Again, Llull serves as the best poetic image, history's own poem. He was stoned to death in Tunis for preaching not just conversion but a union and re-union of opposites that no one could understand anymore. Ibn ʿArabī, no less, is drenched in such contradictions, bred in the old capitals of multiculturalism that themselves had bred, perhaps inevitably, a cultural relativism which, like Llull's pacifism and Ibn ʿArabī's pantheism, would soon be seen as madness.

In the midst of such violent and drastic historical contradictions, the unions of (what seem to us) paradigmatic opposites in the writings of these poets on the edge make far greater sense—certainly not because the differences are thus rendered less irreconcilable, but precisely because in the explicit paradoxes of history we see reflections of the tensions that inform this mystical poetry, and of the images of seemingly impossible unions that fill every contemplative verse of Llull's Book and every line of the poem that begins, after all, by summoning a bird that has always evoked both secular and sacred loves. And peace. In such a critical context, I believe, we can point to the ways in which the multiple ambiguities and paradoxes within the texts are tied in chainlike fashion: the Beloved is always an Other—and the painful love of Others is the painful love of God. This union of love thus constitutes the ultimate challenge to the self (whether the external and transient manifestation of the self is the flesh and blood lover vis-à-vis the object of carnal desire, or the Christian vis-à-vis the Muslim, or the supplicant vis-à-vis the Lord). Within the context of a difficult and fading multiculturalism, the Beloved may emerge as that ultimate theophany, *all* Others. And the Love poetry of the poets of such circumstances may well play back what we can scarcely hear in periods defined by different tensions. Are we almost able to hear Llull, before the first stones are cast, talking about how the peoples of the Book really believe the same thing, ranting about how his Lover is God, about how these are all the same thing?

Clearly, as literary critics we cannot articulate (even assuming we can know) the personal revelations that these texts are meant to provoke. But we can reject the cartoonish misprision which absurdly holds that mystics, and thus their lives and poetry, lie outside the paradigms of history, that they are largely or completely devoid of social and historical dimensions. The dismissal of the final verse in Ibn ʿArabī's poem is just such a misprision: the mystical state is beyond any historical detail, beyond flesh and blood. Possibly it is the final irony in the exegetical tradition of such poetry that while we are so intent on having it "make sense"—conform to the orthodoxies of both rational discourse and standard beliefs (those strange bedfellows, once again!)—we also dismiss historical contingency as that which this kind of poetry somehow transcends. I would argue, however, that the examples at hand (and others at only a slight remove—haven't we been hearing the flapping of the wings of Juan de la Cruz's solitary bird from the outset, hasn't he been watching us from the top of his tree?) suggest that it is in the contingency of history itself that we may be able to get the best grip on what this highly hermetic poetry suggests publicly.

For if mysticism were, in fact, devoid of a social dimension, Llull would never have been stoned, Ibn ʿArabī would not be redrawn to seem so orthodox, and others would not have been tried for heresy, banished as traitors, or locked away as madmen. In restoring the marked and violent and moving historical moment to our reading as the best premise for accepting the apparently contradictory truths set out by the poets, we can begin to see that here we have poets who are neither the orthodox and rational in deep cover, nor hermits who are out wandering in the desert because they know nothing of our—their—world. This kind of exile, too, is a starkly political act shaped by a maelstrom. It is precisely in the often violent nature of those reactions to these poets (and the most violent reaction is perhaps that of rendering mystical and hermetic poetry "intelligible" through orthodox exegesis) that we glimpse the startling power of the Love poetry and the urging of a contemplative and peaceful hermeneutics of the *Book of the Lover and the Beloved* and "Gentle now, doves of the thornberry and moringa thicket. . . ."

The act of hermeticism has a critical social dimension in its refusal of exegesis, since exegetical discourse, then and now, is the language of orthodox powers, the "rational arguments of philosophy," and the "positive religion" that Ibn ʿArabī condemns as incapable of understanding what the real language of Love might be. Conversely, logically, hermeticism is perceived as something to be mastered: a (perhaps) tough nut to crack, to be rendered "intelligible" and subservient to rational discourse. When the world all around is calling for clear distinctions, loyalties to Self and hatred of others, and, most of all, belief in the public and legal discourses of single languages and single states—smooth narratives—what greater threat exists than that voice which rejects such easy orthodoxies with their readily understood rhetoric and urges, instead, the most difficult readings, those that embrace the painfully impossible in the human heart? Marvel, as Ibn ʿArabī says, a garden among the flames! Or, as Llull tells us to contemplate on the 27th day of the year: "The bird sang in the garden of the

Beloved. The Lover came and said to the bird 'If we do not understand one another in speech, we can make ourselves understood by love, for in your song I see my beloved before my eyes.' "

It is just such a Song of Love that has always mesmerized us and that has teased the standard exegetical traditions with its explicit fusion of the many beloveds who people our souls and our love songs, with the highly fractured and lyrical self who has many voices, and with that stark fear of irremediable loneliness that is, too, the bird, love, poetry:

> Set me as a seal upon thine heart, as a seal upon thine arm: for love is strong as death; jealousy is cruel as the grave: the coals thereof are coals of fire, which hath a most vehement flame. (Song of Sol. 8:6)

And in the land of the Kabbalah, this was an emblematic song, part of a cabal of birds who displayed on their treetops how many we are, how many the voices are in a poem, and how they can all fly away when the attempt is made to catch and tame them.

Notes

1. Durán, "Ramon Llull," page 13.
2. González Casanovas, "Llull's Blanquerna," page 236.
3. Lola Badía, *Libro de amigo y amado,* page xxxi.
4. Henry Corbin, *Creative Imagination,* pages 41–43.
5. Sells, "Ibn ʿArabī's Garden," page 289 (emphasis mine).
6. Henry Corbin, *Creative Imagination,* page 27.
7. Monroe, *Hispano Arabic Poetry,* page 321.
8. Corbin, *Creative Imagination,* page 146.

2. The Inventions of Philology

Eu, Dante Alighieri

Florença nunca
mais há de nutrir-me
o corpo que já foi
do rio velame
e das ruas,
um vento distraído. . . .

I, Dante Alighieri

Florence will never again
nourish me
this body that was once
a sail on the river
and on the streets
an absent-minded wind. . . .

Carlos Nejar, São Paulo, 1984
(Translated by Robert Myers)

The medieval—and thus what we call the modern and the post-modern—lyric is invented in bitter exile. And not just the normal and conventional and essentially metaphoric exile that is, perhaps, the condition of all poetry and of its reading. No, here the poet must finally face the harsh winter night when he knows, in that full solitude, that he will never again see the lovely terra-cotta rooftops of

Florence, that he will never be buried in the barren but olive-fragrant soil outside Granada. In that cold and darkness, the solitary voice asks what he will do about it. Among the thousands of different answers that have come with the morning, one singular and unexpected one, the love lyric, has been a powerful and charming defense, a form of resistance commonly taken for retreat.

The lyric that is the common love song. And, yes, love songs have always been sung, everywhere, and gathered, everywhere. Anyone can stroll down the street singing some plain old love song. And yet, and yet, what a marvelous part it has played in the effort to transcend the rustic. The love lyric can undergo the most astonishing of metamorphoses: from vulgar song of simple longings to noble and foundational monument of high culture. And this, so often, because it is crafted—written and sung and collected—from the deep loneliness of exile. It is thus, as one of his various answers to the impardonable pains of his exile, that Dante writes the *De vulgari eloquentia,* a work abandoned, unfinished, and largely doomed to the obscurities of an academic audience for posterity (a fate on the face of it different from that awaiting his other book of exile, the *Commedia*). In their disarmingly detailed book on the *Rime petrose,* Dante's famous early lyrics of unbearably unrequited love—these are the marvelously named Stony rhymes, with their *donna di pietra,* the Lady of Stone—Robert Durling and Ronald Martinez emphasize that in crucial ways these love poems anticipate the poetics of the monument of and to exile that is the *Commedia.* The echoes are so loud, in fact, that at least one early critic was tempted to revise the dates of the *petrose* to correspond to the exilic period, and, moreover, thus read those stony poems as an allegory of a harsh Florence and her terrible rejection of Dante, her unrelieved cruelty.

When is a song of love—we might say unrequited or unhappy love, but how many are of any other kind—when is that love song about a city and not a woman? The issue, Durling and Martinez argue, is the rather different one that there is a congruence in the poetics of the two kinds of poetry: "they share a fundamental parallel in the structure of the poet's relation to the world and to his poetry."[1] In essence, this shift is from the "real world" to that of poetry. Just as the *Commedia* becomes Dante's response to the tumultuous and violent and deranging political world with which, everyday, he is vitally concerned and which has so cruelly reshaped his life, driven him away from his homeland, "the poet's effort to achieve power over the lady is, by the choice of poetry, inevitably *shifted* away from the *practical* goal into the *alternate* universe of art, in spite of the poet's fierce desire."[2] But a powerful question is raised which takes us beyond the parallelism in poetics; the *De vulgari* is written in the midst of exile. And it is—not exclusively, but certainly emphatically—an apologia for the love poetry written in the vernaculars of Europe, not forgetting, of course, that the vernacular was still in so many ways renegade, unstandardized, as vulgar as the unlettered songs in the streets. If it is indisputably true that the searing love poems that are the *petrose* were written before Dante could have imagined the various tragedies of exile, and that the parallelisms of poetics of the *Commedia* and the *petrose* exist because from his earliest writing Dante is grappling with some of the most fundamental issues of poetry, it is also true that at least one of those fundamental issues is raised in the most explicit fashion by the *De vulgari eloquentia.* Why is it that Dante turns to the still-renegade, still-lowly love lyric—and the lyrics of others', not merely to his own—in the moment of his greatest political crisis?

As Ezra Pound says, he who does not know Dante is an ignoramus, and everyone thinks he knows Dante. The Dante we know is mostly Dante of the *Divine Comedy,* and we seem to know as little about his life, his history, as we do about Shakespeare's. The difference is that, for whatever reasons, Shakespeare's life is genuinely a mystery, whereas there are many things that might be widely known about Dante's life, which, while well-documented, seems nevertheless to remain just below the horizon—and at some odds with that almost unsurpassed "popularity" of his. Although it is well-known that he lived out his life in exile, and that the *Commedia* was written in that exile, the fact that an often violent and always intense political life led to that exile seems to be known mostly by specialists. Even among them, the simple fact of Dante's vita activa is often treated as incidental to the real Dante, the scholar and writer, who in the end somehow lay beyond all that. History, in the *Divine Commedy,* somehow transcends bloody politics. In our books, politics—especially deeply corrupt, incomprehensible, and violent politics—is not the true place where sublime writers live. But all sorts of them *have* lived there: from José Martí, whose violent death is the touchstone of political martyrdom for all Cubans on both sides of their revolution and on both sides of their diaspora, to Dostoyevsky, so close to the firing squad, and to many others. And Dante.

Actually, it would be far easier not to evoke the scene of Dante's political involvements, which are at once so complex as to deny any attempt at a clear narrative, and so brutal to mean pain, vicious brutality, and death. At age twenty-four, politically active for some time in an Italy ripped apart by the Byzantine and bloody Guelf-Ghibelline (papal-imperial) struggles, Dante went into battle at least twice, once in the Battle of Campaldino and, just months later, in the siege of a Pisan stronghold. The year was 1289, and elsewhere, in the narrative of Charles Eliot Norton, it was the year in which "Count Ugolino and his sons and grandsons were starved by the Pisans in their tower prison. A few months later, Francesca da Rimini was murdered by her husband. . . ."[3] The years that followed were shaped by an increasingly public life; in a city increasingly factionalized, the more radically pro-papal Guelfs—called the Blacks—opposed the Whites, among them Dante, whose reputation (painted by Dante himself in great measure) was to have been more democratic, more moderate. But both sides indulged in the cruel ritual of expulsion of their adversaries from the city whenever they were able, when their hold on the commune was strong enough, and it is in this vicious, Shakespeare-like circle of retribution that Dante's complex tragedy lies.

In 1297, when Dante was thirty-two, a series of concatenated events began (in which, among other notables, Pope Boniface VIII played a central role); these events are inscribed in bits and pieces throughout the *Commedia* and would lead to the years in exile during which, after a number of other projects begun and abandoned, the *Commedia* was written. Dante was no mere observer from the sidelines—far from it—and these are Dante's personal memories, the contours of the pain that is the template of everything he writes. In these last years of the century the White Guelfs sent the Blacks into exile; then, a papal emissary, favoring the Blacks when he was presumably in Florence to negotiate and equalize, in fact began to turn the tide. In the deadly heat of the summer of 1300, when Dante Alighieri turned thirty-five, he was one of six men elected president of the city's powerful council of guilds. In a classic gesture of desperate reconciliation, these good democrats exiled the leaders of both Blacks and Whites. And among the Whites whom Dante himself voted to send into exile was his beloved Guido Cavalcanti, intellectual and poetic agon, *primo amico* to whom the *Vita nuova,* that outpouring of Dante's heart and soul, had been dedicated. Cavalcanti, in illness and despair—and, perhaps, in bitterness toward a man he had helped make, politically and poetically—died in exile in August of the same year. But for Dante—let us stop and imagine it for a minute, as the backdrop of his own exile—the agony of Guido's death expelled from his home, a death which was a sacrifice to a god of hoped-for fairnesses and peace and nobility that soon proved itself unquenchably bloodthirsty, would be far more bitter. Or, perhaps, a Dante who has been sanctified and canonized by biographers from the outset, instead connived in these expulsions of convenience and did not have the courage of his later convictions. The affair and its darknesses, whatever they may be, must have stared unflinchingly back at him, long and cold winter after long and cold winter, ever farther from Florence. And when he crafts the architecture of Hell, Treason lies at its very heart.

Dante's role in expelling Cavalcanti and the others occurs at the beginning of the whirlwind two years during which he was center-stage in ever-fiercer Florentine politics. The climax came in October 1301. The brother of the French king, ally of the pope and the Blacks, reaches the outskirts of Florence; the Whites, fully aware of the danger at hand, make another classic effort to avert further violence and send a handful of envoys. Dante Alighieri is one of the three men chosen for what will turn out to be a worse than fruitless embassy; he not only was unsuccessful in preventing the Blacks from brutally restoring themselves, but unable, even, to return to Florence. By the end of January of the next year, 1302, when he was not yet thirty-seven, he had been officially banished, at least temporarily; by March, the decree was death, which became, instead, permanent exile. For a Florentine, the difference, at times, must have seemed slight.

The nineteen years that follow, until Dante's death in Ravenna, are years of desperate and unfulfilled desire to return to Florence and of often painful and solitary wandering through Italy. The story, as complex and hard to tell as the years that lead up to the exile, is full of poignant moments. During the first years he is often a fugitive and a beggar and in despair—conspiring, contemplating suicide. He breaks ranks with some of his fellow exiles on the issue of reconciliation and refuses to fight against his native land, in whatever political dress she may have on. Hope is high, going on a decade into the exile, when an emperor is to be crowned by a pope in 1310. Dante is now in his mid-forties. But Florence denounces the emperor. Dante, outraged, denounces the Florentines, and when an amnesty for political prisoners is issued, his name is conspicuously left off. Throughout these and countless other vicissitudes, Dante was never anything less than fully engaged in every scrap of news, in every glimmer of hope, in every devastating turn of further violence and acrimony. Every bit of it was his passion, his hopes, his life. And in the first years of this exile, during the first decade of often almost frenzied political activity and that raw bitterness of a man not yet forty, seeing his life devastated, he wrote the *De vulgari eloquentia*—an essay to champion the vernacular, the language of love and its songs.

Why is it that love poetry is so tightly linked to exile that it constitutes an explicit response to it? The project of the *De vulgari eloquentia,* which was accomplished with incomparable success, was explicitly political if we understand (at least as clearly as Dante did) how powerfully political are our literary canons. While the *Commedia* was to become one of that conspicuous handful of basic texts in the Western tradition, the almost unseen and unheard of *De vulgari* is no less pivotal. It is the foundational text that invents the vernacular European love lyric by creating for it a crucial cultural role, by appropriating for the vernacular, and for lyric poetry itself, a place in the violently contested landscape of the institutions of past and future history. While modern philology, also founded in this truncated work, is one version or another of the love of origins, *De vulgari* understands in crystalline fashion that the origins that count are not those of the "lyric itself" but those of institutionalization. Indeed, Dante's is a dramatically and openly political text, unflinchingly focused on the shape of the future, the language that children will learn, the poems that will be sung and studied and passed on from generation to generation. As virtually every article of the 1990s on the content of the American collegiate curriculum dramatically highlights, nothing is more ideologically powerful and politically explosive than the languages we make official and the texts we imagine our children are reading.

It is also true that central to the narrative of our institutions and of our cultures is the obviously legitimizing belief that these languages and these texts are beyond or above the contingent historical moment, the political arena; that, instead, these are the languages and texts of our culture for transcendental reasons; that somehow they have never had to be established or fought over, that they themselves never participated in such vulgar fights, that their value is thus fully without contingency, lying outside common history. This first and most fundamental step of retrospective legitimation is visible in all spheres. One cannot have won the war just because one was smarter strategically or was better armed; some transcendental value has to be invoked. The pervasive difficulty in understanding the starkly political foundationalism involved in works like the *De vulgari*, and beyond that of the love lyric itself—which will then have to be reimagined as Dante's most powerful weapon—is precisely that we have come to believe so profoundly and actively in the essential ahistoricity of both the poetry and those texts that have made the poetry a part of our heritage.

Ahistoricity here means what I have just sketched out: the sets of beliefs that maintain that high cultural icons—and these include, crucially, the whole range of texts that are seen as derivative, such as "scholarship"—are not contingently but "universally" of value beyond the vulgar politics of history. Ironically, it is this ahistorical view that peremptorily holds up as its chief ideological banner, "History" and "Tradition." History is thus reconfigured to mean something like antiquarianism and values that are beyond contingencies, and literature itself is banished from any construct of history that includes stark ideology, bloody politics. It is as if, because these languages and these texts have ended up surviving and outliving one set of conditions, they are then "beyond" conditions altogether. "History" then becomes (as it largely was in pre-New Critical literary studies) the charming background in the first instance, and the circumstances transcended in the second. The tension in the love poetry of someone like Dante is then construed as the reflex of the struggle between the contingent and the transcendental. On the one hand, there is a real lover or political turmoil ("the practical goal") to be impossibly balanced with the poetry ("the alternative universe of art"). Within this framework, Dante writes the *De vulgari eloquentia,* as he writes the *Commedia,* as *alternatives* to direct or "real" political action, since neither is part of the "real world" struggle with the pope who conspired with the Blacks to overthrow the Whites, those real political acts which led to Dante's real exile from Florence. Are we not the cruel and shortsighted Florentines, the ones who left Dante off the lists of the forgiven, ten years later? We have exiled writing itself from the sphere of the most painful, least transcendent contingencies. But, of course, the reason he was left off the lists is because he *was* a writer, and he had cursed the Florentines in writing.

In his painful exile from a desperately missed Florence—and any sensitive soul who glimpses her even today can hardly avoid falling at least partly in love, seeing those traces of stunning beauty and radiant warmth—Dante fights back fiercely. From the center of the bloodiest arena he moves to the center of the next stage, the one where the struggle takes place for hearts and minds, an arena in which many a war has been won and lost. And in fighting back, in his writing of the *De vulgari eloquentia*—which, as its title openly proclaims, is a work meant to justify a specific strand of culture, its languages and texts—Dante invents the first and most powerful version, although perhaps the least recognized or explicitly understood, of Romance philology. This is the great cult of the vernaculars, the tradition of writing into and around and with the texts that are part of the world of the living. Here, the threatened death of exile can be fought back, and this genre of writing's highly political function can be confronted. It says, unflinchingly: in the face of a brutal and stupid enemy, let us eat away at the very basis of his power, let us make our poems the powerful ones, the ones that survive, the ones that teach children their speech. Perhaps there are ways in which this is somehow not the "real" world, but Dante, at least, would not have accepted such a claim, would have written vigorously against such a construct—as the *Commedia* reassures us on every page. It seems to me that reality—and the real world and real politics—is defined in a very odd and limited way if we remove writing, and especially literature, from that definition.

But obviously to many people who *do* clearly understand the crucial role played by writing in the present and future (and past) fashioning of history, some types of writing fall outside the central arenas: the poetries, notably, of hermeticism, of love, of mysticism, the three so often teasingly intertwined. Perhaps this has convinced people that in the *De vulgari* Dante is enjoying a deserved respite from the uglinesses and the pain of the political scene. In a way that is redolent of the kind of purposefully disguised strength of the mystics, it is the love song that works its magic at the heart of this political party—although Dante is so unlike the mystics in other ways, especially in liking to lay all his cards on the table, and it is inimical to him to fool the enemy by denying him a text that makes sense. It would seem even less likely that philology itself, the branch of literary studies that most loudly cultivates distance from ideology and engagement with the most arcane details, might instead be an authentically—and repeatedly, in one strong voice after another—political activity. But let us look at the starkly, at times even cataclysmic, political and ideological real "real world" foundations of a series of texts which are, in direct response, consciously and aggressively foundational, constructing and reconstructing (for each text begins again) what I will persist in calling Romance philology. I use this term despite the fact that in this most highly personal and often poignant form it has always been idiosyncratic and not normative—practiced by a minority, rather than a majority, of those who might (equally legitimately) use the same term.

Let me begin again. The medieval—and thus what we call the modern and the postmodern—lyric is invented in exile. But this time let us put aside that exile for a moment and go down the slightly different road of invention: that form of inventing literature that takes place when someone like Dante (or Ernst Curtius or Ramón Menéndez Pidal) writes a work like the *De vulgari* (or the *European Literature and the Latin Middle Ages* or the edition of the *Poema de mio Cid*). And I do not mean here simply that transparent form of invention perhaps implied by citing Menéndez Pidal's notoriously "creative" editing of the lonesome and badly mutilated Cid manuscript, a practice now often held up to some ridicule since it supposedly contrasts with the more "objective" editing that we would do today. That case is delicious only because it is emblematic, in a highly conspicuous way, of the perpetual and necessary role of ideology in this most human of activities. No, Dante invents—would it be easier if we said "founds"?—the medieval lyric because his book does everything needed to make it a vital part of institutional culture and literary history itself.

The *De vulgari eloquentia* begins with the celebrated defense of the vernacular. Then, as well as now, the old and the thoroughly classicized—Latin, at the time, Greek, at far greater distance and in considerable dimness—is reflexively valued above the contemporary, the unproven, within the circles of high culture. And we have routinely undervalued the revolutionariness of Dante's argument for his contemporaries: the intrinsic and absolute superiority—the greater nobility—of the vernaculars, over the classical languages (which he cannily describes as artificial constructs, as mere "grammar," an artificial and unliving construct). We are stolidly unable to imagine in a vivid way the breathtaking and youthful impudence of the Dante who writes a book about how the old culture and its language are fossils, and about how the new poetry, until now shunted to the margins of respectable and established culture, is the vital and eminent (and eloquent!) new form of the (new) age. Dante is an angry young man of about thirty when he writes the *De vulgari*—a very different man from the venerable patriarch of "world literature" that is the lasting image we seem to carry in our hearts, that impeccably conservative and stern, clean-cut elder of all those little statues they sell in Florence, that remote and distant patriarch on the frontispieces of our *Commedias.* This Dante is still freshly smarting from the impardonable banishment of the old men and the old hierarchies who wield the institutions' powers to punish him for his many impudences.

In most ways the *De vulgari eloquentia* is at its most startling in its opening, with its headfirst and uncompromising advocacy of the vernacular, the spoken language: "the speech of the common people . . . the language which children gather from those around them when they first begin to articulate words; or more briefly, that which we learn without any rules at all by imitating our nurses" (I. 1). Until then—again, the differences between then and now encourage us to forget that this legitimacy had to be fought for, at times bitterly—that language, the language of women and scruffy street singers, had marginal acceptance as a written language. Dante's claim is not just functional or pragmatic, but it is crafted in full knowledge of the ideological freight, and it is an argument with resounding impact and controversy (even today, in many circles). Dante's claim is that the languages actually spoken by people are superior to those that are merely written and not intimately connected with speech. The first chapter of the work's Book I ends, famously: "Now of the two the nobler is the vernacular: first because it is the first language ever spoken by mankind; second because the whole world uses it through diverse pronunciations and forms; finally because it is natural to us while the other is more the product of art. And I intend to deal with the nobler."

What is stunning and revelatory about the statement is that this is the prelude (the entire Book I is prelude, in fact) to the detailed discussion of the refined—arcane, at times—intricacies of the love lyric in Book II. Indeed, it is in the apparent discrepancies between the global programmatic statements, as in the one just quoted, and the no less transparent implementations of the canonical program in the second part, that we grasp the fullness of the struggle at hand. The first book is in great measure the theoretical overture, and its two movements are readily visible. Chapters 2 through 9 set out the basic premises about language as a uniquely human activity and its development, working carefully toward the second—and obviously principal—issue of concern, that of the existence of both change and variation in human speech, and the specific variations that exist within Italy. This is the shift from the dead to the living.

But the remaining chapters of Book I, the second movement that is chapters 10–19, is charmingly set up for us as a hunt. We roam Italy searching for the variation that is, among the fourteen principal variations, which in turn have so many variant forms that they "not only attain but exceed a thousand" (I, 10), "most decorous and illustrious" (I, 11). Why? Because Italy—which, significantly, is not yet Italy but is XXin a state of murderous disorder and internecine warfare, and Dante, who does not say so directly, is transparently its most aggrieved victim—needs a language to call its own. And now a monumental paradox appears to emerge. Dante concludes first that each and every language of the peninsula is in one way or another impossibly deficient to serve this role; furthermore, that the only language which will do is the construct that would emerge if we took the best bits and pieces, those that the different languages have in common, and, from this, forged a new language, which he calls, famously, "illustrious, pivotal, courtly, and curial" (I, 17). Dante knows perfectly well, no doubt, that on the face of it this is a call for creating another "grammatica" or artificial construct, and that he has just demolished, with wit and rancor, the very "nobility" of the languages of the Italians that his essay was supposed to illustrate. The contradictions pile up.

And this is but the prelude, since this same tension, and potentially severe contradiction, between idealized construct and actual historical practice underlies the entire construction and essence of the handbook of love poetry that almost immediately follows. It is in this obviously incomplete second part (truncated in the middle of chapter 14) that Dante is most foundational; here, he lays out the texts which he thinks must be the new canon and must replace those of the dusty old "grammatica"; and it is here that he will show us, through his old-fashioned explication de texte, that these poems, even though they are written in the languages of nannies and Tuscan street scoundrels, of vulgar singers and Sicilian traitors, are nonetheless great high art. Here, the *De vulgari eloquentia* might well be newly described, in the current intellectual climate, as a model document for effective canonical reformation. First, you take the new and un- or undervalued texts. (And here it is crucial to remember that at that time the vernacular lyric had had only local, socially limited legitimacy and success, which had been highly politically contingent. The two big success stories Dante knew about, and from whose leavings he drew many of his sample texts, had been at the courts of Provence, which had been effectively demolished with the victory of the French in the Albigensian Crusade, and at the court of Frederick II, and there too the climate which had fed and legitimized the poetry also perished with the patron.) Then you "prove" the kind of standing in the high cultural canon that these texts ought to have by treating them *as if they were* already part of that tradition. This proof of high standing is done by subjecting these poems to the kind of rigorous stylistic analysis until then reserved for the poetry that had been used in the formal teaching of the "grammatica." What Dante thus effectively reveals, however coyly, is the high degree of complexity of poetry that was written in a language that at the time was widely believed not capable of sustaining great and complex writing. (The conceit that love poetry is written in the vernacular so that women can understand it has many layers, and Dante continues to play with it, sustain it.) In this entire strategy there is an elaborate and extended version of the choice of Latin for the polemic against its canonical supremacy; it is the necessary reliance on the paradox, of which that first choice of language is but a taste. Dante is *not* preaching to the converted, and he must use, in time-honored fashion, the language and the measuring sticks of the unconverted; he must prove that poetry in the vernacular (and thus the vernacular itself, as he has already given away) is as "grammatical" and thus as capable of being a part of high culture as anything out of the classical Latin canon. And so it would be, although—fittingly, Dante the exile would have agreed, with some grim humor, no doubt—the cultural vision he had and which he pushes so hard in this seminal essay was most powerfully resisted in Italy, last among the daughters of Romania to accept fully that Rome and its language were but a lovely memory.

The ideological freight of this cultural vision is inescapable. If the vernacular and its poems are as grammatical, as subject to analysis that reveals its underlying rules, as the literature of Latin itself, then the difference between the two languages is cultural (or what might be called sociolinguistic) rather than, strictly speaking, linguistic. The cultural difference is the one that Dante first set out as a linguistic difference. It is the difference between life and death, between the culture that is cultivated naturally, that mothers nurture their babies with, and the one kept alive only through assiduous and extremely limited cultivation. While Dante is not interested in suggesting that the old stuff, the paternal cult, be banished altogether, he is arguing strenuously that his culture is in drastic need of being brought back to life and that the grammar books need to be replenished with poetry that is every bit as spectacular as anything ever crafted but that is vitally—maternally and viscerally, rather than from a distance and as a learned skill—tied to its public, to its listeners.

In the paradoxes of his argument much is revealed. Much of the first book, its entire second half, is the search for the elusive perfect language for Italy and the discovery that the panther will not be found, but that instead he must be constructed out of the bits and pieces of all of the different variations that have been scattered. In contrast, the second book, which is indeed the powerfully canonical center of the work, is a virtual catalog of exemplary poetry—real poetry, already written, and not just in the variant languages of the peninsula, but in the languages of *oc* and *oil*. At least on the surface of it, the theoretical construct of the first half crumbles on the pages filled with brilliant poem after brilliant poem. Much later, when the *De vulgari eloquentia* surfaced after a long period of being completely unknown, its authenticity was doubted because of the now-redoubled contradiction. How could this work, this rejection of Tuscan and all dialects as candidates for the national language, have been written by the greatest imaginable writer of the Florentine dialect, whose *Commedia* was the absolute cornerstone of the pro-Tuscan factions in their eternal arguments, with all comers, over what language was good enough to be Italian? And no one was ever more merciless with the Tuscans than that Dante, whose chapter 12 of Book I opens: "Let us now come to the Tuscans, who mired in their vast stupidity, claim for themselves the honor of possessing the most illustrious vernacular." Tough words to take from the man who was being held up as the champion of, precisely, such a stupidity, as the best example of the necessary primacy of Tuscan. And easier to claim that, obviously, the author of the *Commedia* could not have had such an opinion, meaning that the attribution must be scurrilous. But since the text's authenticity was eventually clearly established, Dante ends up arguing with himself: the *De vulgari eloquentia* a key text in one corner, the *Commedia* in a very different one, in the quarrel, at times bitter and irreconcilable, rather ingenuously called the "questione della lingua."

But even before the *Commedia* comes along to shatter the fantasy that a language can be made up—or even that it *has* to be made up—we see in that second book of the *De vulgari eloquentia* that Dante now talks urgently and consistently, and with considerable sleight of hand, of the "illustrious vernacular" that can and is now exemplified with a full range of particular and contingent variants. When he discusses the canzone, the song, the "construction of the greatest elegance," his list of the best examples includes a virtually complete sampling of the Romance vernaculars that he knew, from Guiraut's Provençal to Guinizelli's Bolognese. Any number of essentially hermeneutic explanations might account for the enormous discrepancy, the one that can be rather crudely reduced to theory versus practice. But, once again, it is a pity to abandon the fiercely committed Dante at the level of analytical philosophy when, from a pragmatic and consciously political perspective, this might be seen as yet another version of his cunning, another side of his Trojan horse.

Isn't he trying to convince us of something we might not want to believe? Isn't this what explains the placating and seemingly conciliatory tone of the two-sided argument about the vernacular that is the focus of Book I? First, Dante tells us that all of the vernaculars are essentially vulgar and gross—and he plays out that argument in superb and scathing reprise of the old fogey who takes the single crass utterance to represent the vernacular itself—and consequently that a vernacular worthy of great literature must be constructed artificially, as Latin was. These would be the highly conservative responses that the radical assertion of the superiority of the vernacular would have elicited, and Dante wants the unconverted to be lulled into thinking that, despite the very rash opening statement, he actually does speak their language and that he does not really believe the language of the streets and the uneducated—the language learned from women, no less—has anything to do with the Great Tradition. By the time we get to the second part of Book I, we know he is right-thinking; he respects the high standards of high culture, after all, and his judgments are as respectful and respectable as ours. And when he does those impeccably traditional and very nearly scholastic analyses of those poems, we *know* we can trust him. Perhaps, then, there are a handful of poems in an illustrious vernacular—why it works so much like Latin—that can be let in through the side gate.

Probably no story is more famous in our profession than that of Erich Auerbach's writing of *Mimesis* in Turkey. The German professor of Romance philology—which meant teaching Old French, Old Provençal, and Old Italian—is a Prussian war hero and survivor of the carnage of World War I, but he is also a Jew, and in 1935 the Nazis chase him from his position at Marburg University. In 1936 he goes into exile, to Istanbul, where, in the affectionate recounting by Lowry Nelson (who would be his colleague at Yale a number of years later), he instructs "an audience mostly of well-brought-up young Turkish ladies who needed French."[4] But it is here, in such extreme and redoubled exile—Europe and its cultures are savaging each other, Auerbach the German who writes in French sits helpless at the edge of the desert, looking on, without his languages and without his books—that he takes on Romance philology headfirst. He had begun with a Vico long hidden away, a kind of crazy relative kept in a back room out of embarrassment, and he had brought Vico into one of the living rooms. His translation of the *Scienza nuova* appears in 1924. From there, Auerbach goes where Vico takes him, to that de rigeur entanglement with Dante. His *Dante, Poet of the Secular World,* is first published in 1929 (and if one listens carefully the "secular" in the title should echo the "vulgar" of Dante's essay, that hubris of thinking to bring the dead back to the land of the living). Then his involvement picks up in earnest. First, he writes an introduction to Romance philology in French; then, in 1938, less than two years after the beginning of his exile, he writes the essay that would eventually be his most read, "Figura"; and finally, as the 1953 English translation tells us, *Mimesis* was "written in Istanbul between May 1942 and April 1945."

When I was first told Auerbach's story as a graduate student, I think the moral was supposed to be that it was a truly magnificent scholar who could write a whole book without a library (and thus without notes or bibliography), although, as we later snickered among ourselves, the intent of the moral was certainly not that *we* should write our papers (let alone an entire book) without sources or references. But the story, so rehearsed over the years that it has become something of a small fable, has many morals, and it is only one of many curiosities that, as is the case with its lack of notations and references, we are supposed to admire and not to emulate. And the principal reason is that the book reprises and strongly reinscribes the type of Romance philology whose ancestral text is the *De vulgari eloquentia,* a work by a player overtly contingent and politically engaged, conscious of the stage of History—and very much a part of it—and often at odds with institutions of every sort. These are not the virtues of exile commonly taught in our departments of national literatures. Indeed, and this is where we must begin, the very notion of "national literature" is one of the evils being fought by Auerbach during the war, from May 1942 to April 1945, at his post in Istanbul.

When confronted with the astonishingly broad range of interests revealed in the table of contents of *Mimesis,* most literary scholars and critics today are likely to attribute the huge disparities between Auerbach's curriculum and our own to a highly generalized notion of distance between us epigones and the older generation of cultivated Europeans who were gentlemen, and who spoke five languages impeccably, and who had received a sort of universal literary training which no one receives today. There are vague elements of truth in this classical nostalgia, but as an explanation for the structure of a book like *Mimesis* and for the selection of texts within it, such an attitude actually obscures a great deal more than it reveals. The first thing obscured is, precisely, the combative stance that Auerbach is taking and the fact that he does stand out starkly, in his own context, from the institutional structures of "national" languages and literatures.

The tensions between Romance philology and the national philologies (the latter evolving into what are now, essentially, the structures of the national languages and literatures) are a crucial facet of the very incompletely written institutional history of Romance studies. In a superb study (among the handful of systematically "philological" studies of the discipline's history), Hans Ulrich Gumbrecht allows us to see in rich detail crucial differences between a Romance philology largely reinvented and cultivated by the Germans (who were, crucially, not yet Germans) and the national philologies. Gumbrecht focuses on the French, but most of the principal patterns he addresses would certainly hold true for the Spaniards and only slightly less so for the Italians. We are able to see in that history the simple version of the foundational myth, the setting up of the institutions, of the professorships and the courses, in the nineteenth century. It is the nationless Germans that reprise the effort of the *De vulgari eloquentia* and write its next two chapters. The first "official" texts in the canon of Romance philology are Diez's two books, written in German, on Provençal poetry, *Die Poesie der Troubadours* (1826) and *Leben und Werke der Troubadours* (1829). Key distinctions of the philological posture are there: the choice of language(s) and text(s) that are not correlated with national boundaries (indeed, Provençal is a far from innocuous or neutral choice, since the destruction of *languedoc* had been a crucial part of the foundation of "France" and "French"); the explicit fusion of what would fairly soon begin to be the separate studies of language and literature; and this perfectly interwoven whole quite explicitly a part of historical studies in general.

Auerbach's characteristically elegant formulation deserves repeating. "The field that I represent, Romance Philology, is one of the smaller branches on the tree of Romantic historicism, which as it were in passing experienced Romania as a meaningful whole." Usefully complimentary is the more comprehensive description that opens the commemorative article on Auerbach by Lowry Nelson: "Philology meant, and still ought to mean, the general study of literature, from the most technical matters of lexicography, etymology, and establishing texts by rigorous argument, to the reading and explication of literature on a sound basis of authentication and understanding. *In its original conception and in its best tradition* the 'technical' and the 'literary' aspects were properly inseparable. *Separation came balefully later.*"[5] But not much later.

In fact, the very particular combinations of this strongly foundationalist branch and (at a no doubt unconscious level) its equally particular ideological underpinnings meant that Romance philology, for one reason or another, was always vulnerable to partitioning. Gumbrecht's narration lets us see how French national philology differs crucially from the Romance type of the Germans and how—and in all of this the other national traditions differ precious little—the partitioning of France from the rest of Romania is part of the larger project of particularizing the national ethos and a canon of distinctively French works. The potential antagonism—or at least irreconcilability—is clear. In essence, the German model (and it is uncannily like that of the Dante of the *De vulgari eloquentia*) is that of the outsider entranced with the fragmentation, the loveliness and merits of the scattering of the long-lost ancient empire, whereas the focus of the national projects was something like the opposite—the particulars of the single variety that became its own empire, a new, distinctive, and powerful culture, bound by a specific and particular language. The Romance model—we see much the same thing whether we use the life's work of Spitzer or Pound's *Spirit of Romance* or Dante or Auerbach—begins with the premise that the universe has exploded and that its remnants are dispersed everywhere and may appear at any time or place, in any language. And the philologist is a part of that diaspora, its historian, in exile, an exile.

The strong texts in this Romance philological tradition are clearly marked by an indifference—often a palpable hostility—to the parallel but opposite features in the national traditions: the highly temporal and developmental perspective (how France became France from the ruins and from the primitive dark age); the limitations to a single language, with others in subsidiary positions of "influence"; the neat separation of historical moments that divides in virtually absolute and epistemological terms the "medieval" from the "modern" since the division in national history and consciousness runs along the same fault line. What a departure this nationalism is from the exilic ethos, where medieval and "modern" texts are unobtrusively lumped together and are treated neither as developmentally related (with the medieval as the rudimentary form) nor as epistemologically alien. If we look at the *Mimesis* we have chosen as exemplary, there is telling, loving, and fraternal alliance among Auerbach's Odysseus in the first chapter (an Odysseus further lovingly reevoked through a correspondence between Goethe and Schiller), the Adam and Eve of the Old French *Mystère d'Adan,* "the enchanted Dulcinea," and the Virginia Woolf of the last chapter—to select four examples from the full twenty chapters. It is true that in most of these works (as well as in staple courses of study that are transparently based on the same model) the ordering of the texts is essentially chronological, and in the work of Auerbach he is explicitly interested in the transformations and transmutations as one goes along. But these are, at least in the articulations of these major philological writers, very far from the sort of development and improvement model that is the sine qua non of national literary histories. If we glance at the work of Auerbach's confrère (in most key ways), Leo Spitzer, we are as forcefully struck by the same phenomena. One need look at only the three "chapters" of *A Method of Interpreting Literature:* "Three Poems on Ecstacy (John Donne, St. John of the Cross, Richard Wagner)," "Pages from Voltaire," and—most stunningly for all those who automatically equate the philological tradition with a quaint and arcane antiquarianism—"American Advertising Explained as Popular Art."

Once again, what stands out is the explicit lack of boundaries: periods, languages, and even types of art most others, even today, would consider incommensurate and incompatible. As is the case with Auerbach's book—and in its own way with the *De vulgari*—a highly lyrical, openly personal, and essentially atemporal "Romania" is sketched out, suggested. It is without nation—indeed, it is the product of the explicit scattering of a nation—and it is, concomitantly, written in all languages and at all times. Toward the end of his life Auerbach would bind himself even more tightly with Vico and make the point—and its political importance—simply: "our philological home is the earth: it can no longer be the nation."[6] One of the most obvious effects, quite intentional, of the explicit linking of the most contemporary texts with those that, in the national traditions, are placed at a remote distance, is the one aggressively sought in the *De vulgari eloquentia,* as its title suggests: that of integrating the vernacular, the living and not yet canonized, with the traditions that normally get the respectful explications de texte. In fact, within a context—our own, essentially—in which medieval texts are more commonly treated as artifacts or—at best—relics, the vivifying effects are reciprocal and the medieval text reads, epistemologically, like a "modern" one when it is part of the string of texts and authors that includes Montaigne or Goethe or Góngora's "Soledades." Even more conspicuously, in reading together texts that are normally segregated by national frontiers, the frontier's many weaknesses are exposed, perhaps even erased, at least for a moment.

It is far more than simple, wonderful irony, always enjoyed by the relentlessly acerbic Spitzer, that any article bearing the name "American Advertising" (and proceeding with the kind of analysis Spitzer uses) would if written today be automatically accused of being part of the general decline of standards and the attack on the Great Tradition—a Great Tradition, we are led to believe if we listen to the simplistically nostalgic paradigm, that was preserved for us by men like Spitzer and Auerbach, and Dante before them. But in their own moments, they were often far from preservers. They attacked, at times fiercely and courageously, many of the same versions of the Great Tradition as well as the paradigms of knowledge that defend it. More importantly, they stood against that vulgarly antiquarian version of "philology" that sees the canon as fixed and thus in Dante's first formulation, "grammatical," dead. And, crucially, they utterly rejected those intellectual and professional structures that are rooted in the provincialisms of nations and languages—the petty, warring cities, as Dante so scathingly decries them.

There is considerable pathos all around. Auerbach will watch Europe become little more than a handful of petty, warring cities, from Istanbul, which was Constantinople, which was Byzantium. "An aged man is but a paltry thing, A tattered coat upon a stick, unless, Soul clap its hands and sing. . . ." An Istanbul that had been home to exiled Jews before, in the scattering of 1492. And from Istanbul, into Istanbul, he would see, every day, that spectacular church which became not just *a* mosque but *the* mosque, the most sublime model for a mosque: take a Byzantine church and add minarets. Who can believe in cultural unities, in nations—or even in empires, except as memories—at such moments, in such places? Auerbach in *Mimesis* is inscribing himself seamlessly into the tradition of Romance philology that is itself scattered, that embraces the scattering of peoples and empires, that relishes the linguistic divisions it reveals, that eschews the respect of nations and makes a brutally defeated one—the courts and the Albigensians of Provence—into a sort of honorary, obviously ironic, foundational icon. The measures of the resistance to the standard cultural paradigms are ubiquitous and perhaps—appropriately—most visible in the languages this philology would make its own. Not only is the Provençal that it places on the central altar the most conspicuous "vernacular" that has no derivative nation or national literary tradition around which to structure a canon or fund a faculty, but Provençal is crushed, historically, to make French, French.

This is a church so rashly ecumenical that to call it "Romance" is obviously to make that term, too, necessarily iconic. Virginia Woolf? Goethe? Donne? Homer? American advertising? What definition of Romance is this? And I should repeat that these constellations cannot be read nostalgically as signs of how things used to be. On the contrary, the national philologies, the segregation of medieval from modern, and the strongly classicizing attitudes were all, in different ways and to varying degrees, very much operative. Even Diez's original appointment in Romance philology was opposed on grounds that smack uncannily of "standards" we might imagine of more recent invention; he was manifestly unprepared to teach the real languages of Spain, Portugal, and Italy.

This last issue—the nature of the link (or the partitioning) between philological studies and language(s)—is another complex one that will suffer here the indignity of simplification. As Nelson points out, the original paradigm was based on the dramatic union of the "technical" (the linguistic) and the "literary." In this formulation, too, the *De vulgari* is exemplary and foundational. But, once again, it would be distorting to see the "erosion" of this paradigm as essentially diachronic. Within Diez's own lifetime, and even within Diez's own work, the predictable and wholly natural tensions between the technical and the literary dramatically manifested themselves, and Diez becomes the founding figure of the *other* epistemologically distinct branch of Romance philology, the one in which the "literary" is fully subordinated to the linguistic. Here, literary texts, if they appear at all, are but the documents that carry linguistic information, "the subtext for deciphering sound laws," in Suzanne Fleischman's felicitous description.[7] One need only read the standard Diez bibliography, or the faultlessly detailed celebration of his career and his foundational status written by Yakov Malkiel—another European in exile who explicitly founds "Romance philology" a second time—to see clearly that the full-blown intimacy of the linguistic and the literary modes we see in the *De vulgari eloquentia,* or in the work of someone like Spitzer in the middle of the twentieth century, had been long forgotten by the end of Diez's own career *a century earlier.* In each of the three decades after the 1820s, when he published his two books on the troubadours, he wrote the monumental, strictly linguistic works that would be the cornerstones (and some of the parameters) of most philology thereafter. Between 1836 and 1844 he published the tripartite *Grammatik der romanischen Sprachen* and in 1853 the remarkable *Etymologisches Wörterbuch der romanischen Sprachen.*

This kind of almost exclusively technical work would appropriate for itself the label "philological," and it has always existed in an uneasy truce with the literary studies to which it was linked, tenuously, in an ancillary fashion. Part of what makes any sort of "general history" of Romance philology so difficult to narrate is that while a number of its luminaries, those whose impact has gone beyond the boundaries of the "discipline itself"—the Auerbachs and the Spitzers and the Curtiuses—have effectively married the multiple concerns (and the multiple languages), the great bulk of work in the "field" has been far more particularly focused and is almost obsessively atomizing. In the end, the sort of transition and unity that we see between the first and the second books of the *De vulgari eloquentia* more often than not was deferred in modern (nineteenth- and twentieth-century) practice; we needed the dictionaries and the historical grammars and the critical editions before we really had the wherewithal to talk literature. Romance philology may have mimicked, as a broad disciplinary ideal, that vision of a Romania scattered about Europe, inventing new languages and new literatures at the same time, and thus requiring a focus that brought all these shards together. But in practice, even from Diez on, it became more than accepted practice for any given individual or study to play or puzzle over a single fragment. Paradoxically, this tendency to particularize and telescope is explicitly tied to the notion that the details will come together into a coherent whole, and as an approach it will become ever more deeply ingrained, becoming part of the full range of efforts to define, first, linguistic studies and, then, literary ones to mimic the positivist discourses of the natural sciences.

This divvying up of concerns has powerful heuristic implications. Dante's *De vulgari eloquentia* is as powerful as it is precisely because the discussion about the nature and place of the vernacular is an essential theoretical and rhetorical component of the analysis of the poetry. The work's wonderful paradoxes, and thus its canonical importance, lie precisely in the whole being very different from the sum of the parts—just as a very large part of the grandeur of *Mimesis* is in the explicit joining of texts like the *Roland* with others such as *To the Lighthouse*. It is crucial that the "whole," however, is a constellation of fragments, a songbook, and in this it starkly differs from the "wholes" that are the unified narrations. When Auerbach makes the distinction between "the earth" and "the nation" as the home for philology, he means the wide range of concerns as much as the national division between one literature and another. In very comparable ways it becomes disingenuous (or naive) to see as essentially the same what are two types of "Romance philology" fundamentally at opposite ends of a conceptual and methodological spectrum. One type has largely lyrical premises whose effect is rooted in throwing all the shards on the same table, even though it looks like a terrible jumble. The other often has a strong narrative undertow and takes its strength from the conviction that it is only in the most precise identification of each shard that we can—who knows where or when—put the original vase back together.

This tension, and the fact that the latter view has been the normative one from the outset, puts into even greater relief the real isolation and exile of works like *Mimesis* or individual studies like those of Spitzer, and the irony is that these renegades should now so regularly be held up as exemplary, when their examples, in fact, go against almost all the rules and have always done so. The story of Auerbach's first exile in Istanbul is rarely told with what might be a terrifically kabbalistic first chapter. In 1933 the Viennese Leo Spitzer, forty-three years old, distinguished professor at Cologne, was forced to leave his teaching post and go into exile. He was offered a position at the University of Istanbul, where he was delighted with the magnificent views but struck by the lack of books—especially in this heart of fractured empire, where so many books once had been hidden away. Spitzer later recounted that he was told: "We don't bother with books. They burn."[8] He stayed for three years and then went to Johns Hopkins, leaving the post in Istanbul for the next victim of the Nazi expulsions, Eric Auerbach, who would write, there and then, the most famous book written, conspicuously, without books.

> "This book is not a philological work. Only by courtesy can it be said to be a study in comparative literature.
>
> I am interested in poetry. I have attempted to examine certain forces, elements or qualities which were potent in the medieval literature of the Latin tongues, and are, I believe, still potent in our own. . . .
>
> I have floundered somewhat ineffectually through the slough of philology, but I look forward to the time when it will be possible for the lover of poetry to study poetry. . . .
>
> It is dawn at Jerusalem while midnight hovers above the Pillars of Hercules. All ages are contemporaneous. . . .
>
> What we need is a literary scholarship which will weigh Theocritus and Yeats with one balance, and which will judge dull dead men as inexorably as dull writers of today, and will, with equity, give praise to beauty before referring to an almanack. . . ."

So begins one of the most influential and revisionist works of Romance philology of this century, certainly the one which in its direct impact on the developments of poetry of its own time most closely resembles Dante's achievement through the *De vulgari eloquentia.* And when Ezra Pound first explicitly disavows any connection to "the slough of philology" in his 1910 "Praefatio ad Lectorem Electum" that begins *The Spirit of Romance,* it is clear in the course of the next several paragraphs that he is disassociating himself from the same things that Spitzer would denounce less than a half-century later. While Spitzer would religiously avoid holistic work (and consider any unified book explicitly not part of the kind of philology he did), Pound in this book of strung-together essays is transparently providing a model for what philology *ought* to be. In 1920, ten years after its initial publication, Pound requested that it be accepted for his degree in Romance philology in lieu of the dissertation—his single incomplete requirement—he had projected on Lope de Vega. The department of Romance Languages at the University of Pennsylvania refused the request. The refusal was a weak reading (if any reading ever took place) of a fundamental work in the tradition. As the handful of lines from the preface make clear, it shares all of the fundamentals we have seen in the philology of Dante and Vico, Spitzer and Auerbach; time and structure are lyrical and synchronistic, the present is a living part of the past. The string of essays strongly resembles *Mimesis.* A first chapter on how Romance begins, in which the guiding text, glossed from beginning to end, is the *De vulgari eloquentia,* which he translates as the "Treatise on the Common Speech," is followed (among others) by a central chapter on "Proença," in which William of Aquitaine and his poetry are held up as quintessentially modern; in another chapter, he prefers the *Cid* (again for its starker modernism) to the *Roland.* The longest chapter of all, his study of Dante, along with chapters on Camoens and "Poeti Latini" and a chapter on Lope de Vega, we might assume to be what remained of the thoughts of a more conventional dissertation.

It is here that my statement about the invention of the medieval and modern and postmodern lyric—its exile and its ties to Romance philology—takes on concrete, literal meaning. We see the scattered and powerful bonds of kinship that link the creation of modernist poetry, through its principal editor, Pound, to the *De vulgari eloquentia,* whose spirit is much present and emulated in *The Spirit of Romance.*

There are other exiles of various sorts. In 1907 Pound had abandoned far more than his doctoral studies in a Romance philology he thought had betrayed the authentic and foundational spirit of "the Common Speech" (and living poetry); he had acted on the profound estrangement he felt from the United States and gone into what would become long-term exile in Europe, much of it in Italy. In a literal sense he would mimic the exilic Dante of the *De vulgari eloquentia* and, as is laid bare in the *Spirit of Romance* (a very early work, in the context of the revolutions of modernism about to take place), he would continue Dante's foundational work, his saving of other exiled poets, his restoration of the Provençal texts that we should listen to and make new. The poetry of modernism is thus both the new Romance philology and the desert outside Florence. And Pound's belief, shared with his philological cohorts—and in great measure it is this, too, that sets him apart from the institutionalized philology that so poorly understood him—that Romance philology, as well as poetry, is a fundamental part of the real political universe would have tragic consequences. It is unfortunate that the pathetic episodes rooted in Pound's anti-Semitism and in his ill-conceived public pronouncements during the war are taken—or are likely to be taken—as signs that poets (or Romance philologists) are ill-equipped to muddle about in politics and real history. But this opinion, I think, would be to misconstrue the complex tragedy altogether.

Let me betray my subject for a bit and try to glue the vessel back together. There has always been an obvious poignancy and symbolism in the story that Auerbach wrote *Mimesis* during the war in his conspicuous exile from a culture that had nurtured him and then mercilessly destroyed so much of what that nurturing had meant. But I think something is here beyond the vaguely triumphant irony, something far more purposeful that is less part of the (admittedly vague) myth of the Auerbach-in-exile story. It is remarkable that Auerbach gives surprisingly precise dates for the composition of his book, "between May 1942 and April 1945." But clearly he is pointedly delineating the war, the part of it, more precisely, to which his book corresponds. And the dates he gives correspond precisely to the period that begins with the great resurgence of hope after the first American victory at Midway in the Pacific (in fact, Churchill had proclaimed the war won after Pearl Harbor) and ends with the death of Hitler. Auerbach's dates are slightly off the most conspicuous and memorable events of the war's beginning and end, but they coincide uncannily with the more subtle (and yet hardly arcane) subdivision of the war that is marked by the high points of great hope and joy at either end: the first sure sign that the American entry would make the sort of difference everyone hoped for—the powerfully symbolic end of the Nazi leadership.

The largely unspoken interpretation of the Auerbach story (which I suspect is the normative one, as it would be for the *De vulgari eloquentia*) that *Mimesis* and all it represents—culture, scholarship, the disinterestedness and purity of art, literature, science—is one of retreat from the ugly world of politics into a transcendental world of values beyond such contingencies. I momentarily dwell on these details of the inscribed dates because they seem to me the minuscule but sure indicators of quite the opposite. Geoffrey Green has provided us with a detailed reading of the many ways in which *Mimesis* is meant, and effectively acts as a weapon—not a shield—in that war, a war that (like the American participation) imperfectly overlaps with the full war. This philology is in unflinching sympathy with Auerbach's first two interlocutors, Vico and (through him) Dante. It is an explicitly contingent affair, first overtly shaped by personal and political history, and crucially, in turn, viewing itself as a major player in the affairs of history. This philology—as Spitzer's statement makes clear—is about the historically specific uses of language and—as both Spitzer and Pound would make scathingly apparent—this is something dramatically different from the kind of atomizing and antiquarian practices that, almost from the start, became the rule. As Spitzer never tired of showing, the word, the etymology, the derivation—all these meant nothing by themselves; it all had to come back to the text in which it was rooted, had to reveal the dozens of complex layers of meaning that made it all work and that made it a song to which you hummed or a story which made you cry. And it is itself—this kind of philology—quite consciously a historically specific use of language, a part of the landscape from which it comes, a part of the landscapes it refracts and details for the next generation of readers. Who would care in a different universe—that of the Neogrammarians, that of the New Critics, in a universe of transcendent value—when, precisely, *Mimesis* was written? So radical a relativism supremely privileges History and its Poetry.

This philology not only begins with Babel and its exiles; it is devoted to them. Here, perhaps, personal history and the texts of this philological tradition come together most touchingly. While other branches of literary studies are tied to the grand narratives and to the concomitant, singular coherence that comes from the coincidence of a language with a polity and with a culture, the guiding and sought-for coherence of this philological enterprise lies outside those parameters in defiance of the boundaries of given languages and nations, even of conventional periods. The model, once again, is provided in trenchant terms by Dante. "Real" linguistic unity and its necessary state of fixedness is a transparently Edenic notion (and in its rare achievement is death itself), but in the midst of exile, in the most contingent and fleeting of vernaculars, in life itself, superb poetry is born and bred. Within such a universe the philologist overcomes the pain of exile, not by retreating to a universe in search of the pre-Babelian or pre-Edenic unities, those stable language states tied to national identities (that might be said to constitute the retreat of criticism from the playing fields of history), but by gathering together the kindred souls of exiles, by patching together a community bound by values of a different order.

Within such a context, who is left unmoved by Dante's gesture of bringing together the poems of the diasporas of Provence and Sicily—poetry that within the normal paradigms of national literatures was doomed to the worst exile of all? And who would not be doubly moved by the opening scene of *Mimesis,* the evocation of one of the great scenes of the healing of exile? "Readers of the *Odyssey* will remember the well-prepared and touching scene in Book 19, when Odysseus has at last come home, the scene in which the old housekeeper Euryclea, who had been his nurse, recognizes him by a scar on his thigh." Green brings all of this together in his study of Auerbach and Spitzer.

> The careers of Erich Auerbach and Leo Spitzer attest to the arch sovereignty history wields in the creation of literary criticism. Unlike Curtius and Vossler, Auerbach and Spitzer viewed literary criticism as a broad and integrative endeavor that spanned disciplines, professions, and styles of analysis. Both rejected the notion of history as an impartial chronicle or unavoidable fate. They opted for a dynamic conception of history as being alive in the minds of men and shaped by the power of their imagination. Hence, the past must be created anew. It must occur and reoccur as a vibrant present in the life and experience of contemporary man. And from out of this reappraisal must emerge the materials with which we live our lives, develop our culture, shape our history.[9]

Vico and Pound and Dante—all for better and worse—would listen to such a description and approve it for themselves, saying that, indeed, that is philology, that is the spirit of Romance.

A question still to be answered. What is the Romance in the work of an Auerbach or a Spitzer? What is "Romance" in Virginia Woolf and in American advertising? In Greek and in German? The answer is historical and iconic, and it is crucially related to Dante's moment of vision, that perspective from which empire and its singular culture—the sort that lay ahead of Aeneas—is a lovely urn irreparably shattered, a unified past (if it ever was a past) from which we are permanently exiled. From the perspective of a European history which had its Edenic unity in Rome, it is the shattering *into* the Romance world that is the moment of foundation and the perspective from which exile is all around, the entirety of the universe. Vico will write such a history. And Dante's perspective goes well beyond the simple, nostalgic lament and the longing for a golden past that might well have taken over the first book of the *De vulgari eloquentia* and trivialized the narration of its irreparable shattering into many pieces and many languages. The second book gives us the strong alternative, one that if written today would be accused of postmodernism; it gives us that assertion of the loveliness of the present, after all, and of the high lyricism of the shattered bits all around, and of the strength of the ties that show through and in each of the contingencies, each of the languages, each of the chronologically disparate moments.

Historically, "Romance" and its later spirit is a moment at which the vitality of a lyrical present is affirmed; iconically (in distinct and I think often conscious contrast to the nation-centered modes of seeing literature), it is a mode within which literature is itself a token of exile (exile being one of its icons and one of its remedies). Within this framework, "Romance" is a far cry from any sort of geographically or temporally delimiting linguistic demarcation; rather, it is the highly contingent mimicry of the moment at which it glories in the vitalities and the possibilities of its many varieties and of newness itself. It is a crucial aspect of this spirit—and I think this is precisely the part that is shaped and encouraged by exile and that makes it so sharply political—that "Romance" embrace all the contingencies of exile, and thus the different languages, the different times, even the very different manifestations of culture itself. And it is the strongest—and perhaps the most forceful—ideological component of this view that it thus not only reinvents itself constantly and by definition—Dante is the first to make it new in the Poundian sense and takes up, after all, the cause of the avant-garde—but that it do so in opposition to the structures that privilege constant and exclusive cultures, the kind that one has to be born into, the kind that cannot abide new languages.

The medieval—and thus what we call the modern and the post-modern—lyric is invented in lonely exile. Romance philology creates itself as it carves out a niche for the children of the storm. Dante powerfully transcends nostalgia for lost linguistic unity and begins the task of providing a different kind of home for the many dispersed voices. He knows he is one of them. In this universe the first of the Romance literatures is the most anachronic, the one that becomes the first exile within the diaspora, the one that, when Dante gathers its fragments for his book, already has no home, will never have a nation. It is a charming anecdote from the archives of Romance philology, recounted well by a bemused Curtius, that from the sixteenth to the eighteenth centuries (among "scholars" such as Voltaire) Provençal was accorded true maternal status, "the mother language of the others." This view was later propagated by French philologists such as Raynouard, until Father Diez came along to teach that "all the Romance languages were independent developments of Latin" and that Romania thus had a single father but many mothers. (In fact, the theoretical linguistic issues raised by the contrasting models—and the Ur-question at stake—as to just what is the nature of the source language of the Romance vernaculars, are classically *un*resolved questions in the linguistic area.)

But Provençal *was* transparently cast in the maternal linguistic role for perfectly understandable reasons. This is the heart of Romance; not only is this Romance's first great love (for, of course, it is only the languages that create literature that survive to tell the tale and stand in line in the orders of primacy), but the last love as well, wife and mistress, the powerful progenitrix. A first love is always the sweetest, the last to be forgotten, and this love is doubly so, since we have to remember how cruelly, how badly it all ended. That body of poems, those exiles from the bad end, that Dante shelters from the storms—many of the same storms that had cut him loose from his safe home and from which he, too, needed shelter—would come to define love poetry itself. Although on the surface it is paradoxical, or even incomprehensible, love poetry—and this love poetry most of all, so often seen as the pristine original, at once unbelated and exquisitely in bloom—becomes one of culture's most powerful icons. Not that antiquarian culture of the mode which removes itself from the sites of power and politics and history; quite the contrary. As Dante's choice of it for the *De vulgari eloquentia* makes clear, this is culture as a fundamental player in the political arena. Love poetry, the usually solipsistic song of unfulfillable desire, is clearly lined up by Dante as an ally against the powers that have cast him out of Florence and into the desert.

The notion that love poetry has strong political allegiances (especially the strongly subjective love poetry characteristic of this "courtly" manifestation) always seems to make people uncomfortable. Perhaps that is as it should be. One political peculiarity of the love lyric in its heyday in the *languedoc* (which is what Dante calls both the Provençal community and, tellingly, the "Yspanos") and ever since it has been *suspected* of highly unorthodox allegiances, of consorting secretly in back rooms with the heterodoxies of the day, with Gnostics, with Albigensians, with Sūfis, with kabbalists. As with almost everything concerning political sympathies, what matters is not so much whether a given collaboration took place—the case has never been "proven" one way or another—but rather that the appearance of alliance, of sympathies, has always been there. The love lyric always seems to keep bad company of one sort or another. That is why it came to such a bad end.

What is perhaps the single most famous book written on the bad company kept by the Provençal lyric, Denis de Rougemont's *Love in the Western World,* is one of two works of twentieth-century criticism whose structures and premises are in certain ways a part of those of the Romance philological tradition I have been discussing. But its structures and premises also are strongly negative responses to the foundational ideologies of those other texts, particularly to the part of the ideology that elevates both love poetry and lyricism itself (this latter to be understood as including "postmodern" critical modes of philologists such as Spitzer) as weapons allied against institutions rooted in very different values. In other words, while an almost invariably unconscious denial of the Romance philological mode is implicit in the mode's splinter forms—in the ones that atomize and those that antiquate—there is a far more conscious and powerful oppositional stance in works like de Rougemont's, and most importantly, in Ernst Curtius's masterpiece, *European Literature in the Latin Middle Ages.* These are works that do share the basic global premises about the larger enterprise. Knowing that he is dealing with the most fundamental of historical and philosophical problems that cannot be restricted to artificial "disciplines," neither writer atomizes "disciplines." Each unflinchingly sets out the depths of his engagement with the political and ideological issues at hand and sees his own book as a major player on a very real battlefield, a direct response to the contingencies and sorrows all around. But here we have full-fledged and conspicuously open responses to the cults of the vernacular love poetry, to the political party that made bedfellows of troubadours. In fact, I think we will find here the strongest political reading of works like the *De vulgari eloquentia.* Curtius and de Rougemont understand and respect—and thus battle fiercely—the highly ideological and foundational nature of that enterprise.

The focus of de Rougemont's campaign, famously, is the social subversion implicit in the poetics of what is commonly referred to as courtly love. His book has become an ambiguous classic in the field. Everyone knows about it, but no one admits they actually spend much time reading it because, although it raises and amply discusses many essential historical and textual issues, it is tainted by the openness of its commitment to certain values, to the necessary primacy of marriage and to the negative effects of those concepts of romantic love that blossomed in the medieval lyric. We are embarrassed, I think, by the very direct connection made between love poetry and life and its shaping values. One legacy of "new criticisms" of all sorts, and from all sorts of periods, is the notion that poetry is not real life. Once again I cannot resist the urge to point out that although, most recently, a "conservatism" on the attack argues strenuously that the various movements of the "left" have compromised scholarship—particularly literary scholarship—by making it a part of the political and ideological arenas, a highly "conservative" work such as *Love in the Western World* should provide considerable historical perspective. Not only is it true that the ideology and politics are always there, even if it is in the perpetuation of the myth that there are no politics in the canon and in our work, it is also true that a number of key canonical works, conservative ones like *Love in the Western World* and *European Literature and the Latin Middle Ages,* unambiguously illustrate that when there are great battles to be waged, when the stakes appear to be particularly high, open engagement is an openly displayed virtue and badge of honor, on the right as much as on the left. Indeed, de Rougemont's work fell into its current state of benign neglect precisely because of the ascetic standards of the New Criticism.

And for de Rougemont the stakes *are* extraordinarily high. The values of Western culture—those that have to do with love and marriage, primarily—have been relentlessly shaped by that notion of love which is elevated to magnificence and sublimity (and thus imitability) in that poetry of Provence. This is a Provence, we now have pointed out to us (it was all previously whispered but not much said in the open), crawling with people whose values are essentially subversive to a social order that values—indeed, needs—stability and continuity. And narrative. Other "referential" readings of troubadour poetry had focused (and most of this sort continue to do so) on either the orthodox and conventional aspects of "history" (thus, for example, the most banal manifestations of the feudal system reflected in, say, the seigneurial relationship between Lady and lover) or, on a similar plane, on the unstable and ephemeral detail of personal history (thus, the famous search for the identity of the princess in the Rudel poem of "amor de lonh," or love from afar, a search wittily mocked by Spitzer, who understood that History means something else). But de Rougemont's work ups the ante, bringing us, rightly, into the realm of the canon and its ideology. Like Dante before him, embattled, and Auerbach just a few years behind him, this is a philology that reflects a value-laden notion of what culture is, knowing it is what children read, what languages we sing in, what history will write about us.

What de Rougemont wants to reveal about the love lyric, which became ancestral to most notions of love in Western culture, is that it is destructive of desirable social harmony (by privileging forms of antisocial love) and that this is so, in part, because it is created—or at least reaches a crystalline peak—in the midst of a love affair of its own with heterodox ideologies, which, in turn, privilege a whole range of philosophical postures inimical to the normative Judeo-Christian-Islamic social framework. In other words, de Rougemont is saying, we beat our heads against the wall in our struggle to enhance and be part of the continuum of Western culture because a crucial aspect of our behavior—how we approach love and marriage—is (unknowingly) governed by values that were (and are) consciously inimical to those traditions and their continuation. At every level, our narratives are subverted by this lyric. We pretend to prize marriage and the kind of narrative it facilitates, but all along we have been having a powerful love affair. And the affair is not even what we think—it is not with the official history, with the picturesque and chivalrous knights, who, after all, have become a part of the historical narration. No, he tells us, it is far worse. The real love affair, passionately played out, is with the great heresy of the Albigensians (also called Cathars) that (according to those few who have put aside the crusading institutional narrations) distinctly shaped that rugged Mediterranean landscape.

Paradoxically, one of the achievements of *Love in the Western World* was that it put back on center stage the dominantly heretical culture that was later, after the devastating defeat of the Albigensians (which also allows *languedoil* to consolidate and become a national language)—relegated to footnote status by the "successful" narrations of the dominant orthodoxies. In a spirit not unlike that of Peter the Venerable, who first translated the Qur'ān into Latin (so that Christians, whom he perceived as much tempted by Arabic culture, might realize how black the enemy's heart really was), de Rougemont thus brings to light what the narration of the victors had swept away as brutally as the Crusade against the Albigensians itself did, because he believes that we are otherwise unaware of the highly subversive values and principles of the poetry we have accepted with open arms into the heartland of our culture. The Cathars may have been vanquished in some ways, but not in the most important ones—unless we realize that we bring up our children with a literature saturated with a notion of love that the Cathars (along with other heretics) espoused in clear subversion of Christian principles, the very principles that allow us to see and celebrate and be a part of the continuum, of a Great Tradition that is not scattered but whole and continuous.

It is indeed the case—and it is a part of my argument in Part I of this book—that we have inordinately prized the smooth and official narrations of institutions, and at the same time we have blinked at—given footnote status to—the wide range of phenomena that can be called lyrical. What is stunning when one gets beyond de Rougemont and into the handful of historians who have dealt explicitly in the lyrical, in the underground, is how richly cragged and heretical is the picture of *languedoc* they paint. Since the prejudices against de Rougemont are substantial (largely unjustified, I think, but so be it), let me quote at length the description given in a work of undisputed and monumental authority, in an area whose focus and interest, as we shall see, is radically different from de Rougemont's, Gershom Scholem's *Origins of the Kaballah:*

> Southern France, during the period that interests us here—that is, between 1150 and 1220—was a region replete with cultural and religious tensions. It was one of the chief centers of medieval culture. In order to understand the Judaism of this region, we must see it within its environmental context and not remain content with an analysis of the internal factors active at the time. Provence, and especially Languedoc, was the seat of a developed courtly and feudal culture. An intimate contact was established there (*through channels that are often no longer perceptible or that have only today come within the purview of serious scholarship*) between Islamic culture penetrating from Spain and North Africa and the culture and chivalry of the Christian Middle Ages. There, during this same period, the poetry of the troubadours reached its peak. *But beyond that, southern France was an area particularly characterized by strong religious tension unparalleled in other lands of Christian culture.* In this period, among many circles of Languedoc, especially in the area between Toulouse, Albi, and Carcassone *it was no longer Catholic Christianity that reigned,* but the dualistic religion of the Cathars or Albigenses, whose fundamental character has, not without reason, long been a subject of controversy. Judging from the external forms, one would think that it was a matter of a Christian sect seeking to oppose the corruption of the clergy and of contemporary society by means of ideals held to be more or less those of primitive Christianity. An alternative line of thought, increasingly accepted today, holds that we are dealing here with a religion that, while utilizing certain Christian notions, undermined the very foundations of Christianity. That surely was already the opinion of the Catholic opponents of this powerful her-

> esy, which was brutally extirpated only after a long and extremely bitter crusade by the Inquisition which, as is well known, was originated in order to repress it. . . .
>
> *This* [the fact that Catholic Christianity in its orthodox form was fighting for its very life then and there] *was a phenomenon unique in Occidental Europe.* There appear to have been close ties between many spokesmen of the secular culture—which reached its zenith in the lyrical poetry of the troubadours, seemingly devoid of religious tension—and this radical movement, which touched the hearts of the masses and attacked the foundations of the Church's authority and its hierarchy. Tolerated or even actively encouraged by many of the great feudal rulers and by a majority of the barons, the movement took root; and it required the intervention of the kings of France, here pursuing their own special interests, to bring the Crusade against the Cathars to a victorious conclusion and to break the power of the movement. In the heart of the Occident, a sect linked at least by its structure and perhaps also by its history to the world of Gnosticism and Manichaeism was able not only to gain a foothold but also to come close to a position of dominance in society. . . .[10]

I have allowed Scholem to draw this vivid picture for us for a host of reasons. His authority is not impeached for the reader of a work on Romance literatures; his description, with swift and sure lines, sets out a remarkably volatile and unconventional, almost forgotten, world in which the troubadours were born, flourished, and died—all with stunning precision calibrated to the fortunes of the Cathars (and the world, too, that Dante had seen, at least from a distance, severely shipwrecked and for whose survivors he had built a new ship); finally, because Scholem's own focus is the setting for the rise of a different phenomenon, the Jewish Kabbalah, and because the same landscape described for that purpose is the one in which we tend to believe only (or mostly) normative Christians and essentially Christian troubadours held center-stage. But reading Scholem, we realize with some force that *languedoc*—in Dante's terms, and from now on in this study, to include the great swath of land down past the Pyrenees—bred multiple lyric forms. A whole host of movements inimical to the grand narrative flourished: from the Kabbalah to *canso,* from the *muwashshaḥāt* to the Gnostic prayers, and back again, all in often impossibly confusing eddies.

In some ways de Rougemont understated the dramatic scene at hand: that stony landscape, fragrant with olive trees and sage brush, convulses with unnarratable inventions, the peaks of mystical and Gnostic subversions of *each* of the three great institutions, Christianity, Judaism, and Islam. At the same time—and again, remarkably, unaccountably, against each of the three great classical cultures—the strange new gods of vernacular poetries come to thumb their noses. It is not only that the troubadours were the secular masterpiece of a culture sated with the Heresy and eventually pillaged for it. It is also true that the Cathars were far from alone. They shared time and space and politics and basic beliefs with the Jewish kabbalists who created the great Kabbalah there and then, and, no less on any count, with the greatest of the Muslim Sūfis, including Ibn ʿArabī. None of them, in turn, were ever far from the many places where the three old and revered paternal languages were being shamelessly replaced or (perhaps worse still) made to dance to the rhythms of another.

A hint of the ultimately dizzying interweaving of all these strands can be gleaned from the minuscule and Byzantine story of the woman who became the wife of the young James II of Mallorca. The young James was assigned the equally young Ramon Llull as a tutor—a Ramon Llull whose first métier was as troubadour. Of course—lest stuck in our national language corners we forget—Llull's Catalan *is languedoc,* and in this part of "Spain" that is the language spoken and sung—unless, like Llull, one became more than a poet and then, like him, one learned Arabic. In any case, the young woman is a refugee from the fierce war against the Albigensians, part of a diaspora that sent dozens of troubadours to Italy and most of the Jewish kabbalists to Spain, both with powerful historical repercussions. By all accounts (including the triumphant official ones) the war was unusually devastating and effectively razed that stony, fragrant landscape. But she was not just any young woman; she was from Montségur, the greatest of the houses of Perfects, the high and secret nobility of Cathars. Montségur was that great Albigensian stronghold whose bitterly sought fall in 1244 was "the last act of the Albigensian tragedy," to quote Frances Yates.

What Yates also points out is that this charming connection is no doubt the "missing link" between the ever-enigmatic Llull (whose transition from troubadour to kabbalist-sounding mystic may now seem less unusual in our context) and the *De divisione naturae* of John Scotus Erigena, the ninth century text that Yates is sure provides a significant part of the basis of the most arcane of his theories, those that smack most of kabbalist notions. The *De divisione naturae,* it turns out, was not only a favorite book among the Albigenses; it had been banned by the Church precisely because it was assumed heretical given the kind of readership it had. As Yates points out (although her emphasis and intent is no doubt different from my own), piecing together this puzzle in a sense resolves "the other old problem"—which I left unbroached in the previous chapter—of whether Llull was "influenced" by the Jewish Kabbalah, since the travels and fortunes of the text of the ninth-century, Greek-reading Irishman, Scotus Erigena, highlights the extent to which what flourished in *languedoc,* and was then scattered in the maelstrom, was a whole stable of "kabbalas."

Back we are, then, to counting the ways in which the lyric's birth takes place in radical exile. But let me say, first of all, that to deal with the question of the relationship between the Provençal lyric and the multiple mysticisms of its homeland, as if it were a matter of the poems constituting some sort of exact doctrinal hymns, in exact (and provable, of course) correspondence to specific doctrine, is to demean the constructs of poetry as well as those of the various heterodoxies at hand. Instead, this is a situation to be construed and reimagined against the grain—and in this the issue of the Arabic poetries of the period—just down the road a bit in some cases, in others in the very same court and room—gives us something of a model. What is required is a reversal of our fundamental image of the moment, so that, as Scholem says so well, *it is the orthodox that is struggling to stay alive,* and the streets are filled with singers of all sorts of newly invented songs in all sorts of languages. As scholars as far-flung (and as orthodox in their procedures) as Scholem and Yates and Corbin point out, the natural and obvious sympathies and dispositions—both doctrinal and political—among the different species of kabbalists is remarkable.

But the substantial indications of the teeming life and the unusual openness of this concatenation of resistances to the great orthodoxies have been in considerable measure doomed to remain a dim picture because of the inherently secretive and personal nature of the mystics themselves, and because the historical narration, even in modern times, has clearly favored the institutions, which provide the abundant and unambiguous documentation craved by the narrator. For all too obvious reasons, the totalizing narrative tends only to record the victory and minimize the enemy—and in this de Rougemont's work breaks the rhetorical mold. The astonishingly variegated, and unorthodox (in every sense of the word) situation of *languedoc* in the roughly 150-year period, from the end of the eleventh century until the destruction of the Cathars in the second quarter of the thirteenth, has thus been smoothed out from multiple perspectives so that we have either lost from sight altogether or relegated to distant positions (conceived, usually, as difficult and inaccessible "sources" that had to be found in manuscripts) a remarkable array of characters and sounds and sights and smells that made up much of the stage on which the troubadours stood and sang and heard their songs echo back to them: everyone from the singers of the new songs that melded Arabic with any number of the vernaculars, thus deeply subverting orthodox, high-culture Arabic practice, to the Jewish kabbalists who were then perfecting their version of the cult and worship of language itself.

The first exile of troubadour poetry, then, is both willed and shared, and much like Pound's, a Pound who deeply loved the traces of that devastated land. It is the often painful exile from institutions. And that exile begins with the radical linguistic break from classical languages, from those most fundamental emblems and vehicles for the home, the paternal cultures, and religions, and institutions. In our hindsight I think we appreciate far too little the enormity of the step taken when the vernaculars usurp the rightful place of the languages of power, thus usurping—if the coup succeeds—some measure of that same great power. (In crucial and largely unappreciated ways, this is one of the most profound ties and the natural sympathies that intimately bind the *languedoc* troubadours to the singers of the *muwashshaḥāt*.) In turn, that strong ethos of foundation, the at times delirious triumph of success—and indeed the vernacular songs spread like wildfire and were soon enough being heard in the most unlikely places—is perhaps most evident in the near-worship of language itself that is so strikingly the object of desire and love that it is readily confused with some kind of lover. To say this is to realize that this supremely solipsistic love—the love of the love created by language created by the poet—is in intimate communion—fundamental, not technical—with the kabbalists and their own love affair with language itself. And not far away—perhaps it is the same love, at times—is that most basic of mystical principles, that removal of love from the public (and thus social and institutional) sphere to the inner sanctum, the self thus fractured, made lyrical, both because it is now *solus ipse* and because it is deliberately removed from the narrative.

The love lyric, when it is carved out of that land, did keep the beat and very bad company, the sort of company, in fact, that was eventually—soon thereafter, in fact—brutally persecuted and banished, either destroyed or exiled, first from a *languedoc* that by the end of the thirteenth century was being purified and made easily governable, and then, and well into our own lifetimes, from the story we have been telling. The highly charged political significance of the love song is transparent once we bring back into view the faces and names of its fellow travelers, and once we realize that virtually every aspect of its poetics is an act of powerful defiance of the institutions that would fight back just as fiercely. The way the story is normally told—the way I first learned it and the way I suspect it is still told—the troubadours left Provence during the Crusade against the Albigensians because they lost their sources of patronage when the social and economic bases of that world were so severely undermined. In other words, there was no money left to pay for that great luxury that is pure art, a victim of politics, perhaps, but certainly not a player.

But the great virtue of de Rougemont's book—which bears careful rereading in a critical universe struggling with the political roles of critics and of literature "itself"—is that it reminds us forcefully that the ideological burden of a work of literature, or of a whole tradition, which in this case is a monumental one, "Love in the Western World," has little or nothing to do with crassly overt politics. As de Rougemont points out, what more consequent ideology do we deal with than that which affects a social structure as central to our culture and society as marriage? Like *European Literature and the Latin Middle Ages* by Curtius, *Love in the Western World* explicitly asks to be read ideologically and to consider the fundamentally ideological role which literature always plays. It is an oddly affecting experience to reread Curtius without bypassing his "Author's Foreword to the English Edition" (the English edition appeared in 1953; the original German is from 1948), which, after detailing his earlier studies in Romance (a Romance that, like Auerbach's and Spitzer's Romance, includes a wide variety of non-Romance authors) gets to the point of the enterprise without hesitation:

> Virgil and Dante have long had a place in the innermost circle of my admiration. What were the roads that led from one to the other? This question increasingly preoccupied me. The answer could not but be found in the Latin continuity of the Middle Ages. And that in turn was a portion of the European tradition, which has Homer at its beginning and at its end, as we see today, Goethe.
>
> This tradition of thought and art was severely shaken by the war of 1914–18 and its aftermath, especially in Germany. In 1932 I published my polemical pamphlet *Deutscher Geist in Gefahr.* It attacked the barbarization of education and the nationalistic frenzy which were the forerunners of the Nazi regime. In it I pleaded for a new Humanism, which should integrate the Middle Ages, from Augustine to Dante. . . .
>
> When the German catastrophe came, I decided to serve the idea of a medievalistic Humanism by studying

> the Latin literature of the Middle Ages. These studies occupied me for fifteen years. The result of them is the present book. . . .
>
> *What I have said will have made it clear that my book is not the product of purely scholarly interests,* that it grew out of a concern for the preservation of Western culture. It seeks to serve an understanding of the Western cultural tradition in so far as it is manifested in literature. It attempts to illuminate the unity of that tradition in space and time by the application of new methods. In the intellectual chaos of the present it has become necessary, and happily not impossible, to demonstrate that unity. But the demonstration can only be made from a universal standpoint. Such a standpoint is afforded by Latinity. . . .[11]

De Rougemont, in a book that is also conspicuously framed by the two wars that so unsparingly devastated and then restructured Europe, had sought to confront the same fundamental problem, that of the breakdown of cultural continuity and unity, that scene of moral and social breakdown that must have been an unavoidable and recurring vision from World War I on. In *Love in the Western World* the crisis is perceived to lie, at least in part (the part of it amenable to rational discourse), in the acceptance of a concept of a love that is starkly inimical to the continuity of the social order and to the institutions of continuity and narration (marriage, the Church, and so forth). The last section of the work is thus devoted to a contrast with the texts and the traditions that have privileged those continuums, those unities: love that is agape (and not eros), orthodox (and not mystical), narratable (and not lyric). In the most profound ways, Curtius reads the tragedies that surround him in much the same way. He sits and contemplates the devastated landscape of a Europe that must once have been civilized and unified and not barbarian and fratricidal, as his own nation had become.

His response, his effort to find something worthwhile in the shambles of that civilization come apart, is easily readable in his foreword, as well as in a number of key passages in the book. There is a noble and good tradition that *has* survived all along and that has provided—like an underground river—a unity and a continuum that *will* survive. And this great and powerful unity stands in visible opposition to the vulgar, the vernacular, the secular. Curtius, of course, is writing to the future—as was Dante, as was Auerbach, shortly before him—a future for which he is battling with other forces. And Curtius's stand, like de Rougemont's, is distinctly with the forces of unities and continuations, with narratives themselves, and no less distinctly, thus, in opposition to the Dante of the *De vulgari eloquentia*, and those of Dante's party, in more recent centuries. For Curtius, the *grammatica* that Dante believes is dead and has to be left behind is the single link, the continuum that can make Europe seem civilized, again; for Dante the lyric vernaculars that Curtius leaves aside, tacitly as part of the splintering that has made Europe forget its common civilization, are his allies against the institutions that have banished him from Florence and that want to keep him out of their version of history, too, and out of a canon that excludes people like him. Curtius does not quite come out and say it, but *European Literature and the Latin Middle Ages* suggests it strongly: it is the vernacular and vulgar splintering, the forgetting of that common Latin unity and heritage, that has caused the catastrophes of the war, the barbarities. When Auerbach writes his review of Curtius's work, he notes curtly that the work was "planned and executed in Germany, roughly between 1932 and 1947. . . ." How far from Istanbul.

I think it is this perspective that allows us to see why Dante would and did build a life raft for poets of a culture and ideology for which, in many other ways, he had precious little sympathy, poets who had a poetic ideology that he had in many ways already put aside, in the *Vita nuova*, written before the disaster of the expulsion from Florence. Indeed, the general ethos of the world of *languedoc*, as I have tried to suggest it, is one that would not have appealed to the Dante of the later period of exile, either. The Dante of the *Commedia* eschews precisely the kind of solipsisms (poetic or spiritual) that characterized those that fled Provence throughout the first half of the thirteenth century and, not long thereafter, fled the shattered court of Frederick. But Frederick, too, is a favorite of sorts, although he is radically unlike Dante in many ways. The tie that binds, in the end, in these various cases, *is* politics, the notorious conspiracies of exiles. That is the first reason why the freshly exiled Dante, still fashioning his weapons and sharpening them, would have felt unusually close to these exiles, so different from him in other crucial ways, but in this most important way they were brothers in arms. Despite differences of doctrine and detail, in the scatterings and the dispersals that followed the brutal use of power in Provence and later in Sicily, Dante saw kindred victims of the same forces, or the same kinds of forces.

There is another reason, one no less obvious if we remember how tenuous was the thread by which the new vernacular hung, how slim the chances of its success must have seemed, how huge and powerful and overbearing the tradition it was seeking to replace, the language it was trying to put aside. Here were the handful of allies in that major cause, pleading for help, exiled from their native lands, the courts that had sheltered them burned, destroyed. In the end, whatever differences he had with them could, at least for the moment, be put aside, if he, Dante, wanted to have anyone on that same boat with him at all. And there is, finally, the most particular and special reason: Dante is the truest of believers and he believes (as the *Commedia* will prove) that he can take that whole bag of solipsisms—linguistic, love, spiritual—and make something of them, pull a rabbit out, somehow. From this perspective Dante is building a lifeboat, that *De vulgari,* so that he can save that poetry in all senses of the word, so he can convert it; he will build from their lyrical solipsism and make it narratable, turn their personal revelations into public ones. He does, too. Listen to the converted Arnaut Daniel in Purgatory, renouncing the *trobar clus* and singing limpid poetry.

In a sense, this is a distillation of the Romance philological project as it was invented by Dante and as it continued to be practiced, always sporadically, always idiosyncratically, by individuals with ideologies as wildly varied as Pound's and Auerbach's and Spitzer's. Even those who did not write from exile (and here the strong countercases of de Rougemont and Curtius provide transparent examples), those who were, as a result, partisans of the pre-Babelian *grammatica* and other unities that Dante sets aside in the *De vulgari* as essentially illusory, even they write within the parameters of this exilic genre. "Romance" is an icon—positive for the Auerbachs, negative for de Rougemont—not a limitation; literature is always political and a major player in History; and the critic, the philologist, is always deeply engaged, understanding that what is contested is the future, the language of the songs the children will sing, the notion of love they will take from those songs.

In his informative and clear-eyed account of the history of literary studies in this country, a study focused primarily on "English Studies," but of much direct historical interest to those of us in the other vernaculars, Gerald Graff briefly pauses to note the beginnings of "comparative literature": "the Gauss Seminars of the early fifties did bring together an unusually large-minded group of literary figures. . . . On another level, the seminars brought together native Americans and those European masters of comparative literature who were part of the great foreign influx after the war. Though it has been omitted from my account, it should be noted that the development of comparative literature at this time established an alternative to the old scholarship and the New Criticism, out of which grew phenomenological criticism and later deconstruction. . . ."[12]

As Graff's handful of sentences reveal, the legacy of the exilic Romance philology has been in comparative literature, conspicuously created by the exiled community, and, more important, shaped very much along the same lines. Like the Viconian Romance philology, comparative literature is hopelessly idiosyncratic and inherently lyrical in its structures, as well as aggressively contingent. It has no set languages or texts, no necessary borders, no temporal constraints or narrative shape, and thus it stands in strong and obvious contrast to the narrative forms (as well as the fixed borders and set languages and the totalizing and developmental tendencies) of the national literatures. It is even true that, by and large, it is in comparative literature departments that Provençal, the ancestral and still much-loved mother tongue of this Romance philology, is taught, revealing that "comparative," like "Romance," at times has purely iconic value; it is the literature of exiles, those who have no other homes, or those who do not like staying at home and being absorbed into a longer story.

While the narratives of national literatures are driven (as in the examples of Curtius and de Rougemont) by the search for the transcendent, the lyrical mode of this comparative literature or philology instead accentuates the contingencies of each text and its language. For this reason, among others, the issue of technical linguistic filiation is of no particular interest (unless it happens to be a specific and momentary setting for a text) and why a strong philosophical vein, often explicitly relativist, is often pervasive. Similarly, it should surprise no one that out of a philological mode given speculative shape by Vico should come, in the shape of what is now fearfully (or worse) called "theory," the principal philosophical modes of apprehending literature.

Almost no one consciously understands philology in this exilic mode, nor is comparative literature routinely described in such terms, although, of course, individuals like Auerbach are regularly invoked as ancestral. In a different context altogether, Giuseppe Mazzotta has provided a reading of philology that catches many of the nuances I have tried to articulate:

> How can the method I follow be described? The answer, putting aside the inclination to ignore the question, is that mine is a philological method. The more orthodox practitioners of philology . . . will in all likelihood object to this definition and feel that my use of the term lacks any scientific rigor. And I would have to agree that my understanding of philology has little to do with what has come to be known, somewhat dismissively, as antiquarianism. It has even less to do with the philological positivism that still lurks, in a variety of sociological and ideological disguises, within historicist approaches to literary texts. . . . philology is involved, if I may distort Martianus Capella's title, in a troubled love affair with Mercury; that is, philology is primarily the discipline that accounts for the elements making up for the historical specificity of any text. As Vico (who also knew how unaccountable the power of the imagination is) puts it, nothing lies outside the archives of philology. . . .[13]

The evocation of Vico, the prominent house philosopher of this idiosyncratic philology, reminds us in quick and broad strokes of the remaining features that reveal the carnal filiations between the old philology, invented in the desert outside Florence, and the successor comparative literature invented in the diaspora of World War II. These features are its strong philosophical tendencies and its deeply rooted political engagements. (The other evocation, that of the troubled love affair, reinforces Spitzer's powerful presence in this house—a Spitzer whose astonishing passion in everything he wrote prompted Jean Starobinski to describe his approach as that of a lover whose ardor was kindled by the presence of a rival.) All of these elements are brought together, brought home, in a seminal essay by one of the best-known contemporary heirs of Vico and Auerbach, Edward Said, and it is tellingly called "Secular Criticism." Much of the first part of the essay is a touching reading of Auerbach's *Mimesis* and its exilic condition, and, at the heart of that, of Auerbach's use of the quotation of Hugh of St. Victor on exile. The second part of the essay, moved by the locus of Auerbach's exile, Istanbul, more specifically focuses on the (no less central) issue of critical engagement. The affinities (despite the sharp differences Said himself unflinchingly points out) between Auerbach and Said go further and deeper. And although Vico is not a visible presence in this particular essay, it is in and through his work that Auerbach and Said are joined to each other and to a "discipline" rooted in the dispersions, the exiles, of the lyric, to which Vico always gave primacy over other forms, and the contingencies of history. And, through and in Vico, it is a practice that is what Said calls "secular" (and Dante had called "vulgar"); it is consciously engaged with its own history, and it privileges literature as a powerful weapon in the major battles to be fought. There is significant resonance of all of this in the title of Auerbach's first work on Dante, "Poet of the Secular World."

Auerbach's seminal encounter with Vico and his largely unknown *Scienza nuova* (a text that would remain relatively obscure until Joyceans rediscovered him) lies explicitly at the origins of this philological practice. As Geoffrey Green so aptly puts it, Auerbach becomes absorbed with Vico at an early turning point, when he had left the law "(with its implied continuities to the evolution of Western civilization) for Romance philology (with its textual analysis of specialized milieus)," and he is deeply taken with "Vico's distinction between philology (the relative truth at each particular cultural phase) and philosophy (the absolute and unchanging truth)."[14] Auerbach's first major publication was his translation of the *Scienza nuova.* No doubt he is conscious of the paradox (it is in some ways at the heart of the lovely paradox of deconstruction) that Vico is a philosopher, albeit a very philological one.

For Said, too, Vico is the philosopher who stands against the totalizations of the Grand Narratives and who privileges the stark creationism he had seen in the Dante he loved (and understood in a markedly heterodox way). Said's description of his own early and formative encounter with Vico is translucent:

> The tremendous impact which *The New Science* had on me when I read it as a graduate student was, first, probably due to the scene that he paints at the beginning: of a feral and Gentile man; the giants; the period right after the flood, with people wandering all over the face of the earth, and gradually disciplining themselves, partly out of fear and partly out of providence. That kind of self-making struck me as really at the heart of all genuinely powerful and interesting historical visions (you see it in Marx, obviously, and in Ibn Khaldūn): the way in which a body forms itself into a mind and a body, and then a society. That is so compelling, and so powerful. . . . Second, he was always doing it by skirting around religious notions, of the creation and so on. That oppositional quality to his work—his being anti-Cartesian, anti-rationalistic and anti-Catholic—was incredibly powerful. . . .[15]

That kind of strong foundationalism is precisely the strength and the idiosyncrasy of the kind of Romance philology invented by Dante in the *De vulgari eloquentia.* And Vico will write its philosophical *Muqqadimah,* or prolegomenon. They are each and both committed to a string of fundamental principles that rational discourse, and the normative narrative structures of both philosophy and literary history, will regard as paradoxical: that narrative can be constructed lyrically, that philosophy can be contingent, that history can be anachronic, and that the love song and the hermetic poem can be acts of deep political engagement.

Notes

1. Durling and Martinez, *Time and the Crystal,* page 51.
2. Durling and Martinez, *Time and the Crystal,* page 52, emphasis mine.
3. Norton, "The New Life," page 52.
4. Nelson, "Erich Auerbach," page 315.
5. Nelson, "Erich Auerbach," page 312, emphases mine.
6. Quoted in Said, *The World, the Text,* page 7.
7. Fleischman, "Philology, Linguistics," page 19.
8. Quoted in *Baer and Shenholm,* Leo Spitzer, page 3.
9. Green, *Literary Criticism,* page 165.
10. Scholem, *Origins of the Kaballah,* pages 13–15, emphases mine.
11. Curtius, *European Literature,* pages vii–viii, emphasis mine.
12. Graff, *Professing Literature,* page 160.
13. Mazzotta, "Petrarch's Song 126," page 121.
14. Green, *Literary Criticism,* page 21.
15. In Salusinszky, *Criticism in Society,* pages 135–36.

3. Chasing the Wind

Lanquan li jorn son lonc en may
m'es belhs dous chans d'auzelhs de lonh,
e quan mi suy partitz de lay
remembra.m d'un' amor de lonh:
vauc, de talan embroncs e clis
si que chans ni flors d'albespis
no.m platz plus que l'yverns gelatz. . . .

. . . Ver ditz qui m'apella lechay
ni deziran d'amor de lonh,
car nulhs autres joys tan no.m olay
cum jauzimens d'amor de lonh.
Mas so qu'ieu vuoill m'es tant ahis,
qu'enaissi.m fadet mos pairis
qu'ieu ames e nos fos amatz. . . .

When the days are long in May,
I enjoy the sweet song of distant birds,
and when I go away from there
I remember a distant love
I go about gloomy and downcast with desire,
such that neither song nor hawthorn flower
pleases me more than icy winter. . . .

He speaks the truth who calls me greedy
or longing for distant love
for no other joy pleases me as much
as the enchantment of distant love.

> But what I want is so withheld from me
> that my godfather doomed me thus:
> That I should love and not be loved. . . .
>
> **Jaufré Rudel, mid-twelfth century**
> (Translated by Lowry Nelson, Jr.)

More than twenty years ago the widely admired rock guitarist, composer, and singer Eric Clapton, still in the process of carving out a career, came to a crossroad in his life. Professionally, he had been moving from one group to the next without finding a permanently productive niche. Personally, life had become almost unbearably grim, and madness seemed to be closing in. As the liner notes of one album put it, explicitly in the language of the black music that Clapton had been successfully grafting onto rock, he had "his blues made flesh." Now, as if playing out the lyrical contours of the music he had been cultivating for years, he fell madly and desperately in love with his best friend's wife. (And it is part of the glamour and the poignancy of the story that this best friend was George Harrison, himself at that moment more than a bit at loose ends in the aftermath of the painful breakup of the Beatles.) The story goes on with Clapton tormented by the characteristic impossibilities of his situation: on the one hand, betrayal of a friend (and in this case fellow poet—but it might as readily have been his king or a brother in arms); on the other, obsessive love that fed itself insatiably on obstacles and distances.

Clapton thus began to retreat into a variety of madnesses, including heroin, until he found a way out by turning back to what he knew best, literature and music. In London he began reading the medieval Persian poet Nizami, author of a renowned version of a story already famous in Arabic, one of the most famous of all in a tradition brimming over with love stories. The musical record from this period of his life shows unambiguously, as we shall see, that, in Nizami's *Story of Layla and Majnun,* Clapton found the crucial comforts of literature when it is a part of the living tradition. First, no doubt, there was the solace of explicitly knowing himself not alone in the torments of a love that seemed impossible and literally maddening. Second, and here the grist for the historian's mill, he found the consolation of the classical model that he needed to create poetry from his pain. It is crucial, for my version of this story, to note here that Clapton is *not* part of that small but significant number of rock composers—Sting is the best current example; the special case of Jim Morrison I will discuss below; Bob Dylan is one of the earliest models of the type—whom one would, at this point, suspect of the recherché gesture, the conscious attempt to inscribe themselves into the annals of high literature. What he finds is a translation, a lovely thing, including some remarkable reproductions of Persian miniatures, and transparently meant for the consumption of nonspecialists, that had come out just a few years earlier. He finds this translation by R. Gelpke not as a bit of semischolarly searching; he did not go and dig out something obscure, some antique and foreign text from the British Museum libraries. Clapton, obviously a literate man, was reading the *Layla and Majnun* because a version of it happened to be accessible to him, in translation into English. This was a case of perfectly ordinary accessibility, and I emphasize this in passing because it is a crucial emblem of the great accessibility, often thanks to a translation, and the potential life of literature that is otherwise very "other" and remote—in this case, doubly so, medieval and Persian. And, unsought as an answer, the response of Layla, of Majnun, of Nizami, is visceral.

Clapton emerges from the worst depths of his despair in London, starts to compose again, and then flies to Florida, quintessence in so many ways of the New World, where he finishes putting together and recording, in a whirlwind, and with considerable help from some of his gifted friends in the music business, what would turn out to be universally regarded as one of the most influential rock albums ever. In retrospect, I am both amused and baffled by the idea of what most listeners might have made of the fact, when they read the album cover and the song credits, that the fifth song, "I Am Yours," is listed as having been written by Eric Clapton and some fellow named Nizami. The lyrics of the single stanza are simply repeated three times through, the last verse the same as the first, for seamless circularity, and the whole is sung to an unusually strummed steel guitar, plaintively, to a quiet melody:

> I am yours
> However distant you may be
> There blows no wind but what you send to me
> There sings no bird but calls your name to me
> Each memory that has left its trace with me
> Lingers forever as a part of me
> I am yours.

The song, if we read it as a single-stanza lyric poem, clearly follows in the most conspicuous tropes of the tradition of love songs, a tradition within which the song is what comes of separation and pain, and even in its brevity it gives us distance, birds, winds blowing memories. If we treat the text as critics and scholars and summon up the Nizami text, as the author clearly wants us to (and which I do relying extensively on the indispensable *Medieval Persian Court Poetry* by Julie Meisami, from which are taken all the descriptions that follow), then there is even greater richness in the text's layers and echoes. I thus interrupt the story here to interpolate some rudiments of the story that Clapton had been reading before he composed and recorded that whole clutch of love songs, one of which he feels he coauthors with Nizami, in late August and early September 1970.

Nizami wrote the *Layla and Majnun* (*Layli u Majnun*) in 1188, adapting it from the already-famous story of ill-starred lovers in the Arabic tradition, much as Thomas, about the same time, would have been composing his "courtly" version of the romance of Tristan and Iseut. In the Arabic tradition, the mad lover is the figure of a historical poet, Qays al-ʿAmiri, who came to be known as Majnun. And Majnun, which as a name is derived from the root JNN from which we know the word jinn, means the madman, the one possessed by jinns. Let me steal enough bits and pieces of Meisami's analytic description to provide some sense of the story and its texture. From the start, Majnun's love for his cousin Layli is obsessive. He is the incarnation of the poet who finds the perfect object for his obsessions and poetry come to life.

> He wanders about distractedly, repeating Layli's name and composing verses about his love and the suffering it causes him. . . . Majnun makes a public display of his emotions. His excessive, self-willed suffering and the damage done thereby to Layli's honor, earns him the enmity of her father, who refuses to marry his daughter to such an obvious madman and rejects all efforts to persuade him otherwise. . . . Majnun's reaction is to make a public spectacle of his grief—tearing his garments, heaping dust on his head, repeating Layli's name, and uttering impassioned verses about his grief, before finally falling senseless to the ground.[1]

This romance, far more than most others in the medieval tradition, makes the lyric come to life with little narrative invention (the Lady is not yet married and she certainly is not cruel—Layli is in love with Majnun as well) to account for the obsessiveness rooted in distance. It is the obsession itself which creates the distance here, Majnun's behavior—as a poet, one might add—that will drive them apart.

> Majnun becomes increasingly alienated from his fellow men, and his flights into the desert, where he wanders naked among the wild beasts, grow more and more protracted, as he comes to prefer his isolated state . . . the mad, naked and emaciated Majnun is found in the desert by the Arab lord Nawfal and taken under his protection. . . . Majnun pursues his obsessive quest, manipulating the Arab chief's promise of support to his own end of obtaining Layli at whatever cost. The wars conducted by Nawfal against Layli's tribe result in bloodshed and destruction; ultimately he is obliged to forgo victory, and Majnun, reviling his friend, retreats once more into the desert. . . .[2]

In the end, Layli seeks out Majnun in the desert, but he—too obsessed with the image of her (and with the grand suffering of his passion)—does not recognize her. She dies of grief.

Whether we read this powerful romance in a Romantic framework, within which Majnun's excessive (and willed) passion is the condition necessary to transcend certain realities and write poetry, or (as Meisami suggests it was understood and thus inscribed by Nizami) as a recounting of the destructive aspects and of the abandonment of all moral social responsibilities (and here we have the two models of reading love poetry itself as a canonical force), it is clear why the poem would have so appealed to the love-distraught Clapton. It is true that particularly in the narrative form of the romance—and this is true par excellence in romances such as the *Tristan* and the *Chevalier de la Charrette*—the strongly antisocial ethos of the solipsism of the lyric is nakedly displayed and that Majnun is difficult to cast in a heroic or sympathetic role. This is true for exactly the same reasons that Tristan is a very uneasy hero—and let us not forget the crucial episode, extracted in the *Folie Tristan,* where he plays a madman. Critics have dealt gingerly, too, with the very ambivalent Lancelot of Chrétien's romance.

I have argued elsewhere and will argue again, now in the wake of my discussion of the largest canonical tendencies in Romance philology, that it is precisely in the shift from a lyrical framework (poetry itself, or a critical framework and ideology that are themselves lyrical) to a narrative one (the romances, for example, or the sort of critical framework exemplified by a Curtius or a de Rougemont seeking strong narrative unity) that the solipsism and the pantheism of the poetries that flourished in *languedoc* and al-Andalus in the eleventh and twelfth centuries become rocky impediments to the smooth narratives. It is in the crucial transition from the lyric mode to the narrative one that the ecstatic states which create gorgeous new languages, and transcendental loves, become negatives: impediments to marriage and social continuity (which need both institutions and progeny); the interruptions in traditions; the solipsism that shuts others out and isolates the self irremediably; Majnun wandering out in the desert, unable to recognize Layla herself. But when the lyrical mode is back in place, it comes round. A young poet goes out to the desert to become a companion to Majnun, only to find that Majnun refuses all companionship (including the breaking of bread), so the disappointed young man returns to Baghdad, *"where he recites Majnun's poetry to the admiration of all."*[3] The values, as always, are highly contingent.

It is thus crucial to understand that Clapton's reading of this story, and the seminal and highly influential text(s) he wrote as his reaction to it, are governed by the ethos of the rock tradition itself, both a highly lyrical structure in general and, more specifically, a phenomenon with deep roots and strong kinships, much of it conscious and cultivated, in and with the Romantic tradition. For a lyricist reading and working within a highly lyrical tradition, the story of *Layla and Majnun* is overwhelmingly positive and inspirational: the story of how hopeless love can make great poetry, even if so much else is destroyed along the way. At some level, reading Nizami's text must have reminded Clapton of that essential fact he had known from his years as a singer of rock songs, but perhaps forgotten in the throes of a real passion: if you are a poet and a singer, you can reverse the process of having the blues made flesh. You make the torments of the flesh into the blues. You can kiss Juliet through the bars of a rhyme. Moreover, in the process, there is a strong and sustaining lyrical ancestry established, since, if it is true that no "real" person can commune with the madman in the desert, he can and does commune with those who precede and follow him, those who add bits and pieces, words and rhymes and bits of tunes to his own poetry.

It is clearly in this spirit—these spirits—that the touching "I Am Yours" is written by Clapton and Nizami—and, one might add, Majnun. And in such a context we see that it is at once highly classical and unambiguously rock, at once a part of the omnivorous medieval Arabic tradition of Layla romances and of American popular culture. And it is thus, indeed, that Nizami was brought, first into the rooms in London where Clapton grieved and nearly went mad. He stuck with Clapton during the handful of months of frenetic composition, still in London, but now surrounded by other musicians and lyricists, until they move across the sea and to the sorts of rooms in which so much of this century's new poetry is being made—some recording studios, this time in Florida. Nizami is now no longer just some antique translated author, part of an inaccessible "high" culture, but, explicitly, one of the composers in the rock tradition, smoking dope and drinking, very hard, and making new poetry from old in the long Florida nights with Eric Clapton and Duane Allman. Allman, whose career as one of the best guitarists in rock is made on that album and peaks in the heady following months, would be killed in a motorcycle accident a little more than a year later.

Point of confession number one: The album that was frenetically composed and recorded in a handful of weeks in late August and early September, those weeks during which hurricanes are never far, is called *Layla and Other Assorted Love Songs* and, as that title indicates, the centerpiece is a song simply entitled "Layla." It is a song that everyone in rock—from the least literate listener to the most accomplished songwriters—would unhesitatingly describe as seminal, among the handful of highest achievements in the rock tradition. Anyone within rock who doesn't know Layla is an ignoramus. It is music I have been listening to, and singing with, for more than twenty years and which I would unflinchingly describe as central to my own culture. Yet, it never occurred to me to wonder who or what "Layla" was or meant. This is true despite the fact that it was Patti Boyd Harrison with whom Clapton was in love and that this was common knowledge. (It should be said, too, that after exhausting the lyrical form and bringing it to life in the *Layla* album, Clapton turned to the different satisfactions of the narrative and eventually married her.) I must have looked at the album cover dozens of times and seen the "Eric Clapton and Nizami" attribution without that registering any conscious click. No click at all ever registered until 1990 when, on the occasion of the twentieth anniversary of the recording of *Layla and Other Assorted Love Songs*, a new edition of the album was released, along with a little historical blurb on how the album was made. (Significantly, this process of canonization is everywhere. Rock is now notoriously being classicized in a number of ways: in part as the natural and predictable process that can be readily seen in so many other artistic forms; historically, as a partial consequence of the revaluation process that the technology transfer from vinyl record to compact disc has provoked.) It was in my more conscious contemplation of the historical implications of these new editions (many of them "improved" through remixing of the original master tapes) that it finally fell into place (with verification from the little historical narrative provided in the "anniversary" edition and a lot of help from Julie Meisami's book): "Layla," Nizami, the entire album as a *canzoniere*, a songbook of lyric fragments.

I have provided this little confession because I think it highlights and helps us see the whole range of crucial issues in the literary historiography at hand. The first, clearly, is that I did not see the citation of the "Layla"—and everything that goes with that, as I will come back to shortly—simply because I did not read much of anything in the rock tradition in the way I would read specimens of "high" culture. This bias, in turn, is partly rooted in the (antiphilological!) prejudice against contemporary and popular forms, against that which is vulgar (as in the *De vulgari eloquentia* and, critically, the *Rerum vulgarium fragmenta,* the Latin name of Petrarch's collection of poems in the vernacular). This attitude also exists in part because of our reflexive and often radical separation of the performed, the "oral," from the written. And "Layla" the song, the poem, as well as *Layla and Other Assorted Love Songs,* the album, the songbook, provide a stunning and important example of why these segregations impoverish—in some ways irremediably so—the modes of literary history as we have by and large been practicing them. The first poor gesture we must indulge in is to transcribe, and then read, the lyrics of "Layla":

> What'll you do when you get lonely
> And nobody's waiting by your side
> You've been running
> And hiding much too long
> You know its just your foolish pride
>
> *refrain:* Layla . . .
> You got me on my knees
> Layla . . .
> I beg you darling, please

Layla. . . .
Darling won't you ease my worried mind

Tried to give you consolation
And [———] to let you down
But like a fool I fell in love with you
And turned my whole world upside down

repeat refrain: Layla. . . .

Let's make the best of the situation
Before I finally go insane
Please don't say, I'll never find a way
And tell me all my love's in vain

Layla. . . . (*refrain twice here*)

To sit and look and read the lyrics of a song is a baffling enterprise and a distorting one, particularly if we do know, and know well, what the song sounds like and what the lyrics sing like; when we can hear, for example, the desperate passion in Clapton's voice as he sings this song—the tune is in F but in the middle of her name, Layla, there is a shocking transition to the remote key of the E flat minor, driving the name right through the heart—and the way that Allman's inimitable riffs fill the gaps in between those pained "Layla's." Yet it is precisely this we do, as medievalists, if we study and work with the lyrics of the considerable corpus of songs that we have ended up with, prominent among them the lyrics of the troubadours, on both sides of the Pyrenees. The quick response is that we have no choice. Although that might be true, most strictly speaking, there are ways of reading and ways of reading. One of the relatively few scholars who has dealt with rock cogently claims that the problem is that rock cannot be written, that the writing down of the verses (and, presumably, the reading of them) is inimical to the aesthetics of rock. But this is true, no less and no more, for any other song lyrics. In the case of the Provençal corpus, for instance, I think we have merely become used to the specific sorts of simplicities, disjunctures, and the rest of the wide assortment of peculiarities that are obviously the result of the transfer from song to "poem." But anyone who has just sat and looked at the words of even the most wrenching and spectacular of arias, from an opera tradition that is now unquestionably "high," will admit that the same kind of disruption takes place. The lyrics, read as a poem (and one cannot cheat and sing along in the head), seem fairly rudimentary, even unaccomplished, rarely breathtaking.

Clearly, a whole range of phenomena is part of the music itself and of the way the voice manipulates lyrics (in concert with the music, of course), as well as of the many other variables of performance, that make the lyrics to any piece of music enormously and qualitatively different in performance from what they are as a written text. Part of the difference is phenomenological: music, and music listening, are as different from writing poetry and reading it as they are from any other art. The entire experience of music, as Plato warned, is based on its ability to move the listener unconsciously, primitively, and with its essential anachronicities it ends up at a different pole of ecstasy from most reading. But what we are dealing with here—and I think this creates the confusion—is a song tradition in which language and lyrics are melded indissolubly with music and its very different rhythms and movements. Precisely the way in which the music shapes the voice, and in turn the words, is the crux of the entire aesthetic experience. As Robert Pattison points out about rock, people say the words are so simple and formulaic as to be meaningless, but the fact is that the pure instrumental is a rare thing in rock and the overwhelming majority of rock songs are, indeed, songs with lyrics, and those lyrics that may seem close to absurdly meaningless or flat on the page become highly meaningful. Pattison underestimates how much this characteristic links rock to other traditions. Let us think again of the chasm between our reaction to the words of an aria, alone, on the flatness of the printed page, dependent only on the finesse in construction of a syntax made for other purposes. Then let us think of that same aria, with orchestra or band in full gear, those same words belted out by a fine tenor or by a Clapton, impassioned and making your feet tap and your soul remember the last time you heard it.

The paradox, then, is that the song lyric is a composition keyed to and written for an aesthetic, that of music, that is dramatically different from the aesthetics of writing which is meant to be read; on the other hand, we often are limited to the discourse and the aesthetics of the written and read text both to convey the essence of the song (as in the setting out of the lyrics of "Layla") and to do anything critical with it. The principal contingency of most lyrics is missing: the music and performance that are meant to shape that language and especially the variability that is the hallmark of performance itself, and thus make all of this so intimately a part of the manuscript culture, at least until high classicization takes place when we get into the equivalent of a book culture. In the case of the medieval lyric, the performance is missing irretrievably. In part, a number of the problems related to this phenomenon are at least generally understood because they are linked to other phenomena involved in the shift from oral to written culture, an area that in recent years has received considerable attention. In fact, a relatively small group of scholars has begun the effort, and it will be a large one, to eliminate and reverse the prevalent (and anachronistic) imposition of the notion of a fixed text on a medieval manuscript culture that was instead rooted in variability and in a construct of what even the written text meant that also is based on our own notions of "high" culture and its fixed forms. If we bother to look, we can see that many of the intellectual prejudices against rock are very much those against other oral and performed literatures, or other "unstable" forms; in many quarters the notion that "great" epics such as the Roland or the Cid were orally composed is still met with incredulity, because "high" art is believed above and beyond the sphere of orality and limited to the written medium; in those same quarters the notion that any such "masterpiece" would not have had a definitive text—at least originally, even if it is lost—would seem equally bizarre.

But the case of Clapton and "Layla," and the whole range of issues raised by bringing rock into the same room as the body of songs from *languedoc* that have survived—and here, as before, I will use *languedoc* in Dante's sense, the land in the fat crescent that looks out to the sea, from Provence to the Cape of Valencia—these suggest special problems and peculiar insights to be drawn from the configurations and the examples of rock, which can in some measure help to retrieve bits and pieces of the lost culture of songs that was the medieval lyric. In thus reconfiguring crucial cultural circumstances, I think a handful of the critical issues that have obsessed this branch of philology might be very differently construed.

Origins. The first and last and most enduring obsession of much of the philological enterprise is certainly that of origins. There is probably no better or more famous case of this obsession than that of the origins of troubadour poetry. And there are no origins, we say, mimicking the "objective" sciences, unless they can be proven. Proofs. The second obsession of this branch of philology. And proofs, we all know, must be touchable and readable; they are—if they exist—part of the documentary tradition (what else might they be?). The question one always hears, when the issue is raised of *languedoc* and its relationship to al-Andalus (a decidedly alarming notion to many people—al-Andalus, after all, is where they read backward), is about proofs. It was asked repeatedly at a conference of essentially, or apparently, unalarmed Arabists: how could the troubadours have read the *muwashshaḥāt?* How could they have known enough Arabic? Why don't we have the translations—if translations even existed for them to read?

It is a striking fact, and much has been made of it, that it is precisely in the area of lyric poetry that there are virtually no extant contemporary translations, no songbooks, say, of *muwashshaḥāt* translated into Provençal, to provide the needed proof of such hypothetical origins. And it is a particularly significant fact because it contrasts pointedly with the vast quantities of translations that exist in other areas, most notably, philosophy and the other sciences. There are even other literary genres, conspicuously the collections of framed stories such as the *Kalila and Dimna,* which have numerous surviving versions scattered throughout Europe. Indeed, it is this conspicuous contrast—that fact that translation from the Arabic was a major enterprise from the eleventh century on, but that no translations at all survive of the lyric poetry that might have been a part of the revolution of the troubadours—that has served as the cornerstone of the argument that, in fact, in the most intimate and foundational texts, there was no significant interaction between the poetries of *languedoc* and those of its neighboring al-Andalus.

As my discussion in the previous chapter of the paradigms of Romance philology should in part illustrate, this is not and has never been a small argument, for that first vernacular lyric has immense touchstone value and, for better or worse—whether one sees it as a positive or a negative value—it became totemic of fundamental Western values and aesthetics. And the resistance to accepting the sort of intimacy with a highly Arabized al-Andalus that would have made the origins of Europe's lyrical self so bastard has been predictably strong. The lyric, after all, is not like glass or paper or sherbet, or even philosophical notions (which were, after all, originally Greek, and we are the Greeks' bona fide heirs). What usually emerges in these arguments is the direct distinction between the abundance of translations (and thus what is construed and called "influence") in areas that are basically external to the essential self, all manner of scientific discourse, on the one hand, and on the other, the ultimate discourse of the self, the love song. In this latter there was no traffic—no translations—between "East" and "West" (as northeast *languedoc* is so countergeographically distinguished from its southwestern part, along with the adjacent and ever-moving al-Andalus). The stakes, let me reemphasize, are very high, since we are indeed arguing over the fundamental cultural parameters of our heritage, our "Great Tradition."

So the question is of particular interest. Why are there no translations of the lyric poetry of al-Andalus, of the *muwashshaḥāt* particularly? Or, to ask the same question differently, why does the fact that there seem to have been no translations *not* mean that the first Provençal poets were unlikely to know that poetry? That, of course, is the essence of the proof issue, which, in turn, drives the origins quest. I confess that the difficulty of these questions made me bypass them altogether when I wrote my book on these issues a number of years ago; there, I argued that we should simply suspend the issue of genetic relatedness and study the *canso* and the *muwashshaḥāt* together as an exercise in "comparative literature." I can stand by that answer as such—and it is an answer which urges, essentially, that we merely accord Hispano-Arabic poetry European status and thus consider it comparable without further apology. But, like many others, I have never ceased to be intrigued by the contrast and discrepancy, by that conspicuous lack of translations in one specific area while they flourished in most others. And my simple insight about "Layla" played a crucial role in a derivative and equally simple realization that at the heart of the matter, determining how we construct both "origins" and "proofs" is the most fundamental epistemological notion of what it is we believe we are dealing with when we study *cansos* and *muwashshaḥāt*. Ironically (but in the end no doubt appropriately) it is Clapton's thorough incorporation and adaptation of a textual tradition he knew about through reading a translated text—thus an act of private reading of a written document—that can lead us to the simple but radical reimagination (if it is really and thoroughly done) of the medieval lyric as a cultural structure of songs far more like the rock tradition all around us than like the written literary traditions of which we normally, traditionally consider it a part.

As usual, we might have listened first to the premier Romance philologist, Dante: in the *Convivio,* the other unfinished work of his first years of bitter exile, he tells us clearly why the lyric is an untranslatable genre, why, in other words, any expectation that it could be translated is based on a wholly erroneous notion of what the lyric is.

> E però sappia ciascuno che nulla cosa per legame musaico armonizzata si può de la sua loquela in altra transmutare, sanza rompere tutta sua dolcezza e armonia. E questa è la cagione per che Omero non si mutò di greco in latino, come le altre scritture che avemo da loro. E questa è la cagione per che li versi del Salterio sono sanza dolcezza di musica e d'armonia; ché essi furono transmutati d'ebreo in greco in latino, e ne la prima transmutazione tutta quella dolcezza venne meno. . . . (I, vii)
>
> Everyone should know that nothing that is bound by musical harmonies can be translated from its own language into another, without completely disrupting its sweetness and its harmonies. And it is for this reason that Homer was never translated from Greek into Latin, as were other texts that we have from the

> [Greeks]. And it is for this reason that the verses of the Psalms are without sweetness and harmony, because they were translated from Hebrew into Greek, and then Latin, and in that first translation, all that sweetness disappeared. . . .

In fact, although we do "know" that the Provençal lyrics were songs, as were the *muwashshaḥāt,* for a whole host of reasons we make almost no fundamental alterations in the various epistemological and critical structures we rely on when we read the "poems" or write about them. By and large, our "readings" of the poems are exactly the kinds we devote to poetry written to be read (and not sung and performed), and our notions of the whole range of positivist historical concerns (borrowing, origins, proof, etc.) are also no different. Part of this largely conceptual problem is that, in crucial instances and ways, the boundary lines between the lyric as the words of a song and lyric poetry as the name of the genre that Wallace Stevens wrote are not always unambiguous. In the strictest historical measure, the line *is* blurred. We do not really know when the shift occurs; we are not really sure whether the much-praised *canzoni* of the *Scuola siciliana* were sung (perhaps as part of evenings during which one also undoubtedly heard the *zajals* from Spain, widely preserved in Arabic *diwans* and much the rage at the time); nor do we know whether by the time Petrarch composes sonnets, sonnets were already the unambiguously written form they are today. As the case of Clapton and his Layla suggests, there are any number of individual cases, of given poets or given poems, in which the tensions between the two forms, the written and the oral, are keenly felt and played out, in which the historical dramas of one form replacing the other are conflated.

But as a whole, if we talk about the Provençal *cansos,* and if we study the Andalusian *muwashshaḥāt,* we have compelling reasons to conceive of these types of literature as something fundamentally, and not merely generically, distinct from the written genres that surround them. As Dante says, if it is made into something written, translated, it ceases to be what it really was; the gulf is profound. This is true not only despite the fact that those songs as songs are forever lost to us (unlike rock, which has flourished in the age of recording—although this too affects the canon and begins to classicize it), but it is true perhaps all the more so because of that loss. Steven Nichols pointedly reminds us that the very heart of the innovation—the revolution—of the Provençal lyric *is* that fusion of music and words, of performance and composition. A lot of us have succumbed to a *faute de mieux* posture. Of course, we know they were songs, but what we have got left are poems, and what we can do is read them. And not far beneath this surface lurks a variety of half-expressed assumptions that, in the end, have to do with this being "high culture"; thus, the differences between the written and the performed are not really great anyway. In this kind of cultural monument, after all, the music is soft and refined, and we are supposed to understand the poetry as if it were being read or recited to us. In the end, we come round full circle in our rationalizations, and it no longer seems incongruous that we are historians of the written word and the high culture it bears, and that we are reading these poems that were once "accompanied" by music.

But let me now seriously suggest that we put aside some of our most deeply ingrained notions about literature—perhaps chief among them the silently accepted notion that literature we revere today was always "high"—and reconceptualize the medieval lyric tradition with the model provided by our own living lyric tradition, rock and roll. In an earlier study I suggested some of the ways in which rock is the living continuation of a series of lyrical traditions that have existed at a number of earlier junctures, that rock, in other words, is a part of high poetic structures and experiences that we have already canonized. Now I want to look at the implications of the comparison for the medieval lyric itself. If the model is valid (and I believe it is, almost transparently so, if we can get beyond a series of reflexive prejudices that have to do with often-naive notions of high culture, as well as all of our historical prejudices about what medieval culture could and could not have been), then not only should the "Great Tradition" model alter our assessments of rock, but the model of rock might inform some of our thorniest discussions about that difficult moment of our great and high culture when the troubadours invented the vulgar love song.

I might well begin with an itemized list of all the similarities between the two "schools" of lyric poetry in an attempt to convince the many unbelievers that this analogy is valid. That list certainly would begin with the basic description of a genre whose originality is in the re-creation of the song itself and the making of it a central cultural phenomenon, that utter fusion of words and music and voice—to the point where most people do not really know all the words of most rock songs, even though they listen to them all the time and "sing along" (I will return to this shortly). The genre is both "traditional" (mostly in its largely mythic construction of popular roots for itself) and unambiguously in open rebellion against the forms and languages of a wide range of classical predecessors. It also is centrally true in the two different new traditions (which inevitably draw heavily from predecessors in their modernist posture) that the song (in great measure because of the music and performance dimensions) seamlessly melds contemplation of self—the artist and his creation—with the lyrics of "love" and an extremely strong sense of the tensions among sexuality and poetry and love. For these fundamentals Nichols's encyclopedic comments on the Provençal lyric are refreshingly open-eyed and might as easily and accurately have been written about either the Hispano-Arabic *muwashshaḥāt* or rock and roll.

> The *canso,* then, is alternately a process of resistance to and celebration of physical sexuality. The transfer of the sexual to the verbal incorporates this ambivalence in the speaking subject's attempts to discover (*trobar*) why and how love and poetry are so closely linked . . . the poet fashions the poetic voice as the vehicle for conveying suppressed desire. . . . *Fin' amors* . . . was based on the underlying tension between the real and the ideal, the erotic and the spiritual, the spoken and the unsaid. . . . Even though the early troubadours used complex rhetorical, poetic, and linguistic techniques of the sort we associate with written poetry, their songs were composed for the ear rather than for the eye. . . .[4]

A range of astonishingly similar details of structure (the flexible *canso* structure, with a variable number of stanzas and the virtually obligatory refrain, can be used as an unexceptionable description of the song structure in rock) and theme (the centrality of love and its fusion with the song itself but a host of others as well) makes up the middle of the list. At the end we return to the issue of the complex relationship between the "classical" or classicized (which in this instance would mean forms that are fixed, as in Dante's *grammatica,* and thus a part of the tradition already accepted as "high") and a revolutionary tradition at its peak, before it is classicized and thus made written instead of sung, before its performances have no variability left, before it becomes respectable and high.

At the heart of the majority of objections to the suggested new image would be, not this list (or the counterlist of differences, for that matter), but rather the image itself, the model I am proposing. Although models are problematic from many methodological points of view, we always operate with one, no matter how unconsciously and covertly. In a number of famous cases we have had little way of knowing how a literary tradition might have worked except when, through the process of analogy with a comparable form, we can observe from up close. Until Lord and Parry found some epic storytellers in the hinterlands of southeastern Europe, after all (and, as I said, in many cases still), we read the epic tradition as if it had been written down for us to quietly admire in our book-lined studies. Let me detour a bit through the foundational epic that is the counterpart to the lyric we are contemplating. Even today in the scholarship dealing with the medieval Spanish epic, whose fundamental text has that hero with the Arab name, as-Sayid, the orthodox view is still derivative of a model within which the artist was a monk who studied the French epics and then, in a quiet cell in Spain, wrote the *Poem of the Cid*. As Joseph Duggan has tartly pointed out, this is a model that smacks of a British don's view of himself, a model that conceives of the artist as a scholar.

What is at stake—and this is precisely why I have chosen the analogy with the tradition of rock and roll—is the fundamental model we have of the artist, both as a young man and later on. It is also exactly why the analogy will stick in many scholars' craws—and why the list of conspicuous parallels that I and others have provided will mean little, for, once again, what we are doing, consciously or not, is painting the picture of our venerated ancestors. That they might resemble Mick Jagger or Jim Morrison ("he's hot, he's sexy—and he's dead") is an unacceptable and offensive idea to many. Most of our scholarship, particularly in the medieval area (and this touches on most of the issues I raise in the opening part of this book), is enamored of a model of culture that sees the past as if manuscripts had always been quaint, as if literature were mostly, perhaps always, a learned enterprise, and as if the artist were some sort of scholarly nerd: above the vulgarities of fame and a public, most respectful of the Great Tradition, at home alone double-checking references to those Old French epics or to Virgil. Petrarch was instrumental in helping us carve out such a model, and we are happy to overlook the fact that, all the while, he had been at home, in Provence, the very heart of *languedoc,* wishing he *were* popular and famous and he *was* writing some of the most superb love songs ever written, in a language he never tired of saying was too vulgar to be a part of the Great Tradition. Our model mimics what Petrarch preached but did not want to practice, and, as Duggan noted, it all smacks of the most elitist images we have of ourselves. To have the foundational figures of our culture look or sound too different from us, too different from the academy that preserves them, would present considerable difficulties. Indeed, many of our conceptual problems have to do with the audience—since scholars, in the long run, become the public that preserves, teaches, appreciates, and reveals. Given that, it can seem an appalling idea to equate the high poetry we have to study so hard to appreciate with what are believed to be the mindless and vulgar sounds that issue forth from rock stages. But the less comforting truths are different. Rock's audiences run the gamut (as did Shakespeare's, as did Dante's, as did Lope's, as did Dickens's) from the illiterate to the highly literate, from those who "just" dance, Dionysian, to those who (also) know the "sources," who appreciate the thematizations of the myths, acted out on stage. As the famous parallel cases I have just given suggest, performance is the great leveler. The audiences that heard and danced to and clapped along with the medieval lyrics which we now enshrine in hard-to-get editions included as many uncultured boors as any at a rock concert—and if you don't believe me, listen to Petrarch on the subject, just a few pages below.

It has thus been essential to the rhetoric of the decline of civilization as we know it (in Petrarch's time, too, and, among certain classes, in all times) that the artist in modern times—that is, when we can see his picture and know about his life and hear his songs—so rarely measures up to our standards, so infrequently looks anything like that writer-scholar. Like us. Only dead men look like us, and from there how easy to forget they were alive, that they were at one time young and impudent. Just beneath these images and the problems of conceptualization a variety of crucial oppositions are at play: the classical versus the vernacular; the written versus the sung; the orthodox versus the revolutionary. By and large, we have come to define the culture and literature we study as the former—the classical and the exclusive, the written and the high, the forms with origins that can be proved.

There are various advantages to availing ourselves, in the very central study of the cultural revolution in Europe in the eleventh and twelfth centuries, of the model of rock, which *of course*—if I don't say the obvious boldly, I will be accused of not realizing there are differences—is different in a number of ways but tellingly alike in as many others. From a traditional philological perspective the most rewarding is that it does let us amply account for the lack of translations of the tradition of the *muwashshaḥāt*. This was, first of all, a vigorous sung tradition that in crucial ways thumbed its nose at the most basic rules of classical Arabic poetry and was not written down for a number of generations, partly because its poetics mitigated strongly against incorporation into the written canon. Those distortions can already be seen in the verses of the "Layla" when they are severed from the context that gives them so much of their power and poignancy—Clapton's outraged but supplicant voice, the howling of the guitar in brutish sympathy for the pain, the classical-like piano coda that finishes the lyrical section and takes the listener off into an instrumental meditation—are evident in the way that the *kharjas* (the vernacular codas and refrains) have been preserved. These distorting gaps have strongly shaped the relatively young tradition of scholarship on these bilingual songs that were the cultural innovation and great success of al-Andalus and far beyond her shifting, receding borders. In essence, the written tradition has only with great difficulty conserved the key elements of the *muwashshaḥāt;* a written and classicizing veneer has been overlaid, and it has in great measure obscured the Romance (vernacular and extremely vulgar in this context) metrics and accents of these songs. Most of all, the written tradition has minimized or obscured the centrality of the *kharja,* the vernacular (and a woman's voice, at that) refrain whose rhymes and rhythms drive the stanzas of the poem. And in this specific area, philology has obsessed on the veneers, taking the written as primary, rather than on the remnants of the songs underneath, songs that, because of the most fundamental rules of Arabic poetics, could only be written down—if at all—with great concessions, with thick layers of writing rules laid over.

Crucially, however, what the rock parallels let us see is that this is a literary universe that operates, particularly when it is forming itself and flourishing and forming others, on stages and not in manuscripts, in the hearing of performances and not in the reading of conventional sources. The written texts were not primary, originally, but very much secondary and grossly incomplete. (We might want to remember, here, the notorious problems of text establishment in a case like Shakespeare's where, once again, the primacy of performance makes the written version necessarily secondary.) Indeed, by definition, *the* originality and *the* foundational features of troubadours and *muwashshaḥāt* singers alike could *not* be conveyed in any written form since it is in the melding of the voice and the words with the music that its special phenomenology is rooted. "Sources" for these singers, however learned and intellectual they may be—and here too the rock tradition gives us good examples, as "Layla" shows—are both fully integrated into the song's dynamics and may easily come from sources that have never been written, that are unintelligible when and if they are written. Indeed, even if they were originally from a written source, they are "translated"—transmuted, as Dante would say—into the very different languages of the song. And the vast majority of what we call "sources" and "influences" are, more simply, other songs, other performances, a great refrain, which will be taken from one song to the next. As Samuel Armistead has noted, every oral text potentially echoes every other oral text.

If we did conceive of the earliest Romance lyrics as traditions analogous to rock, a range of thorny problems would either disappear or have to be substantially redefined. The "earliest" texts are uncannily well-developed, not because the first troubadours were preternaturally able to invent something from nothing, but because the developments had taken place outside the trajectory of the manuscript culture and inside what one might call a "stage" culture, and also because the texts that are written down, within this kind of cultural paradigm, are those that do reach "classical" forms, and not the earliest attempts, attempts which would not have survived because they probably were not written down in the first place. By definition, in a culture that is not focused on the written form, what is conserved is what is classical, what is written down is what people want to conserve, what is already highly regarded, what already seems beyond improvement. Or, put slightly differently, orality is a culture committed to change and a dynamic history; when its texts are written, they are the epitaphs of that tradition. Ramón Menéndez Pidal put it famously, succinctly: "Vivir es variar" "To live is to vary." Or, better still, "To live is to be a variant."

Even more alien to an aesthetic culture of this sort is the concept of a formal or written translation. One of rock's most striking phenomena is the range of "reading" that can and does take place when poetry is being articulated on a stage with language, body movements, music, and unusually strong thematic expectations. Here is where rock again provides an exceptionally enlightening example, allowing us to see, in action, the amazing—perhaps at some level incomprehensible—spectacle of people singing along to songs in languages they scarcely know, if at all; or—here the paradoxical variant—being moved by songs whose words they can make out only in part. A gap exists in the transcription of the "Layla" I have given—to take the example at hand—because, listening to the song repeatedly, I could not really make out what the word there was, and this may be because I am not an illiterate enough "reader." This, however, scarcely affects my perception of what the song is about, even if all I can do is read the lyrics; perhaps not at all if I am listening to the song, and thus getting such a high degree of the meaning from the other aspects of the performance to which the words are tied. And it turns out, when I look the word up in a songbook, that I had the whole line slightly off: "your old man won't let you down" is what is in print. (It also turns out that the line is comprehensible—all the lyrics are—in the most recent Clapton recording of the song, an already infamous "unplugged" version. Playing only acoustic instruments, nothing electric, Clapton delivers what can only be described as a mellow version of "Layla," which many have criticized—to the point where it has even been insulted as the Muzak or cocktail music version of what is one of rock's hardest-driving songs. Fittingly, this relatively painless and easy-to-read-and-take "Layla" won the Grammy Award for "Best Rock Song" of 1993.)

Two of the most visible phenomena in rock thus speak richly to the issues of cross-cultural and cross-linguistic relationships: there is, firstly, that ability to appeal and impress beyond the normal frontiers of language and culture, and although there are technological factors involved in this, it is no less true that language barriers are radically reduced when the medium is a song, when the meaning is also being conveyed in music; and this is directly related to the fact that a precise "understanding" of every word in a song is not at all necessary to understand exactly what is going on in the song. Having noted this in the songs of rock, having seen it in concerts, having realized it in our own inability to get all the words down on paper when we can sing the song all the way through, we become aware that very much the same things are true about the other tradition, that of opera, that is clearly linked. Now that we think of it, do only fluent speakers of Italian appreciate Puccini? Or, for that matter, do only speakers of Italian sing Puccini? Do we really know what those middle verses of "E lucevan le stelle" say—let alone "mean" in the sense of being able to do an explication de texte? When we go to watch Shakespeare, how many of us really understand every word? How much could we not repeat verbatim and yet claim to have, in fact, "understood"? Do any of these deficiencies in what is really a *scholarly* standard, and not an artistic one, make us any less good an audience, or be less affected in life by these songs, these performances, and what they obviously mean if we hear and see them performed?

In such a context, I think, the whole lot of questions regarding the accessibility of "texts" between *languedoc* and al-Andalus, are rather radically altered. There was, of course, no reason to have contemporary translations of the *muwashshaḥāt,* and no reason we should even blink at the contrast that provides with the prodigious quantities of translations in other areas: of course you translate philosophy, but why should anyone even imagine doing translations of what those singers were doing up there on the stage? Dante said it explicitly: of course we translate the philosophy of the Greeks—but Homer? Clearly, the discrepancy is appropriate, a necessary difference between two universes with little in common. But the other point is that no translations ever would have been necessary in order to account for other evidence of considerable interaction all along the golden coast of *languedoc,* which at a certain point becomes al-Andalus. If a vital relationship ever did exist between the songs of the Hispano-Arabic world and those of the troubadours—songs whose refrains were all sung in varieties of intrepid new Romance vernaculars—it took place while the traditions were very much alive, in creative and compelling performance, before either tradition had to be studied in its written form or in a translation, and at a moment in the life cycle of the genre in which the power of a driven human voice and in which the wit and triumph of performance are remarkable translators.

So where does any of this take us? Do we now go back and rehearse and repeat every argument and counterargument, each shred of evidence and counterevidence, in the bloody origins question? Precisely not, I think, for what is revealed here (or at least what I think I see, and wish to reveal) is that what is at stake is the fundamental and broad cultural picture we have painted at every level. It is necessary to point out that the shift of the model to the sphere where music is dominant points strongly to the originally Arabic "roots" of a significant part of the vernacular lyrical phenomenon, given the predominance of Andalusian musical instruments, many of whose names are still distinguishably Arabic, and given the undisputed chronological sequences, the invention and success of the *muwashshaḥāt,* and in midstream, the invention of the *canso.* But in the long run the very terms of these discussions miss one of the fundamental insights that the rock tradition, in full-blown operation, can offer: how very frontierless a phenomenon it is, how very fast are highly creative movements assimilated and made unforeign. From the outset, the whole notion of provable, specific, and isolated origins depends on discrete differences. And the origins questions, as originally and traditionally posed, rooted in a model of written texts and all the concomitant mechanisms of high culture and learning, and in the fundamental presumption of gaping differences, have made us ask and shape the questions inappropriately. Within a different conceptualization (a very different imagining), of that world, we lose, first, the frontiers that would have prevented interactions among a singer from Córdoba and one from Barcelona or Montpeiller, and second, crucially, we lose the notion that within such a remarkably fluid and vibrant universe one would be primary and the other secondary, one would be source and the other derivative. What those singers had in common—and the traditional historical facts show us that all of them were flourishing at the same time in contiguous territories—were bonds that unified them in their crucial differences from the institutions against which they were inventing these new worlds, new languages, new songs.

No doubt it is true (although it is not an undisputed philosophical proposition) that there was some specific first instance from which all others derive, but I am suggesting that in indulging ourselves in the pursuit of this largely mythical beast—that, too, is Dante's panther he scours Italy for, to no avail—we have lost sight of the truth of dialects, of the far more complex (and troubling) historical truth that there were far fewer differences than we imagine between the singers, and the stages, of *languedoc* and al-Andalus, in the eleventh and twelfth centuries. The search for that originating instance has obscured the more important, highly productive historical contingencies at hand (and, again, the more disturbing picture, from certain traditional perspectives): the volatile landscape that strongly united *languedoc* and al-Andalus, and the fact that during the span of several centuries a whole fistful of revolutions was taking place, among them a very dramatic and powerful one that made the love song and the new language it was written in—a mother tongue, in so many ways—a crucial ideological icon in the most fundamental of battles. These cultural foundations were being laid in a universe in which the alliances between singers of Mozarabic and Provençal were far stronger than any differences between them. Paradoxically, the largely atomizing discourse of the origins question—rooted in the sharp difference later clearly embedded in a different text—has obscured just this. But the differences that counted were those they had in common with the respective institutions they were defying in their singing, with their beats, with the arrogance of the new language, and in their usually heterodox concepts of love.

refrain: Burnt by passion's flame—
How can I refrain?
    Love has ruined me,
    Lain in wait for me,
    Ambushed, then gone free
Followed me amain,
Split my heart in twain.

    On my cheek the tear
    Made my secret clear.
    This please tell my dear:
Tears all men disdain.
How can I explain?

    Speak to him for me,
    Tell him of my plea
    Do not silent be!
Broken love restrain
From a heart in pain

    Solace to me bring;
    Ease for me the sting.
    Ah such suffering!
Sleepless have I lain,
Love my slumber's bane.

Lovers in distress
Cry for a caress.
My heart they oppress.
Come my darling swain,
Cling and kiss again.

This my love song rings
(unintelligible)
"May true lovers twain
Never part again!"

Samuel the Nagid
(Translated by Raymond Scheindlin)

Love as the answer and the obsession, especially pounded out to a hard backbeat, seeped into every nook and cranny. Even the Spanish rabbis started playing the stuff. Of the many stories of revolution and foundation that come from this world, some poignant, others exhilarating, few speak as eloquently to the turbulences and ambiguities of the moment as the largely unknown and untold story of Hebrew poetry. For to the other stunning lyrical inventions of the time and place, we often forget to add that this also was the golden age of poetry for the Jews. And the fact of this cultural explosion is far more than a critical aside or afterthought; certainly it should not be conceived of as coincidental or as a parallel but essentially (or, worse still, incidental) independent phenomenon. On the contrary, we hear so much that resounds of the familiar, that echoes of the songs of dialogue between old and invented, in what is being brought out from behind the familiar twin shields of obscurity (that is, Hebrew poetry is centrally important only to Jews and those with advanced training in Hebrew) and the strong narrative itself, which here, too, has often smoothed things out. There is a lot to smooth over, a great deal from normative and orthodox stances to be alarmed about and puzzled over. Ross Brann asks the question starkly: "How is it that an entire class of rabbinic scholars could have come to embrace Arabic rhetoric and style to the point of composing bacchic Hebrew wine songs or, more remarkably, lyrical songs of love for beloved 'gazelles,' male as well as female?"[5] In at least one crucial way, the Hebrew songs of al-Andalus—for this too is a strongly stage culture, and that is part of the problem—expose the radical features of the full song tradition, that of the *cansos* and the Arabic *muwashshaḥāt,* with unparalleled starkness because the tradition is cultivated by the class that might have been most alarmed by it, the learned and otherwise unimpeachably pious rabbis.

The struggle between foundation and tradition thus lies quite nakedly at the heart of the literary creation in Jewish culture. And once again I am forced to remind myself, as well as others, that this struggle takes place in the same places, at exactly the same time: the three greatest lyricists of the tradition (Moses Ibn Ezra, Judah Halevi, and Abraham Ibn Ezra) are all contemporaries of William of Aquitaine, for example, and the stages they sang on (or on which others sang their songs) were under the same stars, surrounded by the same olive trees, and the music everywhere was part of the emerging, eclectic canon. As scholars of the *muwashshaḥāt* know, and as I have recounted a bit in the first part of this book, the Mozarabic *kharjas* are first deciphered from a Hebrew text by Samuel Stern. In two separate studies (central to which are the superbly accessible English translations of this branch of the medieval lyrical songbook—translations that read like the lyrics of songs) Raymond Scheindlin lays out the crucial problems succinctly; I will excerpt enough to allow us to see a bit of those stages and those bright stars—and the deep ambivalences they would produce.

> What was unique about the Andalusian Jewish courtiers was the self-conscious way in which they synthesized the dominant Arabic-Islamic culture with Jewish religious and literary traditions . . . sought literary expression in a completely renovated poetry. . . . To the Jews who benefited from the opportunity to join the brilliant material and intellectual life of Andalusian-Moorish culture, which in the tenth century was at its peak, the world must have seemed one great wine party held in the enormous lush garden of Spain—and

> they themselves a uniquely gifted generation. . . . So thoroughly did the Jewish upper classes assimilate the Arabic literary tradition that they eventually synthesized it with their Jewish literary heritage, creating almost overnight a new Hebrew literature that derived many of its concerns, principles, images, and even rhythms from Arabic. . . . They [also] began writing secular poetry. . . . For the first time since the Bible, Hebrew writing in the Golden Age dealt not only with religion and the covenant between God and the Jews, but also with categories of experience common to all mankind, and in terms more or less common to Greek and Roman literature and the secular Latin poetry of medieval Christendom. . . .[6]

In fact, it is perhaps far more important to emphasize that the strongest filiations are with the other songs that are heard on stages everywhere, from the tenth century on, until the fires of the Crusade against the Albigensians to the north, and the successive repressions in al-Andalus at the same moment, extinguish so much of all of that, drive it from public view or to Italy, where Frederick provided a small respite, an island stage, for another quarter century. Reading these songs, we are struck by the echoes, the replayings, the workings out, once again, of love as poetry, poetry and sexuality, the generative power of pain and the inevitability of distance from the lover, the lover's shadowiness, and on and on. We are on the same stage.

But being on that same stage is, in the end, a severe problem.

> To the modern sensibility, undoubtedly the most engaging issue to arise from reading Andalusian Hebrew poetry is the question of what was meant by its love poetry. . . . Did the courtier-rabbis actually dally with maidens and young men, or did they merely ogle them? Or is it correct to regard the entire genre as the product of the literary imagination, and if so, to what end? These were questions of some sensitivity even during

> the Golden Age. The Nagid's son Yehosef, for instance, introduced his father's diwan with an apologetic declaration: the erotic themes in Samuel's poetry are metaphors signifying the love between God and Israel. . . . Had the Hebrew poets somehow been outsiders to Andalusian-Jewish society rather than courtier-rabbis, I suspect that the issue of their intention would not have become so highly charged. The uniqueness of the poets of the Golden Age is that they stood at the very center of Andalusian Jewish society, serving as its scholars and communal leaders. . . .[7]

In other words, this was a culture that had forgotten, but was trying to remember, its own most spectacular moment of song culture, the Solomonic one, with the tell-all name in English of Song of Songs.

We might very roughly translate what both Brann and Scheindlin reveal into the language of the general ideological and political constructs and into recent rock terms and say that this is as if an association of Sunday school teachers began to play rock (and hard rock, to boot, not that soft folk-song branch that institutional Christianity so happily embraced two or three decades ago), instead of unambiguous hymns. Indeed, much of the current ruckus on the issue of cultural decline has been created by perceived instances of this kind of thing: classes of "courtier-rabbis" (such as, for example, the professoriat) embracing rock and other assorted vulgarities. The most curious, highly visible case, in recent years—a small but highly charged, emblematic one—was that of the late Lee Atwater, who had been notorious as a hard-nosed right-wing ideologue and a major architect of some of George Bush's most vicious political campaigns. But it then came out that Atwater had not only been a rocker when he was growing up—in the South, the mythical original home of rock—but that he continued to play it and it was his obviously great love, playing for a rock band. The man who invented the notoriously racist "Willie Horton" campaign used his political success to get himself on stage with some of rock's legendary ancestors, old black men. This threw many into a tailspin. Among liberals and throughout the rock world, both performers and fans, there was vacillation between assuming this meant he really could not be so bad a type after all and that this was a part of his skillful campaign to make out that the Republican right was not so culturally out of touch, so politically backward; among conservatives there tended to be an embarrassed silence, a rapid and dismissive suggestion that this was a bit of childish playfulness left in an otherwise stable grown man. In all cases the series of assumptions reflects the same kinds of cultural parameters and stakes that are very much at the heart of a tumultuous and productive medieval lyric: they help us see the dramatically political dimensions of a whole range of phenomena, from rabbis singing profane love songs, driven to the Arabic beats (which were already highly tainted by the most vulgar of the vulgar, Romance) to Dante's collection of so much vulgarity in a study that claims it is as good as the high-culture, high-priced stuff.

In the end, of course, what the discrepancy of the Hebrew songs and their singers lays out for us are the terrific ambiguities and vacillations within these very dynamic cultural systems, those always lurking tensions between fixed and variable, vulgar and *grammatica,* paternal and maternal languages, sung and written, self and other, passion and distance. Indeed, most of these are acted out within much of the corpus of these songs, so often quite palpably aware of the paradox of modernism they embody, that denial of the past and tradition which is so profoundly historical an act. Or, as Paul de Man said, so pointedly, "The more radical the rejection of anything that came before, the greater the dependence on the past."[8] It is crucial to remember, at this juncture, that the Hispano-Arabic songs, the *muwashshaḥāt,* that, like the *canso,* comprise the heart and soul of the new song tradition, are both uncompromising in their innovations *and* openly conscious of their indissoluble bonds with the traditions from which they are breaking away. One might even argue, although it is an entirely hypothetical exercise, that the great success of the lyric vernacular movements of the eleventh and twelfth centuries comes, at least in part, because they were always conscious of their modernity—that awareness of the strong historical and political nature of their innovation. It is thus, indeed, that the *muwashshaḥa* is structured, that back and forth between tradition (the stanzas in classical Arabic) and flagrant rupture (the vulgar refrain) which produce something literally unheard of before, but palpably and visibly rooted in the tradition it makes dance to a very different beat. "Roll Over Beethoven" is Chuck Berry playing out bits of the Fifth and the Ninth to the backbeat of rock, and it is in that gesture that it becomes one of the earliest "hymns" of the new tradition.

In the Hebrew songs it is the backbeat—the strength of the Arabic music and the ways in which it reshapes Hebrew lyrics that are "set" to it—that is the essential anti-institutional gesture, the version here of the invention of Provençal from Latin or the elevation of the *kharja* to dominance over the classical Arabic verses in the *muwashshaḥāt*. It is instructive to see, once again, that although it has practically vanished altogether, it is the music, and that powerful symbiosis with the voice and lyrics, which produces something very different from any one of the original elements. Paradoxically, one of the remarkable things that music does—and here one does have to hear or see a performance of lyrics that one knows on paper, to fully appreciate this—is to heal the wounds of the fractured self that is, in crucial ways, the hallmark of the lyric and its often pained and lonely voice. Music, the backbeat, the same beat from vernacular refrain to classical stanza, from lover's voice to poet's voice, is the glimmer of hope: that evanescent moment when they all dance together, when the differences, the painful fractures, are momentarily healed. And while the problem of the vernacular and "courtly" love poetry had in some measure been dealt with through the emphasis of the topos of the "dissembling poet"—that is, the construction of a distance to divorce the "real" poet from the poetic voice on stage, singing about maddening and desperate love—the most fracturing and most passionately resisted newness was undoubtedly the one that makes it so much a part of the rest of the universe of *languedoc* and al-Andalus: the song itself, that giving over so much of the power of language to rhythms and voices from such different worlds.

Few stars from this period were as constantly and conspicuously on center stage as the Andalusian Judah Halevi, great and world-famous lyricist, master of the Andalusian songs, who also crafts the great love songs to a Zion who is half-sister to Jaufré's princess in a faraway land and who, in a gesture some might perceive as kabbalistic, decides to shape his own life so that it plays out the plots of his poems. Among the many tropes he writes and acts out so charmingly none tells us as much about these often painful ambivalences than the story of his conversion away from the Andalusian song tradition and his repentance for having been a major contributor to the great success of a movement so corrupting of traditional values. Thanks to Brann's work we can appreciate now that Judah Halevi's work of renouncement, the *Kuzari* (*The Book of Refutation and Proof on the Despised Faith*), gives a remarkably detailed and full picture of the ways in which Hebrew poetry was reshaped into Andalusian songs—all the reasons, of course, why it should not be practiced: the "startling fusion" of sacred and profane; the open cult of lyric language itself, with its problematic hermeticism and ambiguities; and most of all, the imposition of a prosodic system that transfigures the sounds of Hebrew. (Here, Brann specifies "the phonology and rhythmic stress of biblical Hebrew" that interferes with the language so much that it is made ambiguous, whereas the "free cantillation" system of biblical recitation allowed the language to remain both central and clear.) But it is no less clear, from the *Kuzari* as well as from another treatise on meter he writes, that the catch in all of this is that Halevi, like so many others of his generation, is thoroughly hooked, is enamored of what these songs sound like: as Brann paraphrases him, he is unable "to 'shake himself' of the sensory attraction of the 'delightful' meters."

In the end, Halevi knows that his songs not only drive the audience to dance a pantheistic dance, but are in love with themselves: "The verbal form of the Israelite's sedition and hypocrisy may indeed have been highly significant to Halevi, for it suggested the quintessentially Andalusian hubris: the belief in the power of rhetoric and poetry."[9] Indeed, what is really at hand is the danger of the Dionysian song: it leads to a forgetting of the self so powerful that the frontier between self and other is, indeed, ruptured. And Halevi did not sing on center stage for so long without loving desperately, hopelessly, what he could create, and without the very great hubris of all those who walk out into spotlights. It is the perhaps painful paradox that although Halevi understood more clearly than anyone the multiple ways in which this song tradition undermined many of the central institutional values to which he was otherwise committed—those that depend on distinct differences between self and other and on other barriers that come down with such songs—his "conversion" shows us that once the borders are eroded it is very difficult to draw them clearly, ever again. Halevi invents the sea songs, and the Zion songs, as very ambiguous repentance for his sins. But he dies before he reaches his beloved across the sea, because, so the story goes, he stayed on too long in Egypt, up on stage, in the spotlight, singing one Andalusian song after another. What greater passion, what more illicit love.

There is, perhaps, one more deadly passion, one more seductive lover, and the ambivalences created by that one—fame and posterity and the possibility of being a classic, of being buried in Paris at Père Lachaize—are also profoundly shared by the strong lyricists of a variety of highly lyrical moments. And the great desire to be a classic seems at times to be at painful odds with the compelling requirements of the vulgar lyrics to cut away and take your chances, to just sing on the stage and if the leaves end up being gathered someday, well fine, but it is the process and its fluidity and its performances and vulgar communions that are the rules of the day. If the acute modernism of the lyric is in its explicit relationship with the tall buildings that surround it—the past and its narrations, the languages of churches and grammar books—its equally acute canonicity is revealed in a variety of reflexively classicizing gestures, indulged in by the public as much as by the poet.

The paradoxes are seen and heard everywhere around us, and they illustrate, in telescoped fashion, how and why the radical innovations of the eleventh-century lyric came to be fixed cultural icons: there is, to take but one example, already a strong classical period of rock—and there are radio stations that will only play that—from which later generations, clearly and inevitably belated, are supposed to take their models. It is also true, to mention one other conspicuous feature of this process of fixing and stabilizing, that most audiences expect to hear the songs they know played, and played pretty much as they sound in their fixed forms, in their classical recordings. Played the way they sounded when they first heard them twenty years ago, played so they can sing along. In no small measure this is why the new-sounding, acoustic "Layla" is disdained by purists: it is so different in tone and spirit and rhythm from the original that it is practically impossible to recognize the opening riff—that opening riff that is among the most famous in all of rock—and Clapton is no longer overwrought, electrifying, but tranquil, just a bit sad, certainly not desperate. But this is why it is a violation of the rules since, in remarkable ways, the essential anachronicity of music combines, in the song, with the incantatory powers of lyrics that have been memorized, and time—the time of the inexorably receding narrative—is effaced. This is the very medieval universe of memory, and songs out of time, memorized, that structure our hearts, even, at times, our minds. We want to hear "Layla" because we know "Layla," we can sing it ourselves and our bodies recognize its rhythms, and because it comforts us: it is part of a memorialistic structure that takes us out of the inevitable pain, death itself, of the time line. And, indeed, older rock artists often complain bitterly that they are frustrated by this: they have written new songs and they go on the road and the audiences really only want to hear the handful of their classics, those deeply etched in their memories, those that literally make "the past" become "the living." And if, like Clapton, they try and completely remake the song they always have to play, chances are the audience will be unhappy. All of this reveals, of course, the ways in which rock is being, inevitably, classicized, absorbed into a canon of fixed texts that have themselves become a tradition which is dictatorial and powerful, a strong paternal tongue. But these are largely unconscious movements.

The more complex phenomenon revealed by all of this, however, by the tensions between a creative present and a lasting place in the future, is the existence of individual artists who have been painfully and consciously torn between the desire to be great vulgar poets in the present and the compulsion to be part of the respectable Great Tradition, a tradition against which their vulgar songs, of course, seem to be crafted. In other words, there are conspicuous cases in which the largest historical tensions between poetry, as a written and fixed high cultural form, and what some days seems to be its anathema, the vulgar song, torment a single lyricist, a lonely man. The case of Petrarch is well-known, I have alluded to it frequently, and there are only two small details I can add here. The first is the memory of what his complaint is, in his famous letter to Boccaccio about why he has never read Dante: that, when you write in the vernacular, it is open to the gross reshapings of the stupid masses. But let us listen carefully again to exactly what he says, in Bernardo's fine translation:

> what can you expect to happen to our poet [Dante, never referred to by name] among the illiterates in the taverns and squares? . . . these silly admirers who never know why they praise or censure, who so *mispronounce and mangle his verses that they could do no greater injury to a poet.* . . . I can only express my reprehension and disgust at hearing them *befouling with their stupid mouths* the noble beauty of his lines. Here may be the proper place to mention that this was not the least of my reasons for abandoning *his style of composition* [writing in the vernacular, as opposed to Latin] *to which I devoted myself as a young man,* for I feared for my writings what I saw happening to the writings of others. . . . Events have proved my fears well-founded since a few pieces that slipped from my youthful pen are constantly being mangled by *the multitude's recitation.* . . . Each day as I stroll, reluctantly and angry at myself, through the arcades, I find scores of ignoramuses everywhere and some Dametas of my own at the street corners usually *ruining my poor song with his screeching reed.*[10]

What is wrong with writing in the vernacular, more than anything else, is that others can then do whatever cover of it they want, they can sing it in their own accents, in their own rhythms. (Oh, yes, and by the way, to write rock is the foolishness of the young.) In the context of a strong tradition of performance, it seems clearer than ever that Petrarch's allergy is to the mutability of the song tradition, the fact that posterity might like a version different from his own (a perfectly rational fear in the manuscript culture with which he was amply familiar), that the posterity with which he was so obsessed, would get a different version of any given song. It is out of this fear that the *Canzoniere* is crafted: an aggressively written tradition that uses the language and some of the forms of the vernacular song traditions but remakes them in the fixed forms of classics. He is mesmerized by the possibility of change—and this ends up petrifying his forms. It is in some measure ironic, of course, since the healing of the fractured self that Petrarch so lusted after, that so obsessed him—that made him fear the medieval lyric and invent the Renaissance narrative of continuities—is fleetingly, but powerfully, to be had in the pantheistic moments of the dance, the song, the communion among all the selves, all the birds, all the lovers, all the voices, when you can't tell, when it doesn't matter. But it is in this episode, in the acute passion of one man who wanted to make poetry out of songs, that the chapter of the European song lyrics of the medieval period comes to a close. And while it may be true that some wrote vernacular lyrics before him that were not meant to be sung, and while it may be no less true that some of his own poems will be sung, centuries later, it is nonetheless the case that with Petrarch we see the new language, the new chapter, the new lyric modernism: the tradition of the song heretically turned into written poetry.

Rock has had one spectacular and unlikely counterpart to Petrarch in Jim Morrison—or rather, in James Douglas Morrison, as he tried, unsuccessfully, to be known when he wrote poetry, which he did obsessively. Although Morrison was as successful and influential as any lyricist and performer in the rock universe could hope to be, and although, ironically, in many respects, his music and performances acquired touchstone, classic-canon status virtually immediately (and with dizzying universality after his death in 1971, when he was twenty-seven) he believed this to be an essentially insignificant cultural activity, at least compared to the enduring value of "real" poetry: crafted to be read, written down and fixed. In one almost amusing way Morrison is Petrarch's distinct mirror image. He escapes from the public persona and goes home to fill notebook after notebook with "real poetry." In Morrison's case, he was escaping the role of rock star extraordinaire, demonically and quintessentially Dionysian, riveting performer, composer of powerful and hermetic lyrics. And he would go home, night after night, to work extraordinarily hard at writing himself into the canon of the poets who are in the anthologies, who are studied at school. Petrarch, on the other hand, cultivated the most conservative of public figures and most of all a great disdain for the vulgar poetries that were obviously being sung at every corner and at every bar, but he went home to write and rewrite, throughout most of his life, his own covers of those songs, but now made so they could not be sung or changed. The cracks painfully etched in stone now, these poems, too, for the anthologies, for the schools. Morrison and Petrarch are, remarkably, surprisingly, alike: seduced by the notion that the fluidities of the vulgar song are not as noble as the unchanging written poem, impossibly impatient and distrustful of history, unwilling to let history, in its fitful and often treacherous ways, choose and fix the texts it might for posterity.

Morrison's intimate relations with a slew of earlier poets—the English visionaries, the Romantics, Rimbaud, and the American Transcendentalists—are obvious from his earliest gestures with the nascent Doors, a group named for the "Doors of Perception," Blake's words later appropriated by Aldous Huxley. Many of the Doors' most famous lyrics are squarely situated within these poetic traditions, although unmistakably made rock. The first song on the first album begins, "You know the day destroys the night / night divides the day / Try to run / Try to hide / Break on through to the other side. . . . / We chased our pleasures here / Dug our treasures there / Can you still recall / The time we cried? / Break on through to the other side. . . ." The devoted editor of Morrison's poetry insists that Morrison's roots and love were always a very different kind of poetry from the standard lyrics of rock. This is true both in the rock lyrics he did write as well as in the poetry he wrote—far more starkly—so he would be a poet, a real poet, and more than anything else a real American poet like Whitman or Crane—or Stevens, whom I do not believe he knew. Well within that tradition, he was already writing vigorously, when, at age fourteen, he crafted "The Horse Latitudes." He composed trunkfuls of poetry which are still being dug through and edited, and they show all the traces, on paper, of obsessive and incessant rewriting and editing. Just like Petrarch, he wrote every day, day after day, and then another—the *Canzoniere*'s 366 poems tell us there is no day of the year on which the poet does not write and rewrite.

But some of Morrison's worst fears—and in a sense they were Petrarch's exact trepidations—are realized. The two posthumous volumes of poetry are invariably shelved in the "rock" section of bookstores, never with the written poetry. Morrison, dead now for some twenty years, is the perpetual, remarkably vigorous emblem of rock at its most libidinal and threatening, of lyricism as a diabolically corrupting force, the performances and beats and anguished screams among the most powerful rock lyric statements ever performed. The most famous of these is no doubt the apocalyptic "The End" to which Francis Coppola sets the full, spectacular finish of *Apocalypse Now.* But Morrison wanted something he would have said was "more" and (at least in that he has had some satisfaction) he was buried where he wanted to be, among the poets at Père Lachaize. Like Petrarch, he may have been right in many of his dark suspicions of a lyricism that was allowed to fly out the window and that is performed, night after night, on different stages, with different road bands, and of a crude public that cannot understand the magic of Blake or the tinkling of Rimbaud. But the piercing tensions, for both Petrarch and Morrison between the vulgar, lyrical, stage tradition and the high, written tradition of the solitary writer, produced marvelous, pivotal hybrids, the poetic results of the open, painful struggle between the fame of the eternal present, the song, and that of the desired future, the poem painfully rewritten, and then etched in dreadful finality.

If we commune with Alejo Carpentier's work, we know that a rock concert is a baroque concerto. Time is explicitly jumbled, the languages and voices of a whole calliope of moments are seamlessly united, it comes in colors everywhere. This is the great invention of Latin American literature, the breathtaking magic of Gabriel García Márquez. No matter how many new songs the resilient and highly productive Eric Clapton writes, he must always sing "Layla"—and no one cares, perhaps least of all Clapton, that he has been long divorced from Patti Boyd Harrison Clapton. This is the timelessness of the song, the essential anachronicity of music itself, the ways in which memorization so sublimely effaces time, the way in which history, in a lyrical universe, means the other poets playing with the band, the sublime memories of the other nights that "Layla" was played, and the power of the song to evoke them all, the way that even Ibn ʿArabī's Layla is up on stage, sometimes. And every time it is played, "Layla" brings Duane Allman, now some twenty years dead, back to life, his expression of Clapton's pain in that unmistakable guitar riff that everybody knows, everybody wants to learn to play. "Layla" is still "Layla" some two decades later, and the superb story of *Layla and Majnun* has truly been made new, is renewed, each time it is sung, each time it is played. This is literary history at its most elusive, and difficult: Clapton's anguish over an impossible love, over the madness of a certain kind of love, turned into the kind of songs that his kinsman Majnun sang out in a distant desert. These are the love poets whose lovers have all been Laylas and whose poetry has always been the song that deflects, at least for the moment, their madnesses. They patch themselves back together, they make music, healing music, out of the loves that fracture us, tear us into pieces. All that survives, technically, in "classical" terms, is the singular name of the moon-faced lover—which one sees even in the album's cover—the name that Clapton appropriates, with stunning passion, as the name for his own lover. But when he does so, and, then again, every time we hear the song, we hear the complete lack of coyness or falseness, the real lyrical authenticity in the medieval tradition into which he inscribes himself. His lover *is* Layla, and, in renaming her, he reveals that she is that passionate love itself, part of a superb tradition of lovers, of beloveds who can always be brought back, created and re-created, with a song.

Notes

1. Meisami, *Medieval Persian,* page 159.
2. Meisami, *Medieval Persian,* pages 161–62.

3. Meisami, *Medieval Persian*, page 165.
4. Nichols, "The Old Provençal Lyric," pages 32–34.
5. Brann, "Of Rhetoric, Revelry," page 119.
6. Scheindlin, *Wine, Women, and Death*, pages 4–6.
7. Brann, "Of Rhetoric, Revelry," page 129.
8. de Man, *Blindness and Insight*, page 161.
9. Brann, "Judah Halevi," pages 128, 132.
10. *Familiares* XXI, 15, ed. and trans. Bernardo, vol. 3, pages 204–5, emphases mine.
mine.

III DESIRE

Nobody on the road
Nobody on the beach
I feel it in the air
The summer's out of reach
Empty lake, empty streets
The sun goes down alone
I'm driving by your house
Though I know you're not home

But I can see you-
Your brown skin shinin' in the sun
You got your hair combed back and your sunglasses on, baby
And I can tell you my love for you will still be strong
After the boys of summer have gone. . . .

The tent marks in Minan are worn away
where she encamped
and where she alighted
Ghawl and Rijám left to the wild,

And the torrent beds of Rayyán
naked tracings,
worn thin, like inscriptions
carved in flattened stones,

Dung-stained ground
that tells the years passed

since human presence, months of peace
gone by, and months of war. . . .

But why recall Nawár?
She's gone.
Her ties and bonds to you
Are broken.

Desire is the struggle to not always look behind, at what is gone, at what will be gone. But desire is memory, the memory of first love, gone. Desire is poetry, the first language, stark and pained, coming out from the desert. Desire is imagining you have really left that first love, that old language, back out there, more or less buried in the desert, to be scorched by the desert sun, perhaps it will leave some traces, some sun-whitened bones, but not many. And you, you can start all over again, you can write the story from the beginning.

If this book begins on the sea—or, rather, at the edge of the sea, waiting to get on a ship that takes us into exile—it must end at the edge of the desert, that foundational moment of coming out of exile.

It is where Dante stands, at that edge of the desert, when he must write himself out of exile, and founds Romance poetry by inventing the love for those love songs and their new languages. Songs that had come to him, themselves refugees, on small, wind-tossed boats, no sails.

It is where Ibn ʿArabī stands, listening to the doves, it is where he is when he has become that black stone and, hour by hour, they circle his heart, in rapture, in love-ache. It is the black stone from the desert, and it is the desert all the Prophets came out of. Muhammad stood there, when he was forty, when he had spent his forty days in the desert, and he was commanded to recite extraordinary poetry, in a language that was so new it could never be translated, it could never smell of belatedness. He declared the past sealed away and desire perfectly grammatical. And when Ibn ʿArabī wrote, he knew, standing at that edge, knowing Llull would stand in the same place and be stoned for it, that the trick is that desire, even the very object of desire, what it is you want, is so hard to figure out. So he writes, from that very spot in the desert, *The Interpreter of Desires,* his collection of poems where, sometimes, there is no difference between the tables of the Torah, the scrolls of the Qurʾān, the lost Layla.

It is where Eric Clapton stands, and sometimes it is hard to tell whether it is him or Majnun, the madman, who hardly ever does come out of the desert. Poor Majnun he is mad, he has stayed out in the desert far too long and he is blinded. There is a girl called Layla who goes out to see him, sometimes, but he says that she is not Layla, that he is Layla. In this space, at the edge of the desert, it is extraordinarily difficult to say, sometimes, exactly what you desire, what she looks like. Sometimes it looks like her, Layla. Sometimes it looks like that temple with that black desert stone at its heart. Sometimes it looks like a city, just over the next hill, a hill covered with olive trees. Columbus said, Salman Rushdie tells us, that sometimes you cannot tell the difference between ships—money and patronage—and love, a woman. But some nights Majnun does come out, grasps his pain in his hands, he stands at the edge, he sings a marvelous song. And Clapton still comes out, night after night, to that edge, and sings the song, making it sound new as long as there is enough pain in his voice. There is no new song unless there is pain.

And there is pain, and many tears, when the Cid stands there, in that best of beginnings, sublime because it is the mutilated manuscript, no traces at all left of the encampment in the desert, of the past or the reasons for its failure—just start in the middle of it, with wailing all around, the grief for the past and its many injustices, surrounded by that arid landscape, more hills planted with olive trees. Start right in the middle of it because, with the past buried, the language is new, and first we will tell the story of the exile in that desert, that will be the beginning of the story, we start with the tears that let us speak, that let us sing.

It is where that desert love song stands, the Muʿallaqa, it is where the poet of the tribe stands, contemplating the place she once was, the spot where her tribe once had its camp. But now she is gone. Her ties and bonds to you are broken. Are they, really? The traces of the past are hardly ever erased, long past summer, when the streets are empty and the beaches have become frozen deserts, snow and sand in the same handfuls you pick up. The only way to begin, again, is to contemplate the etching of the past, to give the memory a place in your heart, to remember when you heard the song before, to say yes, the tracings are naked, very much there, worn thin, like inscriptions carved in flattened stones. And when you can remember, when you can sing about the moon shape of her face, then you can walk away from the encampment, you can go off, perhaps arm in arm with Rodrigo Díaz Vivar, to tell the story of your tribe.

It is where Auerbach stands, without books, so that what he writes will be as authentic as he is, filled only with the quotations from memory, who knows how many he misremembers slightly, how many his life and his language have made him recite just differently enough so that we can hear he really is reciting. What he writes is what is engraved in him.

It is where the kabbalists stand, when they say that God and the language they had made up, the Sefirot, are one. But the Kabbalah, always a story of exile, is written new after every exile. It must be so. When Provence becomes the memory, and the songs sung there are left behind, deeply buried in that stony ground, then there will be Spain, and the Sephardic Kabbalahs. And when it seems, unspeakably, that there will be no more Spain, that this will become the most painful of memories, the harshest of exiles, the new diaspora, then provisions are made, the dates are set and reset. And then, there will be Italy, there will be Palestine, there will be kabbalists to come out from the desert, there, and say that the Kabbalah is our Tradition, after all.

IV READINGS AND SOURCES

The essays that follow, one corresponding to each chapter above, are written to provide a somewhat fuller sense of the readings that lie behind the main body of this book than traditional footnotes tend to allow. The relatively few direct citations in my text have been footnoted, and these references appear at the end of each chapter. And all references—in the chapters above, in the citation notes, and in these essays—are to works listed with full bibliographical information under Works Cited.

Beyond that, I have attempted to give something like a running commentary on the main text (a very medieval practice), thus fulfilling the legitimate requirement to document one's debts to others but, no less, suggesting the contours of other readings, of lines of inquiry not pursued. I have always written long footnotes in a discursive manner, and I find, as many others certainly do, that they can rather severely interrupt the flow of the narrative. Indeed, footnotes that are more than merely citational constitute, in effect, an altogether different discourse from the body of an article or book, and reading them either disrupts the reading of the main text or it is deferred, and thus it becomes an independent reading experience. I decided to formalize this second practice here.

Separating the reference material and rhetoric from the book's principal narrative has allowed me to write the entire book for a more general audience than might otherwise be the case. In a sense, then, these essays on sources are for the more specialized scholarly readers of any given chapter. Since I cover material from a variety of fields whose scholarly discourses are separate from each other, this means that the Arabist, for example, might be more interested in the essay on the Ibn ʿArabī than the one on Romance philology. Or it might be the other way around. Each essay is meant to be independently accessible, but, inevitably, there are some overlaps and exceptions. I have provided cross-references in as many of these cases as possible.

I thank Sepp Gumbrecht, who, at a pivotal moment in the manuscript's development, encouraged and supported this separation of parts, this small break from a scholarly practice that many have elevated to sacrosanct status. I have been particularly helped by his insight that, in making this kind of division, I am in some measure playing out one of the crucial problems of writing history as I present it in this book: that attempt to mediate, to reduce, the distance between different times, different discourses. As he puts it: "What we normally call 'secondary literature' is not only a scholarly commentary of the 'story' which the author tells, it is definitely an important part of the story which unfolds in the intellectual space *between* the past and the present."

I THE HORSE LATITUDES

When the still sea conspires . . .

Throughout 1992 there were hundreds of commemorations of the two principal "separate" events of 1492, the discovery of the New World and the expulsion of the Jews from Spain. However, I saw no conference, newspaper article, book review, or any other public indication that the two were linked in more than an essentially coincidental way—if that. The expulsion of the Jews, characteristically, was dealt with as if by definition it was of interest only to Jews—and there was virtually no awareness, except among specialists, that the taking of Granada was the beginning of the process of expulsion for the Muslims. Indeed, the conflation of dates is obscured in a *New York Times* article of April 1, 1992, reporting on the "poignant ceremonies" held in Spain on the anniversary of the signing of the Edict of Expulsion, March 31, a ceremony attended by Chaim Herzog and Juan Carlos, King of Spain. The article first notes the date of the edict and its terms, the three-month grace period: "Facing death if they stayed beyond July 31 that year, 100,000 to 200,000 fled the country," but it does not mention, let alone account for, why the commemorations of the Jews' last day in Spain are held on August 2, rather than July 31. Indeed, in the same paragraph in which the taking of Granada is mentioned as one of the "watershed" events of the year, the Columbine anniversary noted is October 12, not August 2.

The issue of why it is August 2—if it is—rather than the date of July 31 obviously meant in the decree is the subject of much controversy. The version of the story that keeps cropping up, that is told by Abravanel, and that I have retold—and keeps being denied, by all sorts of people—is that the postponement, the two-day stay was negotiated by Isaac Abravanel, who had worked for Ferdinand and Isabella and had failed to get them to rescind the edict altogether. (Abravanel is thus a crucial patriarchal figure on both sides of the expulsions. His son Judah, in his exile in Italy, would become Leone Ebreo and write the *Dialoghi d'amore* that made him an influential Neoplatonic philosopher; far less known, Judah wrote a powerful poem of lament, in Hebrew, to his own son, who had been sent to Portugal and was being raised as a crypto-Jew, of necessity. For an excellent introduction to this remarkable chapter in the distinguished family's history, as well as a fine translation of Judah's poem, see Raymond Scheindlin, "Judah Abravanel to His Son.") This story is retold in one of the more sensitive articles on the Expulsions, a piece by Fouad Ajami in the *New Republic,* which manages to work in the "coincidence" of Columbus's departure, although even here the punch is pulled when Ajami says that Columbus and his men left in the early morning of August 3. In fact, some traditional scholarship disputes the whole story, believing it is a conspicuous and spurious rewriting, so that the dates come out right, and it is clear that "public knowledge" more often than not elides the issue.

Yitzhak Baer, the foremost historian of the Jews of Spain, tells it like this:

> On July 31, 1492 (the 7th of Ab) the last Jew left the soil of Spain. The few who weakened and happened to stay

> behind were soon rounded up by the secular and ecclesiastical police, and were either baptized under duress or forcibly expelled from the country. According to a legendary report—among the first to give it currency was R. Isaac Abravanel, one of the men who figured very prominently in the whole chapter of the Expulsion—all the Jews left Spain "on a single day, the 9th of Ab." This is nothing but a fable invented in the bright light of history. On the anniversary of the destruction of the Temple all the Jews of Spain were either wandering outside its borders on land and sea, or were confined in the dungeons of the Inquisition and bound by the fetters of an alien faith which had been forced upon them. (vol. 2: 439)

Indeed, the historiographic issue is straightforward. Isaac Abravanel says the postponement was asked for and granted; positivist historians like Yitzhak Baer, and other scholars in his wake, find it a tough coincidence to swallow, do not know how to account for kabbalistic narrations in a normative historiography, and simply accuse Abravanel of having made it up, "in the bright light of history."

The already vast bibliography on Columbus and the discovery of the New World increased exponentially in 1992. I am grateful to my colleague Sandra Ferdman for her patient bibliographical help when I was in an early stage of this project. I have read with great profit her Yale dissertation, "The Dis-Orientation of Christopher Columbus," which focuses on Columbus both as a reader (and the texts he read) and as the text he becomes in the literary narration of the origins of Latin American literature. Curiously, but in the end not surprisingly, most of the new and self-styled revisionary scholarship in this area did not touch the sorts of issues I have been concerned with here. Indeed, some of them, written by Renaissance New Historians, in effect perpetuate the stereotypes of the medieval world, no doubt unwittingly. The classic biography is still, in many ways, Samuel Eliot Morison's, which was published in both one-volume and two-volume editions, the latter containing the full critical apparatus. Daniel Boorstin's 1983 tome on discoverers is also of fundamental help, particularly because of the extremely broad context within which Columbus is considered. A number of works have more specific perspectives. Tzvetan Todorov's 1984 study, from which the epigraph for this section is taken, is surprisingly disappointing, riddled with the sort of unanalyzed clichés that have yielded such quotations. The specifically (although certainly not narrowly) geographical perspective of Robert H. Fuson, who provides a study and transcript of the log of Columbus, gives this English translation of some of the Columbine writings added value and is particularly sensitive to the log's textual history. (I have not been able to see a more recent edition and translation of the log prepared by B. W. Ife.) In 1990 Kirkpatrick Sale's widely reviewed book, *Conquest of Paradise,* was written with particular sensitivity to what one might call "environmental" issues (although this now banal word hardly does justice to the breadth of his concerns). Felipe Fernández-Armesto's *Columbus* is distinctly hard-nosed and able to evoke all manner of commercial realpolitik, which clearly conditioned the voyages.

Among the most controversial books about Columbus is certainly Salvador de Madariaga's, which, among other things, sets out the evidence for Columbus having been Jewish. Further arguments along this line have been made by Juan Gil, but otherwise they have been remarkably ignored. I saw no newspaper article among the hundreds on Columbus and on the Jews indicating that this was any sort of possibility, let alone a serious suggestion made by a number of serious historians. Sale dismisses the question altogether, although most of the things he does say about Columbus, about his ever-shifting names and scattered personal history, are paradigmatic of the perforce secretive life led by conversos at the time. As obscured as the fact that there are strong reasons to believe Columbus might have been Jewish is the crucial linguistic and textual fact that we do not have the original Columbine texts but rather, exclusively, the Las Casas palimpsest, which is itself a copy of a copy that had been made in Barcelona at Isabella's request by an anonymous copyist. While the occasional work about Columbus will mention this fundamental fact, it is clearly regarded by most as an essentially meaningless (although unfortunate, the piety is always noted) accident, and Las Casas ends up being viewed as some sort of innocent copying machine that also corrects spelling and grammatical errors. Many studies proceed to discuss the "Columbus" and what it says and does not say, as if we had something like a Xerox copy, perhaps slightly blurred (or perhaps, by some people's lights, slightly clarified). For a highly readable description of the complicated history of the loss of the original logs and of how Las Casas came to be the copyist, see Fuson, who on the subject of the "accuracy" of the Las Casas text is enough of an empiricist to wryly note, "we could say that it is all we have" (p. 6). In fact, there is another partial copy of a copy in Fernando Columbus's biography of his father. Fernando also had access to the "Barcelona copy," but Fernando's original also is lost and preserved only in an Italian translation. This same Italian translation is the text that "conserves" another crucial lost original, the *Relación acerca de las antiguedades de los indios* of Fray Ramón Pané. Fuson does go on to note all the reasons why we have to believe that his version is "an excellent synopsis of the copied original," and he provides the most lucid and full accounting of the subsequent philological history of the text.

The issue of Columbus's linguistic particularities is usually treated separately from the textual studies of the *Relación,* for all-too-obvious reasons, and the origin of the peculiar traits in his Spanish has been the principal point of contention. This issue, in turn, clearly relates to his ethnic origins—a touchily mysterious subject. It is widely accepted that Columbus's Spanish was a fluent but clearly not native Castilian, and the disagreements stem from hypotheses about his original language(s), the cause of accentual and other differences. Because Madariaga believes Columbus to be a third-generation Sephardic Jew, he disagrees with the classic linguistic study by Ramón Menéndez Pidal, who argued that extensive stays in Portugal and dealings with Portuguese had colored Columbus's Castilian. Virgil Milani, in his monograph on the subject, argues that spelling mistakes in fact reveal Columbus's Genoese origins. But although a number of technical studies have argued the fine points of dialectal features in Columbus's language, what is undisputed is that he was extensively polyglot, speaking a number of versions of Romance vernaculars, reading with ease, for example, the linguistically very mixed and thus difficult

Milione of Marco Polo. By the same token—and here he resembles the Polo he studied so assiduously, as well as so many other explorers—he is not of the class (as Las Casas was) of the serious writers of any of the "standards" that were just then being strongly and officially codified and transformed from maternal to paternal languages. Finally, on page 167 of Sheilah Wilson's thorough 1978 article on the letter announcing the discovery of America, she mentions, very much in passing, the "rather bizarre episode of Luis de Torres, a converted Jew, entering a village in Cuba speaking Arabic and greatly hopeful of establishing some linguistic contact with the Indians."

Although much has been written about the Renaissance concept of the Middle Ages in different contexts, the best statements of it are probably found in Thomas Greene's powerful and now-classic *The Light in Troy,* with its telling subtitle, *Imitation and Discovery in Renaissance Poetry.* For the issues I am concerned with, Greene's first three chapters, in particular, have proved indispensable. The work of Lee Patterson reviews the same primary bases for depicting the Middle Ages in his stunning article in the *Speculum* special issue of 1990 (see especially pp. 93–99), but he lays a great deal of the blame on literary historians such as Greene, who, it seems to Patterson, continue to perpetuate the Renaissance narrative: "As Greene doubtless knows, his book is itself an act of 'humanist piety,' itself driven by a sense of 'historical solitude' brought about by 'the loss of a precious past.' Having been written within the assumptions about cultural value established by Renaissance humanism itself, it is naturally unable to discover a point outside these terms for an external, self-reflexive critique . . ." (p. 95). (In my 1987 book on the occlusion of Arabic culture from the recounting of European history, I argued something quite comparable, that is, that modern [late nineteenth- and twentieth-century] medievalist scholarship continues the renascent paradigms explicitly in its systematic repression of the role of medieval Arabic culture. That book is useful for further bibliography on these issues as well as for its comment on the project of moving the beginning of the "Renaissance" backward. The original study redefining medieval studies in that direction is the classic *Renaissance of the Twelfth Century* by Charles Homer Haskins.) For a superb summary of the historiographical problem, with extensive bibliography, see Albert Ascoli's article on "Petrarch's Middle Age." Ascoli's rich argument about the complexity of the Petrarchan place "in the middle" has probably added some nuancing to my own perhaps reductive presentation of Petrarch. Ascoli's statement about the relationship between medievalist scholarship and humanist ideology is from a review of my *Writing in Dante's Cult of Truth*—and that, in turn, in many ways continues the exchange of views that takes place behind the prologue to that book. On Petrarch I also have had both important instruction and important disagreement with Giuseppe Mazzotta, and much of what I have to say about Petrarch in this book is in dialogue with the vision of him that can be seen in the series of articles of Mazzotta's *The Worlds of Petrarch*. It is fair to say that we emphasize very different aspects and readings of Petrarch; to be reductive, I see him as in far greater sympathy with the pathos of the Petrarch of the Renaissance, while I am far more enamored of the vulgar bad boy side that Petrarch felt he had to hide or tame, the medieval singer of love songs. Of course, Petrarch's real charm and great power is precisely in the paradox, in the combination, and for that reason Petrarch serves as one of my principal points of reference throughout this book. In "Chasing the Wind" I dwell on his uncanny and unexpected counterpart, Jim Morrison.

Thanks to Marianne Shapiro, there is now a new English translation of the fundamental *De vulgari eloquentia* (about which, surprisingly, there are few full studies) accompanied by a series of contextualizing studies, translations of other relevant contemporary texts, and an excellent bibliography. "The Inventions of Philology" includes an extended discussion of the *De vulgari*. In an article in the *Canadian Journal of Italian Studies* I provide a basic presentation of the complex and often ill-understood *questione della lingua* in Italy, detailing how the theoretical and prescriptive texts of the *questione* have effectively hidden from view a linguistic reality of remarkable dialectal variation. It is of particular interest that while many of the original participants in the *questione* debates (over the fundamental issue of what "Italian" should be) knew they were engaged in arguments over abstract ideals, modern scholarly literature has taken these as documents in the actual history of the Italian language—and thus, once again, Renaissance historiography has overwritten the dialects.

It is noteworthy that Columbus becomes a seminal figure in the narration, by such writers as Carpentier, Sarduy, and García Márquez, of the literary invention of the New World. Gustavo Pérez Firmat wrote a brief but instructive, and typically witty, article on the subject for the *Washington Post Book World* on October 13, 1992—a blessed break from the heavy-handed stuff on Columbus and his many sins that appeared in virtually every other newspaper around that time. The new final chapter of Roberto González Echevarría's revised book on Carpentier spins out the reading of *El arpa y la sombra* that I have appropriated here; it lets us see that authenticity—which for some is threatened by multiplicity and relativisms—is a key issue in Carpentier's last novel.

An aged man is but a paltry thing . . .

Differences in the perceptions of time, memory, and history in the medieval period are reconstructed by two studies, each ambitious and meticulously argued, from different but highly complementary perspectives. Each in its own way appears to reinforce one of the fundamental notions of the Panofskyan view that the medievals lacked historical perspective. Mary Carruthers's provocative *The Book of Memory* deserves far more extended consideration than I can offer here and should be required reading for all medievalists. (Although it appeared late in my thinking on the issues treated here, it has been satisfyingly useful.) Of special interest to historians of literature is her chapter "Memory and the Ethics of Reading," which includes an exemplary reading of the anecdote about Heloise told by Abelard (p. 179) and finishes with an original and highly persuasive reading of Dante's Canto 5, that of Paolo and Francesca (pp. 185–88). Also of interest is the book's brief "Afterwood" (pp. 258–60), which many authors would have served up as a preface. In it, Carruthers tackles the question of the relevance of her work to theoretical issues when she says that recognizing the centrality of *memoria* to medieval literature is crucial to understanding that literature's fundamental theoretical characteristics. Such recognition makes one realize that deconstruction

> is at the heart of meditation and the assimilation of literature. Indeterminacy of meaning is the very character of recollective gathering. Emotions are the matrix of memory impressions, and so—of course—desire moves intellect, as all learning is based on remembering. These themes of deconstruction and psychoanalytic criticism are not socially subversive when we detect them in medieval literature; *they are the tradition itself.* (p. 259; my emphasis)

As Carruthers notes, "temporal relationships typically are a function of their narrator's recollection" (p. 258).

Carruthers is particularly effective in illuminating the vital functions played by *memoria:* the way in which the past was made a part of each individual's most basic memory traces, and the way in which reading (and this includes most functions that we would differentiate as study or scholarship) is part of the larger project of making the past a functional present. She argues that within such a culture, because of its memorialism, the past is radically different from what it appears to be in the Renaissance and the modern periods; while "modern" consciousness struggles to objectivize the past, render it distant, in effect make it like other objects of detached and scientific subjects, in the memorialistic culture that she lavishly details, the past is constituted by the most immediate and powerful memory traces that make sense of the present and the future. In other words, whereas the historiography we have inherited (and in which we tend to participate) believes that the central issue—and problem—is that the past is necessarily mediated by the present (and this is seen as an unfortunate limitation), the desirable and admired conflation of history and memory in medieval cultures effectively reverses the mediation and sees no particular limitation in the fact that the past, our memories, is what allows us to see and read and understand. Carruthers offers an instructive counterexample of how different literary history and the relationship of self to both literature and history can be in a reading of a famous passage from Abelard, in which he tells how a distraught Heloise, about to take the veil under those well-known trying circumstances, breaks out through sobs and cries into Cornelia's lament from Lucan's *Pharsalia.* The standard analysis of this (or any comparable) passage is predictable enough; in this case, we have R. W. Southern's reading, in which Heloise sees herself as the modern Cornelia, just as Abelard would see himself as the modern Jerome. But Carruthers's reading is subtly but radically different: "Since Heloise read in the medieval way, . . . she did not 'see herself' as Cornelia, in the sense of acting a role; rather, Cornelia's experience, given voice by Lucan, had been made hers as well—so much so that she can use it, even, perhaps, with irony, in such an extreme personal situation" (p. 179). But the equally standard analysis of the premise that one—we—can have a relationship with texts that makes them a part of us and our memories is that this constitutes an anachronism. Once again, it comes down to whether we value a theory of literary history that thus defines anachronism.

Approaching a closely related issue from a very different perspective, Anthony Kemp fully develops the issue of "historical consciousness." *The Estrangement of the Past,* a work of historiography that believes in the fundamental textuality of history itself, concludes: "Between the fourteenth century and the eighteenth, the Western comprehension of historical time reversed itself, from an image of syncretic unity and an essential sameness of time, to one of dynamic and supersessive change spawning schism after schism from the inherited text of the meaning of the past" (p. vi). While the vast range of memorialistic practices lie at the heart of the phenomena which Carruthers sets out, Kemp sees the causes of this "history without a plot or narrative, without development or telos" (p. 41), and this "doctrine of temporal unity" (p. 40) as the explicit result of the peculiarities of Christianity: "never before had there been such a peculiar imperative to overcome the separations of time. To keep the world in touch with its monochromatically incarnated savior required a radical denial of the movement, the discontinuity of time" (p. 15).

Perhaps here I should briefly note that while Carruthers and Kemp limit their observations about memorialistic culture and the constructs of temporality to the Christian realm—and in his conclusions Kemp explicitly says that "both of the systems of history described in this study are responses to problems of earthly time and duration that are peculiar to Christian culture" (p. 176)—their arguments would be enhanced by a consideration of the cultures flourishing under the other principal religions during the European Middle Ages, both intimately related to Christianity in a variety of crucial ways. While I know far too little (and in certain areas, such as the nature of Arab historiography, the literature available to a nonspecialist is limited) to draw major conclusions, a number of the features of the historiographic and memorial structures of Judaism and Islam raise interesting points of comparison and consideration, and a number of questions must certainly be posed if we recognize the strength during the period in question of the interaction among the three, which were, after all, competitors for a specific role in the same covenantal history.

At least in part, both Judaic and Islamic historiography are based on the meticulous construction of chains of rabbinic teachers in one and historians in the other, and both lead back explicitly to the key sources—dominant authority or eyewitness historian, each at the beginning of the chain. (See Robert Chazan's 1988 article for a consideration of medieval Jewish historical perspective.) In Islam, these chains of authority (*isnad*) are parallel to the key feature in the *hadith,* the essential tradition of passing down extra-Quranic material regarding the Prophet. In all these cases, the chain relationship is transparently linked, at least in some original stage, to memorialistic practices which must be codified in order to guarantee accuracy. It is also true—and is the case well into the modern age—that in crucial ways Islam is an *overwhelmingly* memorialistic and recitative culture. This is so because the extraordinary status of the Qur'ān (literally the word of God) makes it a text memorized by all Muslims who must, in order to be Muslims (and in crucial contradistinction to Christianity), learn Arabic so that they may know the Quranic text. Indeed, the terrible and poignant tragedy of the Moriscos was their loss of Arabic; see Luce López Baralt's 1985 study (which in 1992 Brill published in an English translation) especially chapter 6, "Crónica de la destrucción de un mundo. . . ." See also Consuelo López Morillas's wonderful study of *morisco* versions of a chapter of the Qur'ān, which begins: "On the second of May in the year 1606, somewhere in Spain—perhaps in one of the aljamas or Morisco quarters of the larger towns—a Spanish Muslim is performing a labor of love and piety: he is copying a translation of the Qur'ān" (p. 13). Indeed, the opening word of the Qur'ān—God's first word to Muhammad, about to become his last prophet, is "Recite." (Medievalists who know little about Islam can profit from the appropriate entries in fundamental research tools, such as *The Dictionary of the Middle Ages* or *The Encyclopaedia of Islam*.) Finally, contrary to the assertion in Kemp, it is not at all clear to me that Islam does not share precisely the same phenomenological problem with time and history since the Prophet ("The Crown and the Seal") provides transcendent closure: he is the last and culminating prophet and there can be no progress beyond him. On some of the difficult fundamentals of Arabic historiography, see the excellent introduction by Fred Donner to the classic *The Rise of Historical Writing Among the Arabs* by A. A. Duri. Ibn Khaldūn, the Arab historian who has most affected European historiography (and who writes his famous *Muqaddima* having seen the once-brilliant Western part of the Empire, the al-Andalus of his forebears, in irreversible decay), is famously quoted as saying: "The past resembles the future more than one drop of water another." For a definitive and reasoned bibliography of the indispensable Khaldūn, and for a rich study, see both of Aziz al Azmeh's studies.

For the issue of the anthropologist and his objectivity, the seminal work is certainly James Clifford's 1988 book. See also the remarkable reading of this issue in terms of the "parallel plots of anthropology and Latin American narrative" in Roberto González Echevarría's *Myth and Archive*, especially chapter 4, "The Novel As Myth and Archive." The work that provided the substantial groundwork for the many "Other" studies is Edward Said's (in)famous *Orientalism*, which is thoughtfully reviewed by Clifford (pp. 255–76). I note here my great debt to the work of Barbara Herrnstein Smith, in whose *Contingencies of Value* the astonishing power of contingency is revealed, first, in the disarmingly personal readings in "Evaluating Shakespeare's Sonnets." Clearly, my own suggestion that we are both free (and, indeed, obliged) to evaluate the value-laden premises of the basic constructs of History, and to choose others to replace them if we wish, is indebted to this crucial book in the most powerful of ways. *Contingencies of Value* has provided an extended and powerful philosophical grounding and justification for much that I had thought, in ill-organized ways, for a number of years. Second, it also has been encouraging in its brilliant defiance of so many of the rules.

While Américo Castro's life work was vast, his strongly revisionary theories about the importance of the Islamic and Jewish components of Spanish history are comprehensively set out in his major monumental work, which went through a number of versions during his lifetime and is available as *The Spaniards*. A representative sample of the work of his intellectual descendants, and of the ways in which he powerfully reshaped the fundamental historical construct at hand, can be glimpsed in the volume edited by Ronald Surtz et al. It is worth noting that the impact of Castro's thought went far beyond the normal scholarly universe and affected key contemporary writers, Juan Goytisolo and Carlos Fuentes among them. In the essay on readings and sources for "The Inventions of Philology," I discuss Castro further.

In many ways, modern historiography has been dramatically transformed by the Annales school, which, schematically, has put aside the notion of the grand récit and embraced the fine details of the history that lies outside that narrative. While I am not proposing an Annales "total history" construct for literary history, it is undeniable that the basic premises of work done by Bloch, Febvre, Ladurie, Duby, LeGoff, and others, have important implications for the literary historiography I am suggesting. For a very effective summing up of the Annales approach, see Peter Burke's *The French Historical Revolution*.

On the *muwashshaḥāt*, the bibliography is vast and, in a great number of cases, of limited accessibility to the nonspecialist. The fundamental bibliographical tools are Richard Hitchcock's *The Kharjas: A Critical Bibliography*, Samuel G. Armistead's "Brief History," Alan Jones's *Romance Kharjas*, and its "counterpoint," Emilio García Gómez's wonderfully titled *El escándalo de las jarchas en Oxford*. For musical and performative aspects, the indispensable source is certainly Benjamin Liu and James T. Monroe, which I discuss further in the essay for "Chasing the Wind." In *The Arabic Role in Medieval Literary History* I provide an overview of studies, particularly those that have a European focus, and in a 1988 article in *La Corónica* I address the state of so-called "kharja studies" and provide a critique of the acrimonious debates that filled the pages of that journal for many years. In both cases I rehearse, from slightly different perspectives, what seems to me the tragedy of the isolationist study, first of the parts of the *muwashshaḥa* itself, and then of the *muwashshaḥa* from the rest of the corpus of medieval love lyrics. (The fundamental problems are those of any intrinsically marginalized literature, and for this issue I have profited from reading the extraordinarily rich "What Is a Minor Literature?" by Gilles Deleuze and Félix Guattari.) Comparable arguments are made in three pieces. Ross Brann's 1990 review of a book in Hebrew on the subject and Susan Einbeinder's review article in *Prooftexts* both lament the exclusivist and fragmenting approaches that seem to dominate the field (and it is not coincidental that they are both coming at the subject from the Hebrew, rather than the Arabic, perspective). See also Mary Jane Kelley's *La Corónica* study. Finally, the original *relación* of the discovery by Samuel Miklos Stern, published in 1948 in *Al-Andalus,* is also available in a 1974 volume, from which I have taken the cited material.

On the conspicuous and scandalous neglect of Latin American literature vis-à-vis peninsular, little has been written and much is widely known. I am grateful to Roberto González Echevarría for having saved the typescript of the stunning talk he gave at the MLA convention in 1985 ("La literatura desde el Barrio de Cocosolo") and for allowing me to use it. His 1986 "Obituary Note" for Emir Rodríguez Monegal reprises a number of the same points. All quotations on Guillén and the Baroque are from "Guillén as Baroque." It is remarkable that a very early connection between the Baroque and Hispano-Arabic poetry is made by Goethe and repeated by Ernst Curtius in chapter 16 of his seminal *European Literature and the Latin Middle Ages,* a work I discuss in some detail in Part II. The connection also is made later, in a famous essay, by Dámaso Alonso, "Poesía arabigoandaluza y poesía gongorina," reprinted in his 1960 collection of essays on Góngora. In a somewhat different vein in 1990, Vera Kutzinski opens her lovely book with an epigraph that resonates strongly of the stark poetic language of the woman in the Mozarabic *kharjas:* "Yo soy la reina de las mujeres / en esta tierra de promisión; yo soy de azúcar, yo soy de fuego, / yo soy la llave del corazón"; in the course of comparing two American writers, one North, one Latin, a number of the issues that arise in the *muwashshaḥāt* also present themselves, notably that of the dialogics of poetry where the male voice of "civilization" contrasts with the female voice of "nature."

The Pisan Griffin was on display at the Metropolitan Museum of Art's al-Andalus exhibit, one of the few 1492–1992 commemorations which focused on the loss of that Spain. I have learned everything I know about the often astonishing symbiosis of the visual arts from the brilliant Jerrilynn Dodds, curator of that exhibit and author of the innovative *Architecture and Ideology in Early Medieval Spain*. Dodds is particularly compelling in setting out the hybridness of all or most art forms in medieval Spain, and her conclusions dovetail with the sorts of conclusions that some of us in literature have come to: the strands are not separable. A particularly effective case can be seen in Dodds's article in the *Convivencia* catalog for the exhibit of the same name at the Jewish Museum in New York on the mudejarism of many Spanish synagogues.

I know this super highway

It would be fruitless and nearly impossible to give any bibliographical accounting of the myriad quarrels that not only have engaged the academic community for a number of years but have spilled out into the public spotlight (and thus, of course, back into the universities and other intellectual arenas with renewed vigor). From cultural literacy to political correctness, from the supplanting of primary literary texts by theoretical ones to the expansion of the canon, these have become (for better or worse) the public intellectual issues of the day. On the direct connection between postmodernism and medieval studies, see especially Lee Patterson's 1990 article, which also gives an excellent account of the Panofskyan view (pp. 93–94). Patterson, as I will discuss at greater length, provides a succinct vision of some aspects of the postmodernist concepts of history that bear on the conceptualization of the medieval period. Conversely, to see "postmodern" used as the worst insult you can hurl at a medievalist—because it is so "anachronistic" a posture vis-à-vis the premodern world—see Mary Speer's article on text editing, which I discuss further in the essay corresponding to "The Inventions of Philology." On the state of postmodernist studies in general, I also profited from the summary but acute characterizations in Richard Shusterman's article in *Poetics Today.*

At this juncture it is necessary to reiterate that the examples at all cultural levels of the strong and enduring image of the medieval period as a "Dark Age" are everywhere, and to cite one or two is to risk diminishing how pervasive the image is, even within academia and, in crucial ways, even among medievalists. It was particularly jolting to hear a national news broadcaster finish a report on an AIDS conference that took place in Florence saying that since "Florence had led the way out of the dark ages . . ." there was hope that, once again . . ., and so forth. I cite this particular example, among dozens of other possibilities, of the generally grim view of this period because at some dim level it reflects the conflation of the earlier, very different, medieval period with the fourteenth-fifteenth-century period when Florence, along with the rest of Europe, was ravaged by the plague (the obvious if unstated point of comparison with the AIDS epidemic). The other comparably revealing prejudicial statement appeared in a newspaper review of the film *Robin Hood: Prince of Thieves* (1991). The reviewer felt compelled to stress that the addition to the story of a black actor, Morgan Freeman, playing a "Moor" who has returned with Robin from a Crusade that took him to Jerusalem, is *not* some ahistorical concession to modern demands to impose multiculturalism everywhere. Clearly, the premises of such a statement—and they are certainly shared by the vast majority of people, regardless of level of education—are that multiculturalism is a modern phenomenon (for better or worse, depending on one's ideology) and that the *last* place it is likely to show up legitimately is in the "Middle Ages," at the other extreme from all that is modern. The real irony and the crucial misrepresentation (from that point of view) in the movie is that one did not have to go to Jerusalem to see "Moors." In the family and the England in which Richard the Lionhearted grew up, the interactions with the full spectrum of ethnic and religious groups of eleventh- and twelfth-century Europe are notorious and run the gamut from familiar (Richard's family, from great-grandfather to sisters, is variously intermarried with "Spaniards" of all sorts) to that of patronage (Henry, Richard's father, housed Petrus Alfonsi, among others, at his court).

Even within our profession the standard view may no longer include words like "darkness," but most curricular and other strong canonical features reveal the fundamental premise that whatever it is, the medieval period is *not* modern (and thus, for example, that its literature is dealt with in distinctly different ways). The case is made eloquently and in considerable detail in Patterson's "On the Margin: Postmodernism, Ironic History, and Medieval Studies." In an essential and thorough critique of multiple aspects of medieval studies, from how the discipline is seen to how it sees itself, Patterson also notes that since the proliferation of academic discourses on postmodernism has left the door open for the inclusion of previously marginalized areas, medieval studies has an interesting chance, but one that may not be taken because of its "patriarchal past" (p. 88). In fact, further on in his argument, after his superb discussion of the ways in which the master narrative makes the medieval "premodern," he notes that the field of "medieval studies has been all too eager to accept this account, and the professional sequestration it entails" (p. 100). This brilliant piece seems to me the best analysis of the fundamental problems of the study of the medieval period, and it ought to be required reading for all of my colleagues. I confess that I read it thoroughly and with great satisfaction when it appeared in 1990 and then put it aside for more than a year; in rereading it after writing the original draft of this chapter, to my amusement and chagrin I "rediscovered" there, often in identical rhetorical terms (such as the trotting out of the thesaurus entry), much of what I had just written; it strikes me that nothing speaks better to the power of this piece in addressing the crucial issues before us.

On the more general and theoretical issue of the modernity of the lyric—about which all the chapters of Part II will have something to say—I have been most affected by Paul de Man, whose brilliant dehistoricizing of the concept of modernity appears on pages 142–65 of *Blindness and Insight*. In *Isla a su vuelo fugitiva,* Roberto González Echevarría also takes up the dehistoricizing approach and defines modernity as the abandonment of poetics as an autonomous and ruling category. In both cases, powerful arguments are made that what History means in such a context is contingency rather than chronology or a simple diachrony. In the case of de Man, the privileging of the lyric as the quintessential modern form in the face of a conventional framework within which the lyric is the very antithesis of modernity has helped my own formulations considerably.

Much has been written about the change in both material conditions and in the overall, compelling changes in general attitudes, from the medieval period to that of the fourteenth-fifteenth centuries. No recent work is more valuable in this regard, certainly, than John Boswell's famous *Christianity, Social Tolerance, and Homosexuality.* In this seminal work, Boswell argues that Christianity's traditional and broad tolerance of homosexuality throughout the medieval period comes to an end during the fourteenth and fifteenth centuries, and he succinctly charts the crucial difference I am suggesting: "Most of the attitudes of fanaticism and intolerance which are today thought of as characteristically 'medieval' were in fact common only to the later Middle Ages. The early Middle Ages, with a few exceptions, had accommodated a great many beliefs and life-styles with relative ease. . . . Almost all historians are agreed that the late eleventh and early twelfth centuries were periods of 'openness' and tolerance in European society, times when experimentation was encouraged, new ideas eagerly sought, expansion favored in both the practical and intellectual realms of life . . ." (p. 269). This is a fundamental work far beyond its immediate focus since it chronicles in astonishing detail (and in a style of exemplary accessibility for those outside his immediate academic field) both the unexpected tolerance of the earlier period (a tolerance for minorities which surpasses that of many "modern" societies today) and the shift away from that tolerance later on. (I am also deeply indebted to Boswell, my invariably generous colleague, for many kindnesses and especially for the typescript of a special class he gave to my graduate seminar on al-Andalus, in the spring of 1992, from which I take the moving statement about our embarrassment at the founding act of "humanism" and of the "modern world": the expulsions of 1492. Boswell's extraordinary eloquence on the subject of the "unhappy family" of the three religions is legendary.)

A vivid description of "a few of the darker landscapes of that age" is given, in the context of Columbus's departure from the Old World, by Kirkpatrick Sale in his *Conquest of Paradise.* Although Sale does not particularly insist on the radical changes these darker landscapes mark from the "Golden Ages" that precede them, he is clearly not generalizing about the medieval period as a whole: "The once stable customs and values of the medieval world no longer held. . . ." Obviously, this is a version of Huizinga's famous thesis of the "waning" of the Middle Ages, and the limitation of the general view in these and many comparable cases is that it holds up "traditions" and "stabilities" as the principles of the earlier, happier time and dissolutions as the consequences of the later, uglier period. Again, the ideological values of the terms used are highly charged, and the vision of tolerance of difference presented by Boswell is not what most scholars imagine when they conjure up the "stability" of the High Middle Ages. Indeed, once again we see a potentially full reversal of the fundamental constructs, since it is in the earlier period that great variety and tolerance flourishes, while in the decline of the fourteenth-fifteenth centuries the forms of strong authority come in. For the Muslims' decline in fortunes in Spain, from the first epoch to the second, see the major history by L. P. Harvey. On the Moriscos and the spiraling intolerance toward them, see Louis Cardillac's now-classic study as well as Roger Boase's eloquent piece in the volume of tribute to Harvey. Finally, in a last speech for the Medieval Academy, sketched out but not given before he died, Archibald Lewis chronicled the decline in relations between "The Islamic World and the Latin West, 1350–1500." Lewis notes important touchstones and ironies:

> The new religious emphasis of these years was essentially hostile to the body of philosophical and speculative thought that had been the glory of earlier medieval Islam . . . (p. 837). Ramon Llull was the last Latin religious figure seriously interested in studying the Islamic religion. And it is worth noting that Ibn Khaldūn,

> the greatest Islamic historian, served for fourteen years at the court of Pedro the Cruel of Castile without anyone ever grasping the importance of his writings, which remained unknown in Europe for centuries. Indeed, this same Pedro the Cruel, who died in 1369, was the last Iberian monarch who had inscribed upon his coinage that he was the (fourteenth) "King of the Three Religions." Under his successor we find the first of those pogroms and forced conversions of Jews which were to disgrace both Spanish and Western European civilization in the future. . . . (p. 841)

Once again, we note that the medieval period is not only tarred and feathered unjustly (and thus viewed as the land of pogroms and forced conversions), but we note it with great irony, since, in general, the tolerance of Jews and Muslims in the medieval period in Europe was far greater than would ever be the case thereafter.

Having noted all this, it is particularly irritating to recognize that the extensive scholarship on various aspects of the "Conquista as Reconquista" by and large traces its intellectual genealogy to Sánchez Albornoz and his view of medieval Spanish history, a subject I have reviewed extensively in *The Arabic Role in Medieval Literary History,* to which I refer the reader for further bibliography. Luis Weckmann's studies provide a good example of this sort of work, ranging widely from the tie to pious and crusading Christianity to the eclecticism of the architectural landscape. The earlier sections of Weckmann's 1951 article, which was based on a talk given for the Medieval Academy of America, are almost unbearably condescending on the simplicities of the premoderns, and the whole of the piece is severely tainted by that Albornozian view of Spain and her civilization ruined by the Arabs and Jews ("Forced to remain long in the background of European evolution . . . ," p. 130) and, bound and determined from Day Two of 711, to get things back on the right path. Nevertheless, Weckmann's observations on the radical variety and admixtures in the visual arts (mainly architectural) perhaps inadvertently reveal a "medievalism" very different from the ideological simplicities and homogeneity he is otherwise depicting. And one small but telling tidbit drops out of his hat: "to the study of Latin that of oriental languages and of native languages was added as the result, I believe, of the impulse given in this direction by St Ramon Llull" (p. 138). While in Spain itself the study of Arabic in the first period after the expulsions could be justified as part of the effort to convert the Moriscos (for this, see James Monroe's indispensable *Islam and the Arabs*)—and this was the reason for Llull's strong emphasis on the need for the study of Arabic—it is far from clear to me how this need to study Arabic is transferred analogically to the New World. This is one more case of the very weak readings of simple details that constitute much of this Conquista-Reconquista argument. Presumably, well into the colonial period in Mexico no one assumed that Arabic would be used to spread the Gospel to the unconverted Indians. Much briefer but pointed statements on the subject, in the context of the nature of "frontier" societies, may be found in the 1989 Robert Burns essay—he too a scholar dedicated to valorizing the Albornozian paradigms. An interesting variation on the theme is to be found in a pair of articles by Abbas Hamdani, where he argues that Columbus's real goal was to affect the end of the Crusades through the final recovery of Jerusalem.

Finally, as discussed in the text, Charles Gibson's article on the subject is an even-tempered consideration of the theory that effectively dismantles most of it, from its Albornozian premise in the uniformity and universality of the Reconquista itself, to a variety of the details that supposedly manifest it, all with particular attention to the primary historiographic texts. Among other things, this reveals that crucial parts of the earliest texts that proposed the connection were immediately contested (thus, for example, Las Casas's vigorous refutation of the views of Gonzalo Fernández de Oviedo, for a time official chronicler of the New World; see pp. 25–26). The other valuable revelation in these readings—although Gibson himself does not elaborate on the subject—is that the notion of Reconquista is close to the idea of *imitatio* in the Renaissance; one, like the other, is rooted in a desire to reestablish a mythical golden age in a remote and distant past, and, again in both cases, because of the strong aversion to the immediate past.

For a deconstructive reading of Columbus's religiosity in particular, see Juan Gil's "Colón y la Casa Santa"; I hasten to add that Gil's reading is closely parallel to the kinds of readings of Golden Age literature of which Stephen Gilman's influential *The Spain of Fernando de Rojas,* is exemplary. Luce López Baralt's moving remarks, in her necrological essay on Gilman, is important testimony to the power of these studies, which taught us to see the tell-tale signs of conversion, whether coerced or voluntary. As López Baralt says: "Stephen Gilman me enseño una lección que retengo para siempre: un texto como el de *La Celestina* hay que leerlo muchas veces à l'envers, echando de lado los reclamos superficialmente aleccionadores de las moralejas pías . . ." (p. 241). Thus, it is crucial to read work like Gil's as a counterbalance to the rather naive acceptance of the simplicity of his faith (and thus his "reconquista" facet) in the work of scholars such as Burns, Weckmann, and Hamdani (as well as many, many others, one must add). Indeed, what Gil does is point out that Columbus's obsessions with Jerusalem, which Hamdani takes to be the ultimate (Christian) Crusader obsession are, instead, deeply rooted in Columbus's Jewishness. And on the interpretation of the detail of the mosque as a point of reference, the Burns's 1989 article includes the following on the resettlement of Valencia: "Many of the secular processes initiated to take control were offered as religious in their effects. Valencia city's major mosque was commandeered immediately as a cathedral, and a dozen mosques in the city neighborhoods as churches. . . . [But, at the same time,] what of the Muslims themselves? Valencia had been their land, and to many intents remained so. Most of the mosques were still in their hands . . . the muezzins still called from the ubiquitous minarets, the cry penetrating Christian home and palace . . ." (pp. 326–27). Even in the fiercest views of the Reconquest, the mosques were simply there, at least for a few more years, some perhaps as churches, others still as mosques.

My meager knowledge of the Inca Garcilaso is part of my education acquired at Yale, under the more or less patient tutelage of Roberto González Echevarría; some of his shaping insights about the Inca are available as chapter 2 of *Myth and Archive,* "The Law of the Letter: Garcilaso's *Commentarios.*" Margarita Zamora's 1988 book is the first full-length study of the "Commentarios" and provides rich readings as well as bibliographic guidance.

This wind of yours Is a perfumed wind, O West

My reading of Carpentier's *El arpa y la sombra* derives from the final chapter of *The Pilgrim at Home,* particularly the new and final chapter on "The Pilgrim's Last Journeys." The wonderful story of the travels of Columbus's bones back and forth across the Atlantic—and the subsequent phenomenon of multiple sites of authentic burial—is one of those reminders we have that literature at times is a pale attempt to approximate the strangeness and magic of life. In its metaphorical configurations the story raises, inevitably, one of the questions begged in this introductory essay: what kind of literary history can we write that might mimic Columbus's bones, cross the medieval with the post medieval and cross the Atlantic, over and back and again, so much that the possibility of "authenticity" is left behind? As I grappled with this question, I found some inspiration in the writing of Juan Goytisolo—both his fiction and, especially, a number of his essays on the subject of the cultural makeup of Europe—for example, those in the *TLS* and in the *Yale Review,* both keyed to the 1492 issue. The "Fortress or Common Land" piece, which appeared in the *Yale Review,* was translated by my colleague James Fernández, who is doing innovative work on the complex relationships of literature on both sides of the Atlantic from a perspective that avoids the old hierarchies of a simplistic diachrony and genealogies. It has been delightful to read his work in progress on "Cervantes and the New World." The very rich volume of studies edited by Gustavo Pérez Firmat, *Do the Americas Have a Common Literature?*, has been enlightening, despite the fact that the barrier not crossed is the one that segregates the medieval; nevertheless, from a methodological point of view, I have learned especially from the essays by Antonio Benítez Rojo on "The Repeating Island"—now a book by the same name—and from Pérez Firmat's own brilliant contribution, "The Strut of the Centipede."

For Halevi, and especially for the crucial question of whether he did or did not repent of his extensive cultivation of renegade poe… forms, see the rich study by Ross Brann, *The Compunctuous Poet*. Without his work, and that of Raymond Scheindlin, I would have little access to Sefarad. (In the essays below I discuss in greater detail a number of their studies to which I am so indebted.) Curiously, Scheindlin has written on the Court of the Lions, which figures so prominently in the Salman Rushdie story; his discussion of the Ibn Gabirol poem, which has been used to hypothesize that the famous fountain is a Jewish artifact, is an excellent introduction to both the remarkable poem and to the polemic that surrounds the primary cultural filiation of the stunning basin and court at the Alhambra.

At a 1991 conference on al-Andalus and medieval Europe, Patrick Harvey noted, disarmingly and movingly, that once again in Europe, for the first time since the sixteenth century, there are communities of *moriscos* (Muslims living in Christian states). They are now in England, France, and Germany. Salman Rushdie is one of them and his complex relationship to Islam and to Anglophonic culture has been playing itself out in the public eye since the infamous *fatwa* was pronounced against him by the late Ayatollah Khomeini. I could easily write a chapter of this book on Rushdie alone. From his evocatively entitled *Imaginary Homelands* (a collection of scattered essays) to his act of powerful resistance veiled as a medieval-like narrative for children, Rushdie's life and works reflect many of this volume's seemingly disparate themes. His marvelous "Christopher Columbus and Queen Isabella of Spain Consummate their Relationship, Santa Fé, January, 1492" appeared in the *New Yorker.*

II SCANDAL

Love and Mercy

Two of Paul de Man's seminal essays have influenced my thinking about the relationship of the medieval lyric to historical contingency and the writing of literary history (a subject central to this chapter as well as to the two that follow): "Literary History and Literary Modernity" and "Lyric and Modernity," both in *Blindness and Insight*. The passage alluded to is his superb reading of Nietzsche's essay "Of the Use and Misuse of History for Life" (pp. 145–53), in which both the impulse to modernism and its strongly historical nature are intimately explored. A number of passages in the essay hold special meaning, I believe, for historians of the first vernacular lyrics of medieval Europe because much of their import within that historical contingency is of a dramatically literal nature, making the modernism of the medieval lyric an overdetermined feature. "The appeal of modernity haunts all literature. It is revealed in numberless images and emblems that appear at all periods—in the obsession with a tabula rasa, with new beginnings—that finds recurrent expression in all forms of writing. No true account of literary language can bypass this persistent temptation of literature to fulfill itself in a single moment. The temptation of immediacy is constitutive of a literary consciousness and has to be included in a definition of the specificity of literature" (p. 152).

The premier contemporary poet of Arabic, Adonis, has a small book of essays somewhat misleadingly entitled *An Introduction to Arabic Poetics*. The pieces are not only perfectly accessible to someone with no specialized knowledge of Arabic, but they are of general interest and provocative in their concern with the theoretical issue of creation and modernism. Adonis writes from a perspective particularly insightful vis-à-vis the creation of the medieval vernacular tradition in Europe. Two of the four lucid essays are of special interest here: "Poetics and the Influence of the Qur'ān" and "Poetics and Modernity." The first is an unexpected and compelling assertion of the ways in which the Qur'ān is a starkly modernist text, radically breaking with preceding traditions, and in which modernism in Arabic has to both mimic the Qur'ān and break with the strongly conventionalizing tendencies in literature rooted in its obsequiousness to the poetics of the *Jahiliyya* (the pre-Quranic period with the stunning name, the "Age of Ignorance"). The second essay continues along many of the same lines with greater emphasis on the writing of the handful of notable modernists within the Arabic tradition (chief among them the remarkable poet Abū Nuwās) and on the problem of the imitation of Western poetry, as an inauthentic form of modernism, in contemporary Arabic poetry.

Llull and Ibn ʿArabī lived and worked at a moment that was crucially different from the period that immediately preceded them—and it is crucial to understand the schematic differences between the two. (The next two chapters deal with many texts from that earlier period.) The cultural flourishing of al-Andalus begins in the tenth century and endures through the eleventh, the period of the Taifas, or city-states, which resulted from the shattering of the Califate and which was a prelude to the military and political encirclement that would end with the fall of city after city during the first half of the thirteenth century; thus, by 1250, as is now superbly detailed in Harvey's history of Islamic Spain, "the new frontier drawn on the map at about 1250 became a frontier of the mind also" (p. 15). Although the kingdom of Granada would survive until 1492, pluralistic Spain as a bona fide and productive entity had come to its end. Harvey's study is an excellent, up-to-date resource on the period after 1250 as well as on the transformations from the earlier to the later periods. On Andalusian cultural and historical developments during the "pluralistic age," I provide a full and annotated bibliography in *The Arabic Role in Medieval Literary History.* Several accessible introductions to the subject for the nonspecialist are the eloquent introductory essay in Luce López Baralt's *Huellas del Islam,* now in translation as *Islam in Spanish Literature.* For a wealth of detail on the height of classical Arabic culture in Spain, see the translation into Spanish of the classic *La poésie andalouse en arabe classique* by Henri Pérès. The year 1992 saw the publication of *The Legacy of Muslim Spain,* a mammoth volume of essays, edited by Salma Khadra Jayyusi, on almost every aspect of Andalusian culture.

At the same time, this peak moment of Andalusian culture is paralleled in the culture of *languedoc:* the "first troubadour," William of Aquitaine (d. 1127), was at the peak of his artistic career from the end of the eleventh century on. The remainder of the twelfth century is the "Golden Age," whose end is foreshadowed with the beginning of the Crusade against the Albigensians at the beginning of the thirteenth century, and which comes to a fiery final climax in the destruction of Montségur in 1244. Meanwhile, the flourishing of the kabbalistic movement in Provence coincides with the Golden Age. The years 1150–1220 are given in the seminal work on the subject by Gershom Scholem, with the kabbalists moving elsewhere at the time that the Albigenses, along with many troubadours, fled from *languedoc.* Most of the kabbalists escaped to what remained of Sefarad, where the Golden Age of Jewish culture was still very much being felt. Indeed, *that* Golden Age, primarily in al-Andalus and practiced by the rabbinical class, also reached its peak during this period; the three major poets were all contemporaries or slightly younger than William of Aquitaine. For obvious reasons, the decline of this age corresponded to that of the rest of pluralistic al-Andalus; thus, it was very much on the way out in that same first quarter of the thirteenth century. Rudimentary biographies are provided in both of Raymond Scheindlin's translations of the poetry of the period. These volumes also constitute a first-rate introduction to the complex poetry of the Golden Age, poetry understandable only in terms of the remarkable symbiosis of the Hebrew and Arabic, a subject I take up again in "Chasing the Wind." (For the work on mystical poetry in this chapter, I also have profited from Scheindlin's observations in "Ibn Gabirol's Religious Poetry and Sufi Poetry.") The monumental work on the social and historical constructs of Jews in Sefarad is S. D. Goitein's five-volume *A Mediterranean Society: The Jewish Communities of the Arab World as Portrayed in the Documents of the Cairo Geniza;* the posthumous fifth volume is particularly helpful, dealing with "The Individual: Portrait of a Mediterranean Personality of the High Middle Ages As Reflected in the Cairo Geniza." A number of studies on the Jews of Spain appeared in 1992; among these Jane Gerber's basic and comprehensive historical introduction.

On that most difficult of phenomena, the Kabbalah, I am indebted most to Harold Bloom, who in his *Kabbalah and Criticism* first made the phenomenon something of interest to those of us outside the rather tight circles of mystical Jewish thought. Bloom's book still seems to me the indispensable starting point on the subject for anyone primarily interested in the Kabbalah as a literary phenomenon. Beyond that, there are two masters of scholarship on the Kabbalah, the late Gershom Scholem (whose achievement Bloom rightly called Miltonian) and his brilliant, revisionist successor, Moshe Idel. Scholem's two classic books on the origins of the Kabbalah and on the general issues in Jewish mysticism are still basic scholarly introductions, although one hesitates to say that they are for the uninitiated. Idel's outpouring of writing on the subject—translated, book by book, from Hebrew into English—involves a dialogue with Scholem's positions on many of the basic difficulties of the Kabbalah. His first and most important question is whether the Kabbalah is an "authentic" Jewish phenomenon—and the root KBL does mean "tradition"—or whether it is a powerful form of mysticism that was (and is) essentially inimical to normative Judaism. The trick question is, what does "tradition" mean for the kabbalists? One approach is to assume that it was not as much of an eccentric outsider as it would come to appear to Ashkenazy post-Enlightenment Jews; the other approach is to see it as an essentially antirabbinical, antihalakic phenomenon (a form of what in this chapter I call mysticism) with an essentially antagonistic relationship to normative Judaism. It is remarkable, and altogether predictable that here, as elsewhere, "origins" is the great obsession, and part of the issue of "origins" is whether the Kabbalah does or does not originate in the extraordinarily fertile land of *languedoc,* under the same sun that seems to have hatched all sorts of other heterodoxies, philosophical and literary. Indeed, one other much-disputed principal area is the relationship—if any—between the Kabbalah and the strongly Aristotelian philosophy that Maimonides is seen to represent. Idel's interests have tended to lie on the fringes of the heartland—he has written a great deal on the period of the "classic" Spanish Kabbalah, as well as on what he calls the ecstatic Kabbalah—another Sephardic phenomenon from the period after the expulsions out of Provence best represented by the Spaniard Abraham Abulafia. While Idel's two books on Abulafia and on the ecstatic Kabbalah are difficult and assume a basic knowledge of many complex issues, his more basic *Kabbalah: New Perspectives* is an essential complement to Scholem's oeuvre.

Thus, the twelfth century, as well as seeing the golden ages of Provence and al-Andalus, provided those contiguous areas with a fertile base for the highly creative and foundationalist vernacular poetries of the troubadours, the Hispano-Arabic world, Jewish poetry in (but adapted to Arabic meters, and/or in the highly ver-ızed form of the *muwashshaḥāt*), and the heterodox movements alists, Sūfis, and varieties of Gnostics, including the Albigen-sians, *all at the same time in roughly the same geographical area.* In the years during which these groups (or the social and political conditions which allowed them to thrive) were disappearing, a small and temporary refuge presented itself in Sicily, at Frederick's court, but this too would disappear by the middle of the thirteenth century. However, in both *languedoc* and al-Andalus a variety of repressions and isolations among the groups meant a virtually complete retreat from the various pluralisms, and it was in this reversal of climate and fortunes that first Ibn ʿArabī and then Ramon Llull did their work. One of this second period's most striking aspects, emphasized and explained in Harvey, was that Granada ceased to be multicultural, and, ironically in many ways, the Arabic culture of the last period, one of continual retreats and eventual capitulation, was far more aggressively and "purely" Arabic than the culture of the earlier period during which multicultural forms flourished.

For the life and works of Ramon Llull, a recent commemorative issue of *Catalan Review,* edited by Manuel Durán, provides a number of cogent résumés, as well as some state-of-the-art scholarship and the most recent bibliography on a variety of subjects. The *Catalan Review* pieces of greatest help for a general review of Llull's life and an overview of his work are the introductory essay by Durán and the article on Llull's *Blanquerna* by Roberto González Casanovas. On the issue of Llull's disputed knowledge of Arabic and Islamic sources (often a highly charged area of discussion), see, first of all, the essay on Llull's "Arabism" by Dominique Urvoy, which provides a straightforward discussion of Llull's extensive knowledge of Arab authors. Many of the special issue's other articles prove a point readily visible elsewhere—the fact that Llull's extraordinarily well-developed Arabism might as well have been completely incidental to his highly unorthodox arguments and procedures, many of which smack conspicuously of the other heterodoxies of the time, kabbalism and Sufism in particular. Urvoy makes explicit the general rejection of the comparison between Llull and Ibn ʿArabī first posited by Ribera and subsequently by Miguel Asín Palacios—that is, perhaps there are "literary" links of a direct sort that may be accepted, but from a doctrinal perspective the assumption of a direct influence is not warranted because Llull may have drawn inspiration from too many other sources. In a number of ways this is exactly the kind of highly prejudiced argument made whenever Arabic "sources" are at stake; if any other source can be found, then that source is far likelier, essentially eliminating the Arabic possibility. ("Cette comparaison a été réfutée par nombre de lullistes; quant aux similitudes indéniables, elles ne sont plus characteristiques d'Ibn ʿArabi et Llull peut en avoir trouvé les racines dans la tradition majorquine . . . ," p. 206.) It is extraordinary to find this kind of argument adduced, even in the case of Llull, who is known to have been as Arabized as any highly educated Muslim. In a related sphere, see Anthony Bonner's piece on Llull and the Dominicans, which gives a strong sense of Llull's struggles with the orthodox Church, struggles in which he was passionately and determinedly engaged throughout the last part of his long life. Bonner's article is particularly useful on the theological and conversionary activities and disputes during Llull's lifetime; it conveys, better than most other quasi-hagiographic (and highly normative, in Christian terms) descriptions of Llull's life and thought, the thorough extent to which he was suspected of heretical tendencies and the extent to which a previous era's general conditions of tolerance were rapidly degenerating during his lifetime.

Among the most remarkable Llull studies ever undertaken are the incomparable products of the Warburg Institute's most distinguished scholar: the two lengthy articles first published in the institute's journal, also conveniently reprinted (along with a series of equally dazzling studies on Bruno) in the 1982 *Llull and Bruno.* In the first study, Frances Yates undertakes the formidable task of understanding the total, underlying structure of Llull's life's work through the prism of the often-impenetrable *Ars*—and in this regard her own work thus lovingly mimics Llull's assertions that the *Ars* was the key to the totality. It is enlightening to read Yates's comments about the difficulties that scholarship has had in dealing with Llull, and the peculiarities in such work as there is because of the limitations of those who are variously involved in the campaign to canonize him. Yates also points to the fact that scholars in other areas who might bump into Llull from time to time dismiss work like the *Ars* as impossibly idiosyncratic. Although Yates's remarks were written in the early 1950s, many of the scholarship's parameters and biases are substantially the same today. The second installment of Yates's studies reveals the text that she believes provided inspiration and foundation for many of Llull's most unusual theories in the *Ars*, the *De divisione naturae* of John Scotus Erigena, a text which also is intimately tied to the Albigensians and to the kabbalists.

On the relationship between mystical and profane love in Llull's poetry, see especially Nathaniel Smith's concise, but fully detailed article. Although at both beginning and end Smith maintains that Llull adapted the language of his "pasada folor" to the more transcendent enterprise of his later years (thus "standing in the great progression from the Old Provençal lyric to the *Divina Commedia . . .*"), Smith provides other insights which suggest that the relationship between the two poetic modes in Llull's thought and poetry is considerably more complicated. (For the incredible complications of the mode of the repentant poet, see Ross Brann's 1991 book.) The basic editions and translations I have consulted are Llull (1985, 1950, and 1946). All citations are from Martín de Riquer's edition and the English translation by Allison Peers. (Note that chapter 5 of the Peers translation is missing in the Riquer edition and that all subsequent chapters accordingly differ in numeration, the Riquer edition thus ending with 365 rather than 366 chapters. I have given the Riquer number first, the Peers number second. This discrepancy is rectified in the 1985 edition of Riquer's translation, which, however, does not include the Catalan text.) Meanwhile, in looking at the more recent translations of the *Llibre,* it is interesting to note that while Peers's translation into English rather neutrally capitalizes *both* Beloved and Lover, Martín de Riquer's widely used translation into Spanish imposes a far more specific reading onto the text by capitalizing, and thus divinizing, *Amado* but leaving *amigo* (and variants, such as "el loco") uncapitalized and thus, obviously and unmistakably, profane.

In Smith's analysis of Llull's views of the troubadours, and particularly in Smith's comments on this issue as it emerges in *Blanquerna* (pp. 5–6), we can see that Llull is most insistent not only that the converted *juglar* is still, first and foremost, a *juglar,* but, even more critically for my argument, that the *juglar,* who is (also) singing about God, is in fact fulfilling his original, divine function. "Courtly love" (and its problems, since it is by definition problematic) has a long and respectable exegetical tradition within which the obstacles are real and external, as well as a tradition that sees the problems as necessary and internal to the poetry. (I will return to these issues in the next two chapters. See also my extended discussion of both the history of the study of courtly love and readings of Hispano-Arabic poetry within that tradition in *The Arabic Role,* chaps. 3 and 4.)

Even the recent quasi-revolutionary study of San Juan by José Nieto, *San Juan de la Cruz, poeta del amor profano,* which suggests that the *Noche oscura* is "about" a profane love, is still tied to the regnant paradigm that sees love as either (fundamentally) profane *or* as sacred. In a different context, work on San Juan de la Cruz is extraordinarily enriching, especially that done by Luce López Baralt. See especially her book-length study of San Juan's mysticism in the context of its strong (and strongly repressed) Islamic foundations. In this powerful work (for which, it must be added, López Baralt could find no willing publisher in Spain, even in the 1980s!) she is at pains to show the unique features of San Juan's mystical and linguistic practices, as a poet, and the extent to which he is outside not only the traditional stream of Greco-Roman sources but also the contemporary mainstream of European Renaissance poetics. In López Baralt's view—and here a distinct congruence exists with many of my own assertions about kindred poets—San Juan is distinctively modern *avant la lettre,* primarily because of his immersion in the linguistic-poetic traditions of Spain's Semitic past. López Baralt carefully and tellingly reveals the cultivation of polyvalence and ambiguity and a purposeful cultivation of hermeticism, all of which are very much in sympathy with the kind of stance I describe for both Llull and Ibn ʿArabī.

On the enormous exegetical problem rooted in a discrepancy of belief between poet and exegete, and the possibility (as I suggest) of "indulging" the poets' "irrational" beliefs, see my extended discussions of the same problems in reading Dante in *Writing in Dante's Cult of Truth,* where I dwell on the gaps in our understanding of segments of the *Vita nuova* because we cannot credit the notion that Beatrice *is* nine. Because of that disbelief, her "nineness" must be allegorically explained in terms of Beatrice being like Christ, although to an unbeliever the latter explanation is no less difficult to swallow than the former. Thus, while in most cases we are happy to suspend our personal lack of belief in another *institutionalized* religion in order to read certain texts (and thus grant, for example, Graham Greene his Catholicism), when we run into heterodox or mystical or otherwise uninstitutionalized beliefs, our exegetical reflex is to allegorize them so that they do end up corresponding to more predictable and acceptable beliefs (the latter, in absolute terms, no more "rational," just more widely accepted). An unsparing critique of the positivist philological mode of which this kind of exegetical discourse is clearly a part is given in Aziz al Azmeh's *Arabic Thought and Islamic Societies.* Although he is particularly discussing Orientalist philology, the fundamental precepts are little, if at all, different in the context of medieval literature, equally marginalized: "This exactitude of information and of designation which fired whatever spirit positivist philologists may have had, was animated by a typical Enlightenment motif, and was aimed at the seizure of the Real without the intervention of Passion. It is a form of vernacular realism. This realism does not yield the truth; it only yields discrete items of information, factoids. . . . Naturalism is fundamentally a censor, a defence against passion, and positivist realism is essentially antiseptic . . ." (p. 10). From only a slightly different perspective, Adonis meticulously sets out the problem in "Poetics and Orality in the *Jahiliyya*": "Today when we read the poets of the past it is not only to see what al-Khalil [an important codifier of early poetic forms] and his successors saw, but also to see what they did not see. We read the blank spaces which they left. Legislation and codification go against the nature of poetic language, for this language, since it is man's expression of his explosive moods, his impetuousness, his difference, is incandescent, constantly renewing itself, heterogeneous, kinetic and explosive, always a disrupter of codes and systems . . ." (pp. 33–34).

On Ibn ʿArabī, Henry Corbin's *Creative Imagination in the Sufism of Ibn ʿArabī* is the fundamental work, difficult and brilliant. See also the far more straightforward study by Seyyed Hossein Nasr, and the 1939 book by A. E. Affifi, both of them still of considerable introductory value to this difficult subject. The story told by Ibn ʿArabī is available in a number of sources in translation: Miguel Asín Palacios (1931), pp. 39–40; Henry Corbin, pp. 41–43 (which is the one I have cited); and Nasr, pp. 93–95. Asín Palacios's classic work provides an abundance of further insights and information. Each of these works provides some biographical and historical detail as well as considerable exegesis of the mystic's vast oeuvre, and both Nasr and Corbin provide extensive and still-useful bibliographies. For many years I have relied on the translation of the famous poem of pantheism in James Monroe's indispensable anthology, *Hispano-Arabic Poetry*, although various translations of it (usually truncated) are found in most of these basic sources. Nasr (p. 118) and Corbin (p. 135) are examples of the omitted final verse of the poem, but they are certainly not alone in this citational practice—in fact, I have done so myself. Indeed, the elegant but basically easy expression of pantheism of the penultimate stanzas is rendered far more complex by the final verse. We are far more ready to accept, it would seem, conventional pantheism—which some readers, in fact, take as an expression of equal disbelief in all religions—than we are to see the explicit and literal conflation between any god(s) and a human lover. On the extremely difficult question of Ibn ʿArabī's theophanic vision, Corbin's brilliant study is suitable, in great measure, only for the initiated, but a briefer and extremely clear exposition of Ibn ʿArabī's thought can be found in Nasr (esp. pp. 116–18). Nasr makes explicit the essential connection between theophany and pantheism that also should be tied to the vision of the Beloved: "every prophet is an aspect of the Supreme Logos and is himself 'a logos' or a word of God" (p. 117). On the general Islamic context within which Ibn ʿArabī is to be understood, *Mystical Islam* by Julian Baldick is accessible and often revisionist of traditional (pious and normative) accounts. It also accords special and admiring status to Ibn ʿArabī; Baldick calls him not only "Sufism's greatest systematizer . . ." (p. 82), but the book is structured in such a way that Ibn ʿArabī's death (1240) constitutes the great divide. Monroe's fundamental *Islam and the Arabs in Spanish Scholarship* provides essential material on the crucial role that

Ibn ʿArabī plays in the development of a canon for the Spanish Arabists of the nineteenth and twentieth centuries. I also wish to thank Roger Boase, who has made available to me his unpublished translation of passages of Ibn ʿArabī's *Risalah ruh al-quds,* a text about which, as Boase says, "it is generally acknowledged that no other document contains such a wealth of information about Ibn ʿArabi and his spiritual milieu."

Finally, of greatest importance to me in my work on Ibn ʿArabī are Michael Sells's publications. I am grateful to be able to use his translation of the stunning poem, "Gentle now, doves. . . ." Sells's *Beyond the Name* places Ibn ʿArabī in a broad and complex context of other mystics: Plotinus, John Scot Erigena, Marguerite Porete, and Meister Eckhart, and Sells's brilliant writing on Ibn ʿArabī's poetry is unique in approaching it as the highly lyrical poetry of a complex philosopher—and respecting the integrity of the poetry as such. His introduction to the poem—which I analyze in this chapter—was immeasurably helpful in my final revisions of this study.

The textual similarities of Ibn ʿArabī's poetry with the poetry of the Zen tradition are striking. Anyone familiar with Zen and its poetry by now will have recognized the considerable congruence of form, function, and content. The poetry is brief and hermetic; stark images are meant to provoke contemplation leading to a spiritual enhancement inimical to intellectual understanding; and empirically unresolvable paradoxes are often emphasized, precisely to elude the traps of the reasonable intellect and its overbearing hermeneutics. A typical example from Isshu Miura and Ruth Fuller Sasaki's *The Zen Koan:*

> I take blindness as vision, deafness as hearing;
> I take danger as safety and prosperity as misfortune. (p. 120)

Or, in a style more reminiscent of the imagery of Ibn ʿArabī:

> Above the budless branches
> The golden phoenix soars,
> Around the shadowless tree
> The jade elephant circumambulates. (p. 122)

This last poem brings us full circle, to the pervasive bird imagery with which I open the chapter and which is such an integral part of a variety of lyrics and one of the central unities (explicitly so) between love and mystical poetry. A succinct but thorough review of bird images in mystical poetry from a broad range of traditions is provided in Luce López Baralt's "Para la génesis del 'Pajaro solitario' de San Juan de la Cruz" in *Huellas del Islam* (pp. 59–97), where she pays particular attention to the whole range of "bird" texts that were particularly known and read in Spain. Among those texts of enduring and general interest, two merit singling out: the extensive and subtle use of bird imagery in the enormously influential Avicenna (studied in another remarkable work by Henry Corbin, *Avicenna and the Visionary Recital*); the other, the twelfth-century Persian *The Conference of the Birds,* by Farid ud-Din Attar, is available in a widely admired translation by Dick Davis. (This, in turn, is a work uncannily like Chaucer's similarly titled *Parliament of Fowls,* although it is also deeply engaged with parts of the mysticism of Islam.) But, as the epigraph from Wallace Stevens suggests, the ties of the bird to lyrical and hermetic contemplation and expression are multifarious. They are even a staple of the lyricism of rock, particularly in suggesting the ever-shifting identities of poet/lover/beloved.

The lyrical and exegetical parallels with the Song of Solomon are apparent, and it is well known that the originally "secular" love song eventually underwent every manner of normative exegesis. Within the medieval Christian tradition it was the "most frequently interpreted book . . ." and a distinct genre onto itself (see the informative book by E. Ann Matter). Normative exegesis is overwhelmingly allegorical. For a good representative sampling of contemporary readings of the Song, see the anthology edited by Harold Bloom. Of special interest in the context of this chapter is Bloom's introductory essay, where he repeatedly emphasizes the ties of the Song to the kabbalists (and, in passing, of the singular fact that Luís de León, descendant of a family that "converts" in 1492, translated the Song twice over, into both poetry and prose); and, crucially, the article by Arthur Green on the ties between the Jewish mystical tradition and the Song. Here we can see the way(s) in which the strong kabbalistic readings emphasize the fractured lyricism of the poetry and eschew unifying allegorization, emphasizing the strength of the language itself. The echoes with the *sefirot* are evident, and Green's succinct explanation is helpful: "the major innovation in Kabbalistic thought, the *sefirot*, symbol-laden stages of divine self-revelation. The static unity of God, a cornerstone of Jewish philosophy, is converted by the Kabbalists into a dynamic unity of one-in-ten. The ten *sefirot* are bound to and leap forth from the One, in the words of a widely used image, 'like a flame attached to a coal,' having all the irregularity and yet the unity of the multiple darting tongues of a single fire" (p. 146). A final telling note: although there is only a brief and truncated direct commentary on the Song in Moses de Leon's *Zohar* (the ultimate text of Kabbalah and, from many perspectives, one of the last major texts deeply rooted in pluralistic and heterodox Spain): "there exists hardly a page in the entire *Zohar* in which the Canticle is not in a broader sense discussed. Quotations from this relatively brief book are everywhere, and even where it is not quoted, its theme remains central to the author's consciousness" (p. 150). Finally, see Giovanni Filoramo's *A History of Gnosticism*, which is not only informative on the Gnostic heterodoxies, some of which thrived during the historical period I have been discussing, but also highly suggestive of the ways in which these heterodoxies are inherently lyrical.

The Inventions of Philology

The most complex reading of Dante as a poet of exile (in the full and broad implications of the word) is Giuseppe Mazzotta's, although I believe that the meaning of the titulary *Poet of the Desert* has been only partially understood; it also has uncanny (and originally unintended) resonances with the stark imagery of exile of the poet and poetry in the literature of the *Jahiliyya*, the pre-Islamic "Age of Ignorance." After I had written the next-to-final draft of this chapter I read Mazzotta's 1993 "The Life of Dante" and was gratified with our general congruence of views on the pain and shaping passion involved in the intolerable exile. (I have drawn dates from the standard sources for my rudimentary narration, including Michele Barbi's classic *Life of Dante*.

The Charles Eliot Norton quotation on the historical events of 1289 that would end up in the *Divine Comedy* are taken from Bart Giamatti's invaluable collection of essays on Dante, p. 52.)

In his *Dante's Vision and the Circle of Knowledge*, Mazzotta has a key chapter, "Theology and Exile," which reprises and expands many of the themes dealt with here. My readings of a whole range of key features of Dante, and the shapes of history in his text (beginning with his various passionate reactions to exile), have been profoundly shaped by Mazzotta's work in these and other studies (even when we are in substantial disagreement). A key passage from *Dante's Vision* speaks directly to the matters I explore in this chapter:

> More than that, this is the point where we can grasp the profound reasons why exile systematically punctuates this stretch of the text [*Paradiso* XXIV–XXVI]. In effect, the occurrence of the fall from the Garden is not given merely as a theme, but is metaphorically rendered as an exile into language. The prelapsarian tongue he used at Creation, Adam states, was extinct before the building of the Tower of Babel. This explanation, as has often been remarked, substantially revises the theory Dante put forth in his *De vulgari eloquentia*. . . . In the economy of the treatise the continuity of the language of grace allows Dante to envision grammar as the tool by which to forge and order from the forest of multiple dialects one national language. . . . In *Paradiso* XXVI there is a drastic deviation from the myth of a persistent prelapsarian language. The Tower of Babel, Nimrod's unaccomplished work, is now the sign of the lovely foreignness of every voice. . . . (pp. 191–92)

This is that "lovely foreignness" of exile itself (famously celebrated by Hugh of St. Victor) as well as the paradoxes of the lyrical: "In the changes that occur in the names that we use to call God," Mazzotta continues, "we confront the lack of any appropriate names available to us. If anything, the words we use for God reveal our yearning for and our distance from him. From this perspective poetry and theology, as Boccaccio had intuited, are linked together both by a longing for the absolute and by the cloud of unknowing hovering over them . . ." (pp. 192–93). In the end, "as a trace, the poet's language, and from Adam's speech we can infer all language, is the allegory of exile, the figure of man's displacement into an alien world . . ." (p. 196). That influential articulation by Hugh of St. Victor of the virtues of exile as an allegory of reading is also cited and discussed in the crucial chapter on "Allegory" in *Dante, Poet of the Desert* and it is worth quoting again: "Finally, a foreign soil is proposed, since it, too, gives a man practice. All the world is a foreign soil to those who philosophize. . . . The man who finds his homeland sweet is still a tender beginner; he to whom every soil is as his native one is already strong; but he is perfect to whom the entire world is a foreign land. . . . From boyhood I have dwelt on foreign soil, and I know with what grief sometimes the mind takes leave of the narrow hearth of a peasant's hut, and I know, too, how frankly it afterwards disdains marble firesides and panelled walls" (pp. 272–73).

This is one of the handful of passages from medieval texts that has been embraced, and frequently quoted, outside medievalist circles. Tellingly, it is often adopted by Edward Said, eminent exponent and practitioner of what he calls a secular criticism; it is openly autobiographical and rooted in the conditions of his exile, as a Palestinian, and it is a criticism that privileges not only the contingencies of history but the roles that literature plays within it. Aside from his many published works—*The World, the Text and the Critic* is the most pertinent in this context—see the revealing interview with him by Imre Salusinszky (pp. 123–48); also see more on Said, especially on his relationship to Auerbach and Vico, below.

On the exilic condition of the *De vulgari eloquentia* itself, Marianne Shapiro's *Dante's Book of Exile* plays many roles (although, incomprehensibly, in her far-ranging discussions she ignores the kind of broader questions of exile and literature raised in Mazzotta's work). Shapiro provides an accessible historical-textual introduction and the first really fluid translation of the *De vulgari*, from which all my quotations are taken. She also offers an introduction to (and limited translations of) the most important other "grammatical treatises" of the period, which serves to highlight the profound originality and foundationalism of Dante's text. In addition, Shapiro's work provides an accessible narration of the events leading up to Dante's banishment from Florence and pertinent to his exile (at least leading up to the composition of the *De vulgari*). Some of the same material is covered in the remarkable work on the *Rime petrose* by Robert Durling and Ronald Martínez, which also provides a new translation of the second part of the *De vulgari eloquentia.*

Because my assertions here go very much against the grain, it is necessary to note that although Shapiro states that the Provençal was already canonized and "high culture" by Dante's time, I think this view is radically undermined by, among other things, the very existence of the *De vulgari eloquentia.* Indeed, on this issue of Dante's self-constituting authority in establishing the vernacular as the new prestige language, my premises are largely complemented by Albert Ascoli's complex meditations on both the *De vulgari eloquentia* and the *Convivio* (1989 and 1990); both articles are informed by his ongoing consideration of the problem of change and perspective in the writing of history, which is obviously of central concern to me here. I believe that the widespread belief that Provençal was *already* canonized at that time, and that Dante's act, consequently, is one of reverential piety rather than of revolutionary foundation, is part of the general blurring of the transition from vulgarity to classicism that we strongly revert to, since we do not want to believe either that what is vulgar today might one day be classical, or, vice versa, that what we now privilege (and reserve for the selectively educated) was once the property of the streetwise. Further direct evidence of Provençal's lack of prestige is provided by Petrarch, writing decades later and still obsessively concerned with what the vulgar street rabble will do to his songs—distort them as they have Dante's, of course. (See the final section of my next chapter, "Chasing the Wind," for the quotation from Petrarch's letter to Boccaccio on this subject.) What was most visible to Dante's highly prejudiced eye, no doubt, was the destruction of the original environment, the home that had sheltered those renegade poets, and the exilic condition of the poets and poems.

Although for a long time Dante's linguistic views, especially those concerning the artificiality of Latin, were somewhat patronizingly regarded as either quaint or coy, in crucial theoretical ways he acutely grasped what historical linguists have only relatively recently "discovered" and accepted: that classical Latin is not the mother tongue from which the Romance vernaculars descend, but rather a *grammatica* much as Dante describes it; the vernaculars develop, instead, from a spoken Latin (often called vulgar Latin) which was, for a considerable period, coterminus with classical Latin (rather than "descended" or "degenerated" from it), which was probably dialectally fractured from quite early on. I further discuss some of these issues, as well as the corollary issues that become the "questione della lingua," in an article in the *Canadian Journal of Italian Studies*. In this context, two other notes are called for. First, I use the terms "language" and "dialect" understanding that from a linguistic point of view there is no hierarchy (and at times no such distinction is needed or desirable), whereas language is sometimes used to designate the dialect that is politically privileged and thus whose usage will extend far beyond its original geographic dialect boundaries. Dante would muse, no doubt ironically, that Italy, among the countries of Romania, was the last to fix a standard national language and remains the country with the most persistent dialect boundaries. It also should be remembered that, after Petrarch, much of Italian culture dramatically retreated from the vernacular, and for several hundred years Latin again became the dominant language of high culture, far more universally so than in other countries in Europe.

Much self-described "old-fashioned" criticism—the sort that tends not only to believe in "the text itself" but believe that, in so proclaiming, a historical mission is being performed—equates both diachrony and transcendency with history, whereas in a different philosophical frame (Dante's, I will argue, but also a broad range of others' from Vico to Richard Rorty) both of these concepts are radically ahistorical. What is noteworthy is not which side "owns" history, but the fact that in versions of this argument that are currently center-stage in our culture, the view of history and tradition that banishes contingency and engagement has effectively positioned itself as "historical" and "traditional." Gerald Graff in *Professing Literature* provides an outstanding history of the struggles that have shaped and driven literary studies as an institution since its inception in this country. Graff's study is a model of lucid analysis, setting out the continual shifts and tensions among the different models of literary study: critic versus scholar, vernacular versus classical, teacher versus researcher. In the course of his discussions, he also offers rich documentary evidence that proves the truth of *plus ça change. . . .* Indeed, Graff has published an ancillary volume, the *Documentary Anthology,* which is a gold mine of crucial documents from the various archives of the institutions that have housed literary studies and in which one can read such things as a speech, "The Dark Ages," given by the great Dantista Charles Grandgent. The Dark Ages in his speech, it turns out, are Grandgent's present—what are now mourned as the good old days—when standards of education and scholarship are declining, and so forth. Both volumes ought to be required reading for everyone in literary studies; those who cannot get beyond the first essay in *Professing Literature,* "The Humanist Myth" (because they believe in the myth too strongly), can simply turn to the anthology and read "the historical evidence" for themselves. Two chapters of Barbara Herrnstein Smith's book are crucial for these discussions, and they thoroughly inform my work: "The Banishment of Evaluation" and "Contingencies of Value." Finally, a recent discussion of John Dewey's work (and a salutary reintroduction to an often dismissed philosopher of remarkable accessibility) by Richard Rorty, with the great title "Just One More Species Doing its Best," includes a pithy discussion of the issue and of the basic point of disagreement between what can roughly be called pragmatists (who in some incarnations often have been labeled relativists as well) and others. "Williams speak for the vast majority of analytic philosophers . . . when, following Locke, he insists that physical science is less bound up with human interests than are, say, chess, novel-writing or the munitions industry. The question of whether any area of human culture could be less bound up with human interests and needs than another—whether there is such a thing as seeking truth for its own sake, without any admixture of practical deliberation—is the central issue between pragmatists and their opponents" (p. 5).

For Auerbach, I have used the following editions of his work:

Auerbach (1946) 1957, *Mimesis;* (1948), *Introduction to Romance Languages and Literatures;* (1959), *Scenes from the Drama of European Literature* (I use the 1984 edition here); and (1949), the French version of the philology book. The details of composition appear opposite the title page of the 1953 Princeton University Press version and are reproduced from it in the 1957 Doubleday paperback. The twenty chapters in *Mimesis* are as follows: (1) Odysseus' Scar, (2) Fortunata, (3) The Arrest of Peter Valvomeres, (4) Sicharius and Chramnesindus, (5) Roland Against Ganelon, (6) The Knight Sets Forth, (7) Adam and Eve, (8) Farinata and Cavalcante, (9) Frate Alberto, (10) Madame du Chastel, (11) The World in Pantagruel's Mouth, (12) L'Humaine Condition, (13) The Weary Prince, (14) The Enchanted Dulcinea, (15) The Faux Dévot, (16) The Interrupted Supper, (17) Miller the Musician, (18) In the Hôtel de la Mole, (19) Germinie Lacerteux, (20) The Brown Stocking Epilogue. Although in the brief epilogue, where he mentions as if en passant the hard-pressed circumstances (lack of libraries and journals, among other things) of the time when he wrote the book and suggests that for those reasons the book contains the lacunae it does, the very nature of his project is transparently of a fractured, lyrical sort.

Note also that the English translation (*Introduction to Romance Languages and Literatures*) of *Introduction aux études de philologie romane* (written in 1943, not published until 1948, and translated into English in 1961) rather tellingly drops "philology" from the title and substitutes the "languages and literature" locution. Moreover, the book's original introductory section, an extraordinarily revealing thirty or so pages on what philology is ("La philologie et ses différentes formes" with subsections on critical editions, linguistics, and literary studies, as well as the explication de texte), is also eliminated from the later English version. This statement is, as advertised, an introduction to the fundamentals of "how the Romance languages became the Romance languages" and is of a very general and nontechnical nature—predominantly a historical narrative. This, in turn, is followed by an introduction to the literature of Romania that covers the full range of countries, languages, and periods from medieval to present. In another "I wrote this in Istanbul" preface, Auerbach is acutely aware that this is not much of anyone's philology anymore, and by the time it was published in English, few would consider that sort of nontechnical historical overview (particularly one that ranges well into the modern period) a part of the "philological" enterprise. One need only look at any random issue, from those years, of what had almost completely taken over the "Romance philology" mantle, *Romance Philology*, to see how out of place Auerbach must have felt.

The American journal *Romance Philology* was first published by Yakov Malkiel in August 1947, making this, too, part of the Diaspora and its philological reaction, although Malkiel is conspicuously the heir of the Diez who is the founder of Romance linguistics. Although he was prolific, Malkiel never wrote what we would call a book; he believed in the (functionally) Diezian paradigm of Romance philology, within which, most of the time, linguistic and literary studies were tied to each other under a figurative umbrella. The journal's first issue published "A New Jewish-Spanish Romancero" (S. Griswold Morley); "Nouvelles études de lexicologie française" (Paul Barbier); "Problemas del diccionario etimológico" (Juan Corominas): "Colloquial French Verb Inflection" (Robert A. Hall, Jr.); "Recent European Progress in Old French Studies" (Raphael Levy); "English 'scatter,' 'shatter'" (Charles H. Livingston); "'Bougre' as Expletive" (John Orr). Indeed, it is reasonably clear that Malkiel had some difficulty in accepting Spitzer and Auerbach into the fraternity of Romance philologists. His necrology of Spitzer, both unusually long and unusually unforgiving in its detailed inventory of Spitzer's many sins, begins with the scorching sentence, "Spitzer may not have been the greatest Romance philologist of all times, though he himself not infrequently gave the impression of believing he was." Even more tellingly, Malkiel goes on to ask the only partially rhetorical question of how and why someone as brilliant, rebellious, and ambitious should have chosen a specialty so "inconspicuous" as Romance philology. The answer given by Malkiel has to do with the way in which this had been a far more vibrant métier in old Germany, but it is all, to him, still within the realm of scholarly and gentlemanly excitement. I do not believe Malkiel understands the Dante-like, Vico-like, correlation between Spitzer's (or Auerbach's) enormous ambitions and the choice of philology. Malkiel's evaluative necrologies in *Romance Philology* make interesting (and revealing) reading, as follows: Curtius 1956 (remarkably perfunctory and even dismissive); Auerbach 1957 (where he stunningly—and very aptly!—calls *Mimesis* "a string of essays" and does not mention his book on "Romance philology" at all); and Spitzer (1961). Finally, see a 1975 lament written by Malkiel, "Scholar, Philologist, Critic, Analyst, Essayist," in which he decries (p. 39) the fact that "learning" and "erudition" (the properties of "scholar" and "philologist") are giving way, in appreciation and popularity, to words such as "critic," "essayist," and "analyst" which are part of a cult of "spontaneity, immediacy and creativity."

When one contemplates the whole of the scene in Istanbul, it is hard to avoid envisioning Auerbach in terms of someone like Gibbon—Gibbon sitting among the ruins and, at one level or another, contemplating a response. Indeed, the contemplation of ruins and the reconception, then, of what the original whole was, is not only the archaeological motif that (among other things) gave me the terms of the title of this book but is also the most powerful of the Petrarchan meditations on History. In the cases of Auerbach and Spitzer, the contemplation of the incredibly layered fragment of empires one still can see in Istanbul must have been powerful, indeed, and cannot but have helped shape their notions of the fragmentariness of experience and of History itself. Another famous *History of Rome* reflects in my account no less clearly the pressing and passionate concerns of the moment, particularly of the nineteenth-century struggles to create a German nation—a struggle which ended up producing Romance philology. I am grateful to Sam Armistead for pointing out that Theodor Mommsen's monumental *History of Rome* is conditioned by the same contingencies that created the most distinctive "modern" version of Romance philology.

The discussions of Auerbach's work I have most depended on and cited are many conversations with Hans Ulrich Gumbrecht, who seems to know all the telling details and is invariably generous with them; a number of details in this chapter I know only through him. Also important to me is Lowry Nelson's 1980 memoir, which is both informative and poignant, written by one of the handful of scholars I know who defines (and practices) Romance philology in Auerbachian/

Dantean/Viconian terms. The essays in Nelson's *Poetic Configurations* share that same lyrical structure and idiosyncratic range of languages, texts, and periods; a glance at the table of contents reveals the book's range: Provençal Poetry; Cavalcanti; Sidney and Shakespeare; Civic Poetry; Vico and Gozzi "as innovators in poetic criticism"; Lomonosov, Wordsworth, and Leopardi; Baudelaire and Virgil; and Ivanov's translations of Petrarch. See also Valesio's introduction to *Scenes from the Drama of European Literature.*

The lengthiest study of Auerbach (and Spitzer) is Geoffrey Green's admirable *Literary Criticism and the Structures of History,* which attempts to understand their writings in the context of the complex historical contingencies by which they were initially shaped and in which they consequently worked. Green provides the most detailed and sharply focused reading of *Mimesis* as a direct and purposeful response to the war, and I am grateful that his far more detailed study has ratified many of my own readings. Also of exceptional interest is Edward Said's reading of Auerbach in the context of his "secular criticism." Finally, Albert Ascoli's "Boccaccio's Auerbach," with its lovely reversal of the conventional terms of narrative framing and perspective, has been useful for my own thinking in that it conflates a reading of Auerbach and his readings of Boccaccio with the larger historiographical question of the medieval/Renaissance dichotomy's epistemological effects. Indeed, I understand Ascoli's argument to be that Auerbach's characteristically charming reading of the Frate Alberto story has been dismissed because it appears to reflect that older view of a Boccaccio "renascentista" (sensual, natural, realistic) which has been mostly replaced by a Boccaccio "medioevale" (allegorically and symbolically informed, morally and aesthetically aware). Instead, the story is better understood in an Auerbachian perspective, which, having no particular concern with that epistemological break, actually mimics Boccaccio's own perspectives of narrativity and temporality, perspectives he has used to define his own relationship to Dante:

> Even more strikingly, one should notice that Boccaccio's treatment of the *Commedia* is, at one important level, a critique of historiography, of the perspective from

> which one writes history, that is certainly applicable to Auerbach's own literary history, and perhaps to that historiography, our own historiography, which still attempts to judge the difference between Middle Ages and Renaissance, as between Boccaccio medioevale and Boccaccio rinascimentale. As Dante isolates sinner, purging souls and saints each in their own definitive moment of experience; so Auerbach isolates a single definitive passage from individual works across the Western tradition and orders them from a perspective that claims to stand outside and above that which it judges. In order to focus in on the essential narrative line along which change appears, the literary and historical context is reduced, carefully excluding the possibility of alternative, contradictory or irrelevant, accounts of the *Decameron*'s historical significance. But if the chapter on Boccaccio is any indication, the excluded context, like the repressed, returns to disrupt the orderly flow of history and compromise the critical narrator's claim to objective distance and transcendent interpretive powers: Auerbach no longer judges Boccaccio, Boccaccio judges Auerbach. . . .

My principal demurrer to this argument is that it is Auerbach's intent to have a disrupted and disruptive narrative, and it is that which accounts for the lyrical structure of the book, the "string of pearls."

Of special interest here, as well as in the next chapter, are the remarks in Stephen Nichols's introductory article for the special issue on "The New Philology" of *Speculum* (the journal of record of the Medieval Academy of America) that caused much hue and cry when it came out. Nichols's general recounting here of the work of Auerbach, Spitzer, and Curtius largely complements my own and forcefully reminds us that "philology was once among the most theoretically avant-garde disciplines" (p. 1). The focus of Nichols's interest, however, is on the crucial differences between the philology of the fixed texts and that of variation in a manuscript culture to which he feels we must (at least in part) return, thus reprising the superb wo quiglini. I will return briefly to the issue of variation in cru sition to the stable classicized text in the next chapter. detailed and impassioned response to Nichols's definitions ogy came—appropriately enough—in a special issue of *Romance Philology* edited by Charles Faulhaber and Jerry Craddock. Although the editors claim that the volume's "apparent conjunction" with the *Speculum* issue is "entirely fortuitous" (p. 5), the disingenuousness of such a claim is apparent from the opening words of the editorial preface: "If, 'in medieval studies, philology is the matrix out of which all else springs' (Nichols 1990:1) then textual criticism is the matrix out of which springs philology itself." Well, yes and no, as I think my extended remarks in this chapter make clear. Texts themselves—and thus their "establishment"—is indeed the original "matrix," that is, the parent form of philology. But this is so in a historical and political context within which the text is the most powerful cultural icon—at times, even a weapon, and the whole concept of establishing a "trustworthy" text, to use Faulhaber and Craddock's term, is so severely conditioned by all manner of historical contingencies—now, and then, and always. Indeed, this attempt to view the text as an essentially neutral enterprise ("objective" is the high-priced word we usually use) is itself little more than a reflection of its own effort to make textual criticism part of the discourse of linguistics, which in turn mimics the discourse of all the sciences. Thus, one ends up with the weak (in Bloomian terms) response to Nichols, which basically is to accuse him of not being a textual critic at all. Besides, "*it is simply easier* to produce 'best-manuscript' editions than those based on exhaustive collation of witnesses, determination of their stemmatic relationships, and reconstruction of the most distant attainable archetype . . ." (p. 3).

Within this special issue, Mary Speer's lengthy piece on "Editing Old French Texts" is the most direct rebuttal of the basic premises of the "new philological" posture, although she mostly attacks Cerquiglini's antecedent work, seeing him as the wrong-headed source of many of the ideas in the *Speculum* issue. In essence, Speer accuses Cerquiglini and those in his camp of the classic sin of anachronism: they are postmodernist and want to see the medieval period in those terms. Postmodernism, clearly, to hear tell, is as far as you can get from medievalism: "Cerquiglini accuses traditional philologists of attempting to conceal or vanquish the variability of medieval writing, that very trait of which postmodernists are enamoured (p. 16). . . . Despite the hyperbolic post-modern rhetoric on pre-modern esthetics (p. 19). . . . Cerquiglini's post-modernist manifesto . . . (p. 23)." Since a response to this type of argument is rehearsed at length in Part I of this book, I add here only that in Speer's insistence that text editing *should*—somehow—lie outside its own cultural paradigms, she is suggesting a model that would have been openly rejected by those foundational practitioners of Romance philology I have been discussing.

As is abundantly clear from my frequent citations, I have profited enormously from Hans Gumbrecht's seminal 1986 article in *Romance Philology,* many of whose fine points I have had to present in a reductive fashion. For example, I have largely elided Gumbrecht's contention that the first stage of national philology was modeled sufficiently on the Diezian paradigm that, while predominantly French in focus, it still strongly enunciated some of the features of the Germanic concept of philology such as broader theoretical interests. However, even in its limited adaptations to "Frenchness," this first stage did not fit into the basic parameters of the national literary enterprise; thus, the model of Gaston Paris is eventually replaced by the far more comprehensible and limited (in national terms) paradigms provided by Bédier. See also Gumbrecht's more general reflections on the problems of writing literary history in his article in *New Literary History* and in his collection of essays charmingly—and revealingly—entitled *Making Sense in Life and Literature.* In this philological mode, life and literature are not separable. (It also should be said that in this, as in a number of other ways, Harold Bloom is actually wonderfully medieval.)

Howard Bloch's piece in *A New History of French Literature* is a brief but helpful discussion of the sometimes odd French-German relationship here, framed and strongly conditioned by major hostilities and strong nationalistic sentiments. Bloch's essay is particularly strong in showing us the direct connection between the foundations of medieval (French) studies and ideological and nationalistic rivalry with an emerging Germany. This reference is sometimes told of through the story of how the Germans tried to invent the French; as Bloch says, "at the center of medieval studies from the beginning lay the troubling suspicion that French literature may in fact be German . . ." (pp. 11–12). Bits and pieces of this complex and fascinating story used to be part of the general "cultural" background of Romance philological studies, and I distinctly remember how perplexed I was when I told William Roach, the eminent editor of Old French texts with whom I was studying Old French, what my graduate course of studies was going to be, and he said: "So, you are going to do *romanische Philologie*" [German pronunciation obviously overemphasized]. It took me years to realize the crucial distinction he had been making between what *he* did (which, although it was "philological" in the sense of being text editing and focused on medieval texts, was still part of the institution of French national literature) and what I was proposing to do, Romance philology, a different kettle of fish. As his unfailing use of the German term for it indicated—he always called it *romanische Philologie*—Romance philology was something not only invented by the Germans but was extranational, extra-Romanic, not a part of the trajectory of those languages we continued to speak in the department's hallways. Bloch, again, is helpful: "the founding discourse of medieval studies [French] allows no distinction between explanations of the genesis of France's earliest linguistic and literary monuments and the identity of the nation . . ." (p. 13). In such a context it is self-evident why the Provençal lyric, which originally had been at the beginning and center, was displaced by the old French epic (an epic which, among other things, ratified the legitimacy of a number of nineteenth-century French territorial claims over the Germans). The eradication of the troubadour-producing courts of *languedoc* in the Crusade against the Albigensians was a crucial historical step in the unification of *languedoil*. Provençal was not only outside the national parameters, but had served as something *against* which such definition had taken place. It is thus that the study of Provençal poetry so often comes to fall outside the "old French" chapter of French national literary studies and to be studied, more often than not, under the auspices of the handful of remaining programs in Romance philology or in comparative literature programs.

In his 1991 study, Gumbrecht also has illuminated the ideological contours of Hispanism—it, too, in some branches shaped and directed by the Germans. Although this chapter has not gone into this topic in great detail, it is evident that the work of the most influential Hispanists is powerfully shaped by this political context. The remarkable Ramón Menéndez Pidal is an obvious case in point, and for some time the effects of the burdens and promises of the world of Menéndez Pidal on the creation of the modern versions of the *Cid* has been widely recognized. Of greatest interest for me in the context of the next chapter, "Chasing the Wind," is the fact that Menéndez Pidal's vision of Spanish literature (and thus of the desired shape of the Spanish nation) is so strongly rooted in elevating variation and orality to a high cultural status: "La tradición, como todo lo que vive, se transforma de continuo; *vivir es variar.*" ("Tradition, like everything that lives, transforms itself constantly. *To live is to change.*") This stunningly simple and relatively famous articulation is from his *Flor nueva de romances viejos,* a work with an uncannily pre-Bloomian title. In this, medieval Hispanism, at least in the person of Menéndez Pidal, more closely resembles Romance philology than it does the national philologies; indeed, it never elevates the Lachmanian model of text editing to a norm of prestige. Even more conspicuously (and more influentially, for my own work), we should see the strong historical conditioning of Américo Castro's major work, *España en su historia* (*The Structure of Spanish History*). It seems to me necessary to read this massive revisionist project as the wounded but hopeful response to the tragedies of Europe in the 1930s and 1940s. Castro is, like Auerbach and Spitzer and Malkiel, an exile from the chaos, although his own condition is different in its detail. He is a Spaniard exiled from the many bitternesses of the Civil War. Before that, however, he had imbibed a bit of what the German model of philology was; he was responsible not only for the 1914 edition and translation of Meyer-Lubke's *Introducción al estudio de la linguística romance,* with its extensive notes and additions, but in the early 1930s he did a stint as the Spanish Republic's ambassador to Germany, in which position he wrote some of the work from the middle period of his life. However, it was in his post-Civil War exile, first in Argentina and then in the United States, that he would write and rewrite his monumental work that reconceived and redefined the past of a nation now become odious in its unified form. This work is what makes Castro the most controversial of Hispanists. It is a reconstitution of the very notion of what History might be (and that includes a rejection of standard periodization) and of an image of medieval Spain that goes solidly against the concept of the nation-state which had triumphed, an image that instead said: No, Spain—medieval Spain—was once a spectacularly pluralistic society, and those years were the years that were golden and civilized. The Curtius to Castro's Auerbach is, notoriously, Claudio Sánchez Albornoz. Thus, in my simple paradigm, Castro goes into exile, is appalled at what is produced by the working out of a culturally unified nation, and writes a new history within which the nation was glorious only when it was a beautiful calliope of peoples and languages—a songbook—that shaped each other and yet remained distinct. (Sánchez Albornoz, on the other hand, mimics the triumph of the nation-state of 1936, and writes about the single, authentic Spain, ruined in its manifest destiny and potential greatness by foreigners.) To the best of my knowledge, there is no study of Castro's work along these lines, but see Edmund King's introduction and the bibliography in the centenary volume edited by Ronald Surtz.

Two other studies are of direct interest here, and to some extent they tell us a bit more about what is the other side of the coin, the linguistic branch that, from Diez on, was breaking off: Malkiel's "Friedrich Diez and the Birth Pangs of Romance Linguistics" and Peter Hanns Reill's "Philology, Culture and Politics in Early 19th-Century Germany," both of which show Diez rather decisively (although this may not have been the explicit intent) as the often reluctant founder of a Romance linguistics divorced in its individual and particular practice from literary studies. As my discussion of the journal *Romance Philology* and the work of Malkiel suggests, this rival version, in which linguistic studies *themselves* are divorced from literary criticism but are "linked" to them under the same "disciplinary" umbrella (thus, as philologists we read both types, presumably, but only write one of the two), became the normative one in this country (against which the work of a scholar such as Spitzer conspicuously sticks out).

For Spitzer, I have cited from Spitzer 1949 and Forcione 1988. (For additional observations about Forcione's edited collection of Spitzer's essays, see my review in *Hispanic Review* [1991] 59:207–9.) The famous and emblematically very powerful article by Spitzer on "American Advertising Explained as Popular Art" is published in both volumes and transparently sets forth the De-vulgari-like purpose of the text at the outset: "Can the linguistically minded literary historian, who harbors no snobbish feelings towards this genre of applied art, give an explication de texte of a good sample of modern advertising, in which he would proceed from the exterior features to the 'spirit of the text' (and to the spirit of the genre), just as he is accustomed to do with literary texts? Let us try the experiment" (1949, p. 103). In the Forcione re-collection of essays, see especially John Freccero's foreword, which gives a wonderful taste of what life in a Spitzerian universe was like. (I am also pleased to be able to thank John Freccero who, for many years now, has both amused and informed me with his invariably charming and revealing memories of Spitzer.)

Of incomparable value is the analytical and descriptive bibliography of Spitzer's life's work, *Leo Spitzer on Language and Literature*, published by the MLA. It is from the introduction to this bibliography that I have taken Jean Starobinski's characterization of Spitzer as a lover with a rival in the vicinity (p. 1); this introduction is a useful complement to Freccero's prefatory essay in *Representative Essays*. Finally, this reference work allows anyone to see at a glance exactly what constituted Spitzer's notion of a book: not only a collection of essays, but a collection of essays spanning the broadest possible range of languages and topics, time periods and themes. Of the forty-nine items listed in the first section, "Books and Monographs" (the last in this is the posthumous collection edited by Forcieno et al.), one can see not only the stunning range, but the way in which he used to craft his collections—his songbooks, so to speak. Certainly exemplary is the 1959 *Romanische Literaturstudien, 1936–56*, with its range from French (beginning with Marie de France and up through Proust) through Provençal (including his very famous piece on the *amor de lonh* of

Jaufré Rudel), Italian (from the *Ritmo cassinese* through Verga), Spanish (where his range extends "only" up through the Baroque), Romanian, and Latin. The individual pieces themselves are written in German, English, French, Italian, and Spanish.

The central interpretive problem posed by the vast, scattered, and highly disparate corpus of Spitzer's work is to discover its underlying "unity," and this subject too is addressed in Freccero's foreword. As Geoffrey Green writes, "our perception of Spitzer's work has been that it would constitute a whole on the basis of its accumulated components, once a person was found who would be able to undertake such a task. Since Spitzer did not seem to be concerned with producing a unified body of work [Wellek had noted the obvious, that he 'had little interest in composing his own papers and did not write a single unified book'] it was assumed that he lacked a holistic perspective, that each particular critical act was isolated and not concerned with an authorial thematic consistency" (pp. 83–84). Green's long essay, which is the double of his essay on Auerbach, amply merits reading; he provides an exceptionally helpful recounting of Spitzer's education in Germany and his flight from there in 1933 (when as a Jew he was no longer welcome at his post at Cologne), which included several years in Istanbul preceding Auerbach. Green makes a powerful case for a unity of Spitzer's work based (I would argue—Green does not really use the same terms) on the old philological principles that are manifest in Auerbach and articulated by Vico: the power of the imagination and the unities that *are* lyrical, that *do* transcend the normal lines of division. The terms of Spitzer's philology are also unmistakably personal and—despite impressions to the contrary—deeply engaged with the often devastating world all around, a world which, after all, had made him an exile and had proved itself capable of abominable terrors. As Green puts it: "Since Spitzer believed that words and ideas were inseparable, his response to the oppressive developments of history was to attack the words which had initiated the dubious ideas" (p. 163). Green (p. 74) also provides the invaluable remarks that Auerbach made about Curtius's book.

The Pound quote is from the opening pages of his *Spirit of Romance*. The full table of contents reads: The Phantom Dawn; Il Miglior Fabbro;

Proença; Geste and Romance; Psychology and the Troubadours; Lingua Toscana; Dante; Montcorbier, alias Villon; The Quality of Lope de Vega; Camoens; Poeti Latini. I have written extensively about Pound and Eliot and the "miglior fabbro" in *Writing in Dante's Cult of Truth* (esp. pp. 90–129), in which I also provide further bibliography. See as well the extraordinarily original *Ezra Pound and the Monument of Culture,* by Laurence Rainey, a work I am grateful to have been able to read (at least sections thereof) in manuscript and which I was not able to acknowledge in my 1991 study. For the astonishing way in which the Dante-Pound modernism has been influential and shaping in recent years, see the Brazilian Augusto DeCampos's volume, *Verso reverso controverso,* a post-Poundian collection of the kind of poetic translations (many from Provençal and old Italian poetry) that Pound had openly used and encouraged in his project of reviving American and English poetry, making it new. With its crucial non-narrative structure again openly ascribed to Pound, this series of studies and translations is a seminal text in the fertile area of contemporary, modernist Brazilian poetry. I am indebted to a number of my students—Miriam Ayres, Lucia Bettencourt, Kim Mrazek Hastings, and Robert Myers—for bringing these and other crucial Brazilian texts to my attention.

It is important to note here the one crucial—and unique—exception to the generalizations about the project of national literary histories. And it is explicitly the exception that proves the case. *A New History of French Literature,* edited by Denis Hollier, is conscious of all the issues I have raised here, and in the context of its exilic nature—a history of French literature being written outside of France by exiles and by others who are not French at all—it explicitly adopts all the modes and structures of the exilic Romance philological style. Thus, the structure is starkly lyrical, eschewing both comprehensiveness and narrativity; there are brief essays instead of longer, comprehensive ones, and although they are ordered chronologically, "both individually and cumulatively they question our conventional perception of the historical continuum . . ." (p. xix). It is heartening that this work has received a number of public accolades. The fact that it is characterized as postmodern—either praise or damnation, depending on one's views—unfortunately obscures its strong kinship with the philological tradition to which it is so closely related. Of course, if we could bring ourselves to call Auerbach postmodern—or Vico or the *De vulgari*—then the terminology would be, indeed, fully revelatory.

For Ernst Curtius and Denis de Rougemont, I have worked only with their principal texts, *European Literature and the Latin Middle Ages* and *Love in the Western World.* I am aware that the other influential scholar whom I might have considered in this section is D. W. Robertson, who like de Rougemont is put out by the notion of courtly love—and his famous reaction is, in essence, to say it never existed. Like Curtius, Robertson believes that the role of scholarship is to reveal the fundamental unity of Western culture, and for him that lies in scriptural exegesis in which all medieval literature is rooted and without which it cannot be understood.

For the "underground" history of Provence and *languedoc* beyond the Pyrenees, a number of sources are available. I discuss some of these in the essay for the previous chapter, "Love and Mercy," as well as in *The Arabic Role.* Here, I have relied first on the remarkable Gershom Scholem, as unmystical and hard-nosed a positivist historian as one is likely to encounter, and secondly on Frances Yates, the "high priestess" of the Warburg Institute and of equally unimpeachable orthodox credentials.

Finally, let me anticipate issues that will be central in the next chapter, "Chasing the Wind," and point out that on the subject of the widely assumed apoliticalness of poetry (at least that poetry not overtly political) we can see in the way that rock has become a politically charged and powerfully iconic phenomenon how a solipsistic love poem can bear, in certain contingencies, all sorts of political weight. During the Vietnam war it was well understood by all sides that, even in the least overtly political songs—in some cases those, most of all, that sang about love—rock was a powerful antiwar icon and weapon. Thus, even a seemingly innocuous "child's" song like "Puff the Magic Dragon" could be understood (and was, by all sorts of people without advanced degrees) as a sharp critique of the war and its ideologies, as a strong statement in favor of a very different cultural mode. In a rich and often rewarding book on rock, Robert Pattison rather astonishingly fails to see the overtly ideological role played by rock. He recounts the following story, one worth retelling: "A family from Cape Cod brought their car abroad for a tour of Eastern Europe. Driving through Hungary in the fall of 1967 at the height of the Vietnam war, they found their way blocked in a market town by a banner-waving demonstration against bourgeois American imperialism. They watched helplessly as the crowd surrounded their car, expecting at any minute to be lynched as reactionary jackels [*sic*]. Instead someone in the crowd pointed at their license plate, and the demonstrators burst into a chorus of the Bee Gee's 'Massachusetts,' then the most popular song in the world. The crowd sent the Americans on their way with cheers and returned to their socialist demonstration. *Rock is not logical or political . . .*" (p. 174, emphasis mine). I am not sure I know what politics is if that is not it. Exegesis of the story's principal components would certainly include noting that Hungarians *knowing* an American rock song as well as publicly singing it in the midst of an anti-American political demonstration are starkly political behaviors. Indeed, the singing of it is openly *meant* to be read that way, as a political statement—obviously, the singing of "Massachusetts" is meant to say to the Americans that they are OK, that they share a common bond, that it is only the evil institution(s) that are the enemy, and so forth. Clearly, and this is the point, neither "Massachusetts" nor "Puff the Magic Dragon"—"the text itself" (to go back to that principle of ahistoricity)—is political, but, sung in a given contingency, it can become richly so. I am suggesting that while when we read a Provençal love song in our studies it may seem far removed from the highly charged (and ultimately deadly) political maelstrom of Provence, when that body of songs was written and thrived, much as rock does today, we could well imagine, if we tried, all sorts of circumstances under which a performance of the same song would be highly political.

Although Vico is the hard-core house philosopher, Nietzsche is certainly the other, and the one who often mediates Vico. Nietzsche's own career and intellectual development tie him powerfully to these paradigms. He began as a philologist with that de rigeur interest in the Provençal love song and then devolved into a philosopher; his interest in what one might call the intermediate stage, the stage which one sees in *The Birth of Tragedy,* is clearly that of a philologist moving from philological into philosophical discourse. The link, in many cases, and certainly in Nietzsche's, is through the love of origins—and I am grateful to have read Robert Harrison's article "The Ambiguities of Philology," which has reminded me of a number of Nietzsche's philological ties and contemplations. Indeed, in Nietzsche's pragmatism we see this commitment to explicit values that has been more or less ignored in the standard explications and understandings of the work of philologists such as Auerbach and Castro, Spitzer, and Menéndez Pidal.

Vico's Dante is best understood and set out in Mazzotta's collection of *Critical Essays on Dante;* see the introductory comments (pp. xvii–xix) as well as the translated excerpt of Vico's "The Discovery of the True Dante" (pp. 58–60). Vico's reading is (what else?) quintessentially Viconian: "Vico, the philosopher of the imagination . . . [discovers] in Dante a kindred spirit, the sublime poet who grasps the extent to which all rational practices are encroached upon and are constituted by the imagination. From this standpoint, Vico enunciates critical principles that mark a genuine watershed in the history of the interpretation of the poem. Vico believes that the visionariness made available by the poetic imagination is more than just an element of the poem; it is the poem's essence . . ." (p. xviii). Vico thus directly attacks the Renaissance (Platonic, and thus also often normative in modern criticism) subordination of poetry to philosophy. As Mazzotta puts it, Vico goes beyond such things, and as a result he remains largely unread and obscure—or read and then thought highly idiosyncratic. I also have read with great pleasure and profit Lowry Nelson's characteristically learned essay on Gozzi and Vico as Dante critics, an essay which first appeared in Italian but is available in English as a chapter in *Poetic Configurations.*

Edward Said appears to break with the visionary aspects of this philology, and the brief epilogue of *The World, the Text and the Critic,* which stands to balance the introductory essay on "Secular Criticism," is a sharply worded critique of the tendency he sees in criticism (writing in the early eighties) toward an abandonment of the secular spirit and a new embrace of "religion." But in this argument Said is forgetting, or allowing to remain blurred, that the difference between totalizing institutions (which may in some technical sense be "secular") and the sort of individual lyrical act that may, however, be "religious" (because it is mystical, for example, or kabbalistic) is a crucial one that creates the sort of paradox from which this philological structure is built. Within this philological house, a kabbalist may be a strong secular poet, very much in the Viconian sense of the word, and a Marxist may be a religious poet. The other crucial blurring here has much to do with the kind of philology practiced as well as to do with the text at hand—and this point the author of *Orientalism* understands better than most other critics. Within such a context, the hermetic poem is what the philological mode makes of it: either a retreat from the "secular" world or a profound defiance of institutional practices. Finally, I think Salman Rushdie and his "retreat" from a certain kind of openly "secular" literature into the explicitly lyrical (and for most people "escapist") provides a superb example of precisely the sort of contingent reading that Vico urges on us. The story of Columbus and Isabella, which I read at the end of Part I, is anything but a retreat from the painfully urgent issues at hand (Rushdie's threatened life) but instead a lyrical meditation on precisely how lyricism—love poetry and prophetic dreams—shapes and writes history. And Rushdie's publication of *Haroun and the Sea of Stories,* ostensibly a collection of children's entertainments, his first publication after the *fatwa,* is very far from the act of retreat and respite it is made out to be.

Chasing the Wind

Most of the information on Eric Clapton is public knowledge. I also have used some of the narration on the making of the album provided in the album notes of *Derek and the Dominos: The Layla Sessions, 20th Anniversary Edition.* The lyrics of the songs are my own transcription, initially; for the complete "Layla" I have used the songbook *Eric Clapton Deluxe.* I am also indebted to Jeffrey St. John, a composer and performer, for a number of particularly productive discussions about the musical structures of "Layla," as well as for sending me in the direction of Leonard Bernstein's *The Unanswered Question;* and to Lee Calhoun for many insights into "Layla's" structures.

The full album *Layla, and Other Assorted Love Songs,* like a number of other seminal albums from rock's "classic" period (two conspicuous examples are *Pet Sounds* and the album it notoriously influenced, *Sgt. Pepper's Lonely Hearts Club Band*), shows distinct signs of mimicking the kind of songbook arrangement that is characteristic of a number of medieval collections, notably Petrarch's own *Canzoniere.* (It is also the kind of arrangement called the song cycle in classical music, cycles of *lieder.*) Roland Greene's book on the post-Petrarchan lyric sequence explores the ways in which the intrinsically fracturing effects of the lyric are counterbalanced in different kinds of arrangements (for which the *Canzoniere* itself is the archetype) by the fictionlike arrangements in which they are organized. In passing, it is tempting to understand the arrangement of chapters in books like *Mimesis* or *The Spirit of Romance* in this way—or, for that matter, the far larger structure of a work like the *New History of French Literature.* The larger sequence is what tells the story, whereas the individual lyrics embedded within it provide only splinters of vision or insight and remain in productive tension with the implicit narrative of the outer structure.

While perhaps most rock albums are more simply collections of songs, a strong songbook structure is apparent in *Layla, and Other Assorted Love Songs,* beginning with that title so evocative of the Petrarchan "assortment" of love lyrics. As the album's title suggests, virtually every song is a love song; in fact, they all are songs of problematic or unfulfilled or in some other ways unhappy love, and it is remarkable that although they work seamlessly together, a number of the songs were written by composers other than Clapton (for example, the album includes a cover of a famous Jimmy Hendrix song, "Little Wing"). I cannot do a full analysis of its sequential features here, but I will point out that the album begins to build tension, from the beginning, with one song of despairing love after another. These songs are interspersed with a handful of quieter, but still bittersweet, respites—the first of which is Nizami's "I Am Yours." The most openly narrative song—the telling of the story within the songbook—is the hard blues, almost spoken, "Have You Ever Loved a Woman?" written by Billy Myles:

(Have you ever loved a woman / so much you tremble in pain?
Have you ever loved a woman / so much you tremble in pain?
All the time, you know / she bears another man's name

But you love that woman so much / it's a shame and a sin
You just love that woman so much / it's a shame and a sin.
But all the time, you know / she belongs to your very best friend.
Have you ever loved a woman, oh, you know you can't leave her alone?
Have you ever loved a woman, yes, you know you can't leave her alone?
Something deep inside of you won't let you wreck your best friend's home.)

"Layla" is long-delayed climax, the penultimate song. The song that immediately precedes it is a strong but even-tempered bluesy piece called "It's Too Late" ("It's too late, she's gone") that sets the stage for the overwhelmingly powerful opening of "Layla" whose famous first riffs explode out of the blues background that has set it up. And the last song, following "Layla," is the shortest and quietest piece on the album, "Thorn Tree in the Garden," which resonates unmistakably of the sitar-type sounds of "I Am Yours" and provides expired, and resigned, almost prayerlike closure: "There's a thorn tree in the garden, if you know just what I mean, and I hate to hurt your feelings, but it's not the way it seems, 'cause I miss her. / She's the only girl I've cared for, the only one I've known. And no one ever shared more love than we've known, and I miss her. / But it all seems so strange to see, that she'd never turn her back on me, and leave without a last goodbye. / And if she winds up walking the streets, loving every other man she meets, who'll be the one to answer why? Lord I hope its not me. / And if I never see her face again, I never hold her hand, and if she's in somebody's arms, I know I'll understand. But I miss that girl. I still miss that girl." The song is credited only to Bobby Whitlock, who is Clapton's coauthor on a number of other songs on the album (among some of the most wrenching, "I Looked Away" and "Why Does Love Have to Be So Sad?") and only Whitlock sings it, softly and raspily, while Clapton, as if utterly exhausted from the ordeal of "Layla" and its soul-baring to which he built up and gave his all, strum-picks the single, plaintive, guitar accompaniment. You can see the last lonely birds flying away, from the thorn tree in the garden.

After the tragic death of his young son in 1991, Clapton gave a poignantly candid interview to the *Rolling Stone* (October 17, 1991, pp. 42 ff.), which included a lengthy discussion of his relationship with George Harrison, mediated, of course, by the passion for Harrison's wife that had created this iconic song. He discusses his passionate and long-term relationship with Harrison, affected by the affair, but far from destroyed by it. At the time of the interview, in fact, Clapton was about to go on the road as part of the back-up band for a long-delayed tour by Harrison, and at a remarkable point in the interview he is asked: "So you will be playing 'Layla' on the tour?" Answer: "Yeah. [Laughs] That's always been a bone of contention. Every time I play it and he's in the audience, I've always wondered what the hell goes through his mind. But I don't know, we could play it. We've got a sense of humor about it. . . ."

I am deeply indebted to Julie Meisami's wonderful *Medieval Persian Court Poetry,* from which I draw the analytical description of Nizami's romance. Meisami's book is of particular value as it is explicitly written to be accessible to literary scholars outside Persian studies, and it is very strong in providing a medieval framework, as, for example, in a number of apt comparisons between *Layla and Majnun* and the romances of Chrétien. On the shifting concepts of love in the Arabic *qasida* and *ghazal,* and from pre-Islamic to Islamic, I find that Andras Hamori's *On the Art of Medieval Arabic Literature,* published in 1974, is an unsurpassed study, especially for the non-Arabist (although it is not written explicitly for such an audience), and medieval Arabic literature is seen in the context of other literatures. The first two chapters, "The Poet as Hero" and "The Poet as Clown," discuss the shift in concepts of love from that of the pre-Islamic *qasida* to the starkly antisocial ones of the medieval love songs.

The translation of the romance which it seems evident that Clapton read is Gelpke's, which, like many other translations, restores the Arabic "Layla" for the Persian "Layli." The literary resonance of "Layla" is complex and widespread—indeed, in the chapter "Love and Mercy," Layla is prominently evoked as a "lover." Among other things, the name means "night" and is the repeated word in the title of the *Thousand and One Nights, Alf Layla wa Layla.* Sam Armistead has reminded me that it is the hymnotically repeated refrain in innumerable Arabic and Turkish traditional songs: "Ya laili, ya laili, ya laili," and "Layla" has all the evocative powers that "Juliet" does in English. Thanks to the work and personal generosity of the most perceptive and influential scholar of Ottoman literature, Walter Andrews, I now know something about the remarkable Turkish tradition of lyric poetry (a tradition thoroughly "influenced" by the Arabic tradition that reshapes Persian literature as well), where exile is explicitly equated with madness and unhappy love. Majnun, the lover crazed in desert exile, is always the template. A late fifteenth- or early sixteenth-century poem, a gazel, begins with the stunning verses:

> Alas that I have become a stranger alone
> in the land of exile
> An outsider without heart and soul
> troubled and crazed . . . .

And ends, after several verses on the beloved:

> If Necati [the poet] dies from longing for you
> you might say
> Alas stranger and alack stranger! How strange!
> Oh woe, how strange!

A gazel from the middle of the sixteenth century makes the connection through an explicit linking up with the Layla and Majnun tradition; although it is stunning to read it in full, I will give only a handful of verses:

> What if I am bewildered like Mecnun [Majnun]
> in the wilderness of bewilderment
> For a time I have been separated from intelligence,
> thought and patience

I fell in love and the tumults of the world
  flocked about my head
In this world my heart could not
  be separated from tumult. . . .

Ottoman poetry draws fruitfully from the rather simple allusion to Majnun—and understands that he evokes not only madness as such but, at least as significantly, the profound sort of alienation from society which is the common bond between a certain kind of love and exile proper. I am grateful to Andrews for access to his unpublished work as well as for his permission to use his translations. Finally, I note the irony and oddity that Nizami is referred to by Curtius in his chapter on "The Book as Symbol"—having been led to him, one surmises, by the Goethe who opens the chapter and describes, in passing, the baroqueness of Arabic poetry. The irony is contextual: Curtius cites verses of Nizami that associate literature with writing and the book.

Although much is written about rock in all sorts of media, few studies treat it as a part of the literary canon. The well-known *Lipstick Traces* by Greil Marcus, for example, deals with it exclusively as part of the universe of popular culture. More recently, Andrew Ross has taken on the relationship between "intellectuals and popular culture" with some fruitful insights, particularly, as the title *No Respect,* suggests, the highly ambivalent and ideologically charged relationship between the two. Disappointingly, however, rock, whose centrality in contemporary culture seems to have escaped him, plays a barely perceptible role in Ross's considerations. Indeed, he seems to buy many of the most transparent (and ludicrous) foundational myths about rock; he thus claims, for example, that rock's "classical, or vintage, years were already over by the time O'Hara [Frank O'Hara's poem on the death of Billie Holiday] is writing his poem in 1959" (p. 67). (Origins, not surprisingly, is one of rock's obsessions, and its myths are constantly spun out; on the variety of origins narrations about rock, see Albert Goldman's article, "The Emergence of Rock," and *The Triumph of Vulgarity* by Robert Pattison, who is excellent at taking the different myths apart.) Ironically, what Ross ends up doing (at least in the musical arena) is laying out the bits and pieces of "popular culture" that intellectuals not really into popular culture at all have always had some romantic attachment to, thus the Billie Holiday and black jazz Beat scene, and its purported primacy over later rock.

For a limited inventory of the thematic parallels and overlaps between rock and earlier schools of poetry, see my article in *Profession 88*. My colleague Ralph Hexter brought to my attention a charming predecessor to my own study, "Minnesang and the 'Sweet Lyric,'" in which the author carefully details the many ways in which the constructs of Cole Porter's music are very much those of the Minnesänger. I also have profited considerably from reading Pattison's very able book, *The Triumph of Vulgarity.* With a phenomenal grasp of the rock corpus, Pattison does an admirable job of tracing and detailing a number of the major literary features of rock; its creation of a powerful and detailed origins myth and its deep ties to, and resonances with, the Romantic tradition are fully explored.

I believe, however, that Pattison is mistaken in several crucial ways, and I mention these because they bear on my argument. First, although his title suggests some of what I have been arguing in this chapter, Pattison seems to believe that vulgarity is always vulgarity, and he thus writes about rock as if it were an essentially static phenomenon (and this implies the same thing for the other end of the cultural spectrum, that what is high culture was always high culture). What I find far more interesting—and which he would seem to disagree with strongly—is that one can see rock becoming classic, becoming fixed, becoming, in certain ways, no longer vulgar. This, in turn, sheds considerable light on the highly mobile process of canonization which may be unusually fluid in the area of lyrics but which also is notable in other areas—Shakespeare could certainly be mentioned as a notorious case. As part of this general conviction, Pattison believes that the subsections of rock that are amenable to high-cultural analysis are thus not really rock. No doubt he has people like me in mind (and, I fear, I might be seen as one with someone like Andrew Ross) when Pattison makes the following point: "But the editors of these anthologies are hard-pressed to find rock lyrics that meet their needs. Like most literary critics who discuss popular music, they draw from a small pool of rockers who do not irreparably offend transcendent taste. Dylan, the Beatles, and Joni Mitchell are anthology favorites. . . . The rock purist would argue that Paul Simon is not a rock lyricist precisely because his words do make 'a respectable showing on the printed page' . . ." (p. 199). A number of responses to this argument emerge in this chapter, but I note that the best refutation is found in Pattison's own book, in his own dozens and dozens of quotations from rock lyrics that serve (quite intentionally) precisely to reveal rock's deep ties to earlier pantheisms, to visionaries like Blake, and to the strong tradition of Whitman. Despite these areas where I strongly differ with him, his is an unusually fine study in an area that is in many ways a tabula rasa.

More recently, Anthony DeCurtis, a senior editor at *Rolling Stone* who also has academic connections, has edited an eclectic collection of essays. Of particular interest are David Shumway's article, which tries to come to grips with the problem that rock is not really any single/given genre for which we have standard (more or less) critical practices. He ends up focusing, perceptively I believe, on the performative aspects of rock and he notes many of the telling parallels with opera that I have noted:

> the central similarity between rock and roll and opera is that both are practices which are most often identified as music, but which are not purely musical: they communicate through a variety of different sign systems of which music is only one . . . in spite of the ubiquity of lyrics and the fact that they do seem to receive the lion's share of attention in most rock criticism, it has long been a widely shared aesthetic principle that lyrics are not the most significant aspect of the genre. . . . Sociological studies have claimed to show that rock lyrics are routinely ignored by many listeners. . . . But neither in opera nor in rock and roll are the lyrics merely an expression of music. In each case they contribute to the meaning of the performance even if their meanings are not immediately understood. Even if the listener does

> not know what the words "Celeste Aida" mean when the tenor sings them, the opera *Aida* is still understood as narrative. . . . (pp. 123–24)

His conclusion, incidentally, is that we must treat the performers in rock and roll as the texts, "perhaps even the primary texts of the form" (p. 129), a proposition he then intelligently elaborates. For some years Nancy Vickers has been making innovative presentations that begin, I think, with the same assumption—that it is the performance that is the genre—and she thus has focused on the lyricism of the rock video. See her 1988 article, "Vital Signs."

The classicization of rock is a well-known process that involves the necessity of performing certain songs and the increasing restrictions on how they may be played. Once in a great while, one can see a quivering death throe in classical music. The example of pianist Glenn Gould is well-known. Gould, who gave up concert performances in favor of studio recording, famously noted that in the setting of an essentially invariable regime of performance (the concert where the audience expected a set piece) lay death. This reasoning led to his line that classical music performance had become "the last blood sport." See Otto Friedrich's appropriately titled *Glenn Gould: A Life and Variations.* It is true that by this—or by Dante's standards—what we call "classical" music is quite dead, unequivocally a *grammatica.* (And it is not clear to me that most people understand it was not always thus—far from it.) Not surprisingly, in the field of music proper the hierarchies are parallel and value weighted in the same way, that is, the canon of high music culture is what is fixed and authored (close to the same thing) and the rest is perhaps legitimate but certainly inferior. I am indebted to my colleague at the Yale School of Music, Martin Bresnick, for some of his observations on this subject, and for an unpublished paper of his on the matter, "Authentic Music Is Synthetic Music," where he begins with the disarming comments: "I began working with the Waterbury Ethnic Music Project in 1986. . . . My previous training and ideas as a student of 'serious' music and of cultural theory did not prepare me adequately to understand the music I encountered . . . I have since come to feel that critical standards of aesthetic evaluation in support of 'high culture' are based on both a poor reading of even European music history, and on an often hidden social agenda. . . ."

A controversial issue of *Speculum* is primarily concerned with reestablishing the philological enterprise in open recognition of medieval culture being a manuscript culture characterized by variants and a material artifacticity that differ strikingly from printed culture and are closer and more akin to oral culture, although distinct from oral culture as well. In his introductory essay, Stephen Nichols notes: "It is that manuscript culture that the 'new' philology sets out to explore in a postmodern return to the origins of medieval studies . . ." (p. 7). He goes on to itemize various ways in which this kind of philology differs in focus: thus understanding the full manuscript folio with all of its different systems of representations as a vital and energetic unit; thus understanding what I call the "lyrical" qualities of medieval culture. He concludes with a statement with which this study is in full sympathy: "If we accept the multiple forms in which our artifacts have been transmitted, we may recognize that medieval culture did not simply live with diversity, it cultivated it. The 'new' philology of the last decade or more reminds us that, as medievalists, we need to embrace the consequences of that diversity, not simply live with it, but to situate it squarely within our methodology" (p. 9). Indeed, an understanding of the manuscript culture, and particularly of the centrality of variation and diversity that are the "original" mode—history itself and not just the residue of history left for a good text editor to restore to an original, single form—is an indispensable adjunct to understanding the high degree of mobility and variability of the song and stage culture I describe in this chapter. Moreover, I would repeat that the rock model, with its high visibility and easily verifiable features, helps us see many of the mechanics of such a culture in action; the valuing of variation and improvisation and the lack of fixed forms are the single best example.

In this context it is curious to note that although the incomparable *Singer of Tales* long ago revolutionized aspects of the way in which medieval culture was perceived (as have the superb studies in subsequent years by Ong on oral culture), these appreciations of orality have had virtually no impact on studies of the courtly lyric—for reasons I discuss throughout this chapter and which are mostly self-evident, even determining the title we still use: the courtly lyric is poetry that is not of the popular or oral-formulaic types, such as the epic, the ballad, and so forth. Despite the claims of Paul Oppenheimer's study that the break between song and poem (and thus written and oral) is clean and neat—the invention of the sonnet by Giacomo da Lentini—the line is in fact exceedingly blurred, and it is clear (as my quotation from Petrarch's letter to Boccaccio, near the end of this chapter, reveals) that while Petrarch was intent on making the sonnet a classical form, fixed and written, that it was by no means fully so. Oppenheimer's book, with the provocative title *The Birth of the Modern Mind,* is an almost shocking example of the kind of prelapsarian views on the medieval period which I detail in Part I: "the modern mind" is invented in and with the written sonnet, and it is modern because it is written (and not sung). Writing, of course, is the vehicle of self-consciousness (a faculty denied the medievals) the sine qua non of modernity, which, of course, comes after the break from the dark ages.

One of the few scholars who does pay more than lip service to the "songness" of the Provençal lyric is Stephen Nichols, and it is a pleasure to read and quote the brief but to-the-point exposition from the lyrical *New History of French Literature.* To Nichols's comments may be added some of Adonis's very complementary observations on poetry born as song: "it developed as something heard and not read, sung and not written. The voice in this poetry was the breath of life—'body music.' It was both speech and something which went beyond speech. It conveyed speech and also that which written speech in particular is incapable of conveying. This is an indication of the richness and complexity of the relationship between the voice and speech, and between the poet and his voice; it is the relationship between the individuality of the poet and the physical actuality of the voice, both of which are hard to define. When we hear speech in the form of a song, we do not hear individual words but the being uttering of them: we hear what goes beyond the body towards the expanses of the soul . . ."

(p. 13). In the opening essay, "Poetics and Orality in the *Jahiliyya,*" Adonis understands more clearly than most critics of the troubadour tradition the relationship between lyrics and the song's other aspects, and how the latter inexorably shape the former. His short essay provides a remarkable exposition of what he at one point calls "the aesthetics of listening and delight" (p. 27) and the consequences for the lyrics of such an aesthetic. Of incomparable value, I think, is Adonis's extended analysis (esp. pp. 30–33) of the classicization process, that transition from the song to written poetry, and from fluidity and variability (inherent to performance) to tyrannical paternity, the fixed form, the model for all subsequent poetry, concluding with a statement that could well be (should be, I might say) written about the medieval Romance lyric tradition: "In other words, although oral and written poetry involve two different physical activities, the same critical standards were applied to both. Thus the critical discourse which pre-Islamic poetry generated in the past, and continues to generate, is the very thing which obscures that poetry from us" (p. 33).

In the realm of other forms of oral poetry Joseph Duggan's book is a superb study of the Cid. It is a rare example of a reading of a work of literature that is rooted in an understanding of the work's orality and yet deals with it using the same appreciations of finesse, complexities, tensions, ironies, and so forth, that are believed not to be relevant in any significant degree to "popular culture." (Indeed, isn't that what so often implicitly separates one from the other in our paradigms? Even some of its apologists, such as Ross and Pattison, make precisely such a distinction—rock is just havin' fun.) Duggan also makes us think more subtly about the equally complex question of the audience and its levels, whereas we more often simply dichotomize the audience in the same way that we separate types of texts. Either it's high or low; either it gets the allusions or it doesn't. What intelligent and sensitive studies such as Duggan's show is how intricate the situation is, how the layers of audience apprehension and appreciation are wide and variable. Rock also is a picture-perfect example, both in something as simple as the demonstrable demographics of the audience—from the top to the low mid-range of the socioeconomic-educational spectrum—to the appreciable difference in "levels" of appreciation (and how little difference that makes). The fact that I now know the literary allusions in "Layla" makes me appreciate the song differently and, in the terms of the high-cultural paradigm, in a richer way. But before it clicked (to use Spitzer's wonderful conceit) and for those many, many listeners for whom that knowledge will never be revealed, it was still a remarkably powerful love song; it still meant the mad pain of Majnun, it still evoked the worst desperation of love from afar.

On other oral forms, which are ancillary, and their theoretical problems, see the thought-provoking review of scholarship, "Orality and Reading: The State of Research in Medieval Studies," by D. H. Green, who highlights the largely unmodeled and unresolved problem of when composition and performance are different and when, contrary to one of the most fundamental principles of the Lord-Parry structures, memorization does play a vital role. (For this, see also Ruth Finnegan's book, where, among other things, she points out that oral poetry is so varied that many forms of it differ significantly from the Lord-Parry model.) Once again, the rock model allows us to see both of these features in operation and to observe, then, their effects on such things as the stability (or lack thereof) of a text. On epics and ballads the major historian and critic is Samuel Armistead; any of his numerous papers on the subject will provide exhaustive bibliography. See, in particular, the 1986–87 *La Corónica* article, and the 1987 review article in *Romance Philology* on a book by D. G. Pattison on the epic, where Armistead tears apart the basic premises of the so-called "individualist" attitude toward a variety of medieval genres, of which the most appalling is the one about the lack of real artistry in any "popular" (that is, performed and variable) work: "Again, we find in P.'s 'Conclusion' the recurrent individualist misconception that, if a poem attests to 'artistry'—if it is inventive, if it is, in fine, an artistic success—then, of course, it cannot possibly be popular or oral or traditional. Perish the thought! Traditional poetry would seem to be the exclusive province of artless, uninventive, insensitive clods. Only us literates have artistic sensibility. *Los demás: asnalfabetos*" (p. 342). Indeed, as Armistead says, the real chimeric search is for that of the fixed texts, a point originally made by Menéndez Pidal in the *Romancero hispánico.* Finally, see the extensive work of John Miles Foley, especially "Reading the Oral Traditional Text: Aesthetics of Creation and Response" and his comprehensive *Theory of Oral Composition: History and Methodology.*

Of tangential interest is the still-strict association between writing itself and "civilization" (as opposed to just culture) in a work such as William Harris's book on *Ancient Literacy.* Harris explores the pitfalls of dealing with cultures (the Greeks, in this case) in which, we supposedly "know," some significant chunks of high culture fall squarely outside the realms of writing and literacy—and yet, we deal poorly with the implications of this fact. The strong Platonic threads in these virtually reflexive privilegings of philosophy over poetry (and making poetry subservient to philosophy, if we must deal with poetry at all) are not hard to detect, but we should consciously realize how (unconsciously) pervasive they are. Joan DeJean, in a paper on "The Death of the Author" for the 1992 MLA meetings, points out that at the heart of the *Querelle des anciens et des moderns,* that is, the issue on which the line between the ancient and the modern was schematically drawn, was "Homer"—was he a real author or was he, as the Moderns insisted, not one author at all but "a collection of fragments by different authors that had been joined together by someone else." The Ancient camp, which in twentieth-century scholarship on medieval poetry has its very close equivalent in "individualism," reacted with high indignation. Nicolas Boileau said that it was "one of the falsest things ever maintained to argue that there had never lived a man named Homer who was the author of the *Iliad* and the *Odyssey.*" It is a significant curiosity/coincidence that, as DeJean puts it:

> The battle over Homer's existence affords us crucial insights into the institution of literature, as it was defined on the eve of the Enlightenment. . . . When two generations of Moderns argued that Homer had never existed and that the epics attributed to him were really collections of anonymous fragments, this protoformulation of what our modernity has termed the death of the author prompted the Ancients to join forces to pro-

> mote, if not the birth of the author, at least a vastly increased prominence for the authorial function, a factor in the production of literature whose importance had previously been either underestimated or taken for granted.

In other words, as we have seen from other, slightly different historiographical perspectives, the central notion of the individual author as the sine qua non of high literature—and the commensurate devaluation of whole ranges of poetry which are not primarily tied to either fixed author and/or fixed text (this latter the inevitable evolution out of the fixed author paradigm)—is invented at a more or less specifiable point in the history of literary history. Like everything else.

It is well-known among Arabists—those who are familiar with contemporary Arabic culture—that the song tradition of the Andalusian *muwashshaḥāt* did not ever die out and continues to exist rather vigorously in the modern oral tradition. For this question, see the excellent study by Benjamin Liu and James Monroe, which selects a number of songs from the contemporary tradition and presents them explicitly as the continuation of the medieval Hispano-Arabic tradition (otherwise completely lost, as far as music is concerned) as well as in terms of the broad Mediterranean song tradition. This invaluable study includes full transcriptions, music, and translations, as well as a setting out of the strophic structures so that the connections with the medieval tradition are clear.

In a study of "Ibn Quzmān on I'rāb," Monroe gives us an original and remarkable analysis of the difference between "illiterate" poets and those literate ones "who write artificially in colloquial diction" (p. 52). He writes more persuasively than ever on the strength and pervasiveness of the song tradition in the vernaculars in al-Andalus and on the extent to which the "authentically popular" was later incorporated—was the very basis for—a poetics already more complex and more "artificial" in the sense of being *conscious* of the cultivation of a form that was *originally* "illiterate." Within such a context, Monroe brilliantly sees Ibn Quzman—who by and large has been viewed as the tail end of the tradition and as a part of the "decadence" into far greater use of the vernacular than one sees in the *muwashshaḥa*—as, instead, a poet out to restore the by then essentially mythical ancestral form "to its pristine linguistic vulgarity" (p. 54).

By now, anyone familiar with the vicissitudes of rock will have laughed out loud in recognition of a familiar mode and pattern. The trajectory is acted out in perfect detail. There were black roots at the beginning, the music is then elevated and purified, co-opted by the white intellectuals who only mimicked (what else could they do?) those authentic "illiterate" southern roots, and then someone comes along—someone authentically southern and thus almost illiterate, gritty, and redneck, thus closer to those black origins, like the Allman Brothers Band or ZZ Top—and the original sound and authenticity is restored. In a study dealing with tangential issues, Mary Jane Kelley raises the question of why all medieval female poetry (*kharjas,* as well as *cantigas d'amigo,* as well as others) have been preserved in "poetic contexts that are wholly male" (p. 1). To which the surprisingly breathless answer is that "when men began to write in the vernacular [in medieval Europe, after the classical period] they imitated the popular female voice" (p. 8). Well, yes and no—yes, of course, in the sense that, in the process of making the vernacular part of the written tradition, the trajectory is from the orality traditionally associated with women, who could sing, to that associated with men, who could write. But Kelly is a bit trapped in the literalness of what is at times metaphorical and openly mythical; here, too, we have a striking parallel with rock's myth of black origins. Indeed, too much of the article is (mis)cast as a lament for the loss of "authenticity" and all those other good primitive things that only women (we might as well add black slaves to the formula) can do in poetry: "when read in the context of the *muwashshaḥa,* the *kharja* inevitably loses the charm of a would-be popular, spontaneous, authentic expression of female emotion and becomes instead a literary image of woman, created by man, in the service of the male *muwashshaḥa* poet" (p. 2).

In my entire discussion of the Hebrew poetry of Spain, I am unusually indebted to the fine work of two perceptive and articulate scholars and, no less, to their considerable personal generosity. I hasten to say, and this is not the conventional trope but a real fear that they may be suspected of encouraging or holding any of my heretical views, that Ross Brann and Raymond Scheindlin have given me many leads and a lot to read that I would not have found without them, but they may well share none of my views on these subjects. Brann's rich study of the "Dissembling Poet" allows us to see, with wonderful detail of contingency, how and why the poets of the Hebrew tradition had very particular recourse to the classical distinction between the "truth" of some discourses and the "lie" of poetry. Here, as in the parallel piece on the "Compunctuous Poet" (now as the central part of his book on Judah Halevi), Brann allows us to see the special circumstances of medieval Europe (al-Andalus, Provence, later Christian Spain) and the myriad ways in which Jewish poetic culture was shaped. Many of the same issues are richly tended to by Scheindlin in *The Gazelle,* the sequel volume to *Wine, Women and Death,* and in a study of Moses Ibn Ezra's work of poetic theory that also explicitly seeks to make us understand the various dimensions of cross-cultural fertilization. On Judah Halevi, besides the sources just enumerated (and particularly on the sea poems), see Andras Hamori (1985), Marc Saperstein, and Harris Lenowitz. In the end, Halevi's enchantment with a poetry he had to give up—this forbidden love—is really an enchantment with music, although the dichotomy between the right and wrong kinds of poetry usually disguises the true nature of the forbidden passion.

Jim Morrison came back to life (as he does regularly, but this time with a vengeance) in 1991 with Oliver Stone's movie on the Doors. One hesitates to say there has been a revival, since the Doors' music has never not been a fixture of the active rock canon, at the top of rock radio playlists, but certainly there was much revived interest in the legendary rocker. Dozens of articles of every sort were published, and in classic Dionysian poses from 1967, Morrison graced the covers of a number of magazines, including *Esquire* (March 1991: "Roll Over Elvis. The Second Coming of Jim Morrison") and *Rolling Stone* (April 4, 1991); he had made *Rolling Stone*'s cover ten years before with the witty headline "He's Hot, He's Sexy—and He's Dead." But in all of this hype, scant (and then dismissive) attention was paid to Morrison's ambition to be a poet of the written tradition, and even less attention focused on the poetry itself, although his poems are available in two volumes, *Wilderness* and *The American Night.*

I am grateful to David Shiang for bringing all sorts of material about Morrison to my attention, including the interview with him by Bernard Wolfe published in *Esquire* in 1972, from which the remarkable quotation about Nietzsche's separation of music and poetry is taken (p. 182). Morrison also delivers some unvarnished truths about the fusion of sexuality/desire with music/lyrics in rock (much as described by Nichols) and how far down it can get stripped to basics (and thus, incidentally, why he wants to be a different kind of poet). Here is his analysis of the infamous night in Miami on which he was arrested for exposing himself on stage at a concert that reached one version of real Dionysian excess: "it's very, very hard to just get up on a stage and sing a song when you're a sex symbol. They didn't come to hear my mouth, they were all ogling my pants. *The way they refuse to grant your mouth when they've been taught you're all below the waist is very frustrating for a poet. You come forth with your fine words and they keep on staring at your pants.* I decided for once to give them what they were in the market for . . ." (p. 185, emphasis mine). (There are a number of popular books on Morrison—and as evidence of his popularity one need only note that two were on best-seller lists in March 1991: the now almost classic *No One Here Gets Out Alive,* by Jerry Hopkins and Danny Sugerman, in paperback, and *Riders on the Storm,* by John Densmore, the Doors' percussionist.) Virtually the lone campaigner in the effort to canonize Morrison with the same sort of company he has at Père Lachaize is Frank Lisciandro, who has edited the two volumes of poetry and whose extremely perceptive and forceful unpublished paper on Morrison and his poetry I have read with great profit. Lisciandro—predictably, along with Morrison and Petrarch—believes in that strict hermeneutic separation of the oral and the written modes of lyrical poetry, and of their concomitantly hierarchical value, as the title of his paper unambiguously indicates: "Jim Morrison: an American poet and an American rock lyricist." I am pleased to thank Lisciandro for his exceptional generosity, with his time and his memories and his analyses, which I hope to repay in a far longer study of Morrison's poetry that—and in this I do agree with Lisciandro—is of an unusually passionate quality, intense, provocative, and much of it very finely hewn.

One final, odd note about music and the loss of self so feared by Plato. Oliver Sacks, the noted neurologist and writer, has published the remarkable story of a patient blind and gravely disabled neurologically by a huge tumor of the pituitary gland. The young man had virtually no memory (as we would understand it) and, as if tied to memory itself, no affective consciousness, except that, eventually, it was discovered he did respond to music, and, more peculiar still, he responded astonishingly to a specific kind of music, that of the Grateful Dead. Sacks eventually was able to make the patient come back to life, as we know it—that is, shaped by memory and affect—by making elaborate arrangements to take him to a Grateful Dead concert. (The arrangements, as it turns out, were facilitated by Mickey Hart, the group's percussionist, who has written a book suggestively entitled *Drumming at the Edge of Magic;* this is a thorough account—informed by the musicological work of Fredric Lieberman and the work on myths by Joseph Campbell, both of whom were collaborators on the project—of the relationship of percussion instruments in particular to a whole range of practices that involve degrees of loss of self: magic and shamanism.) The multiple layers of irony are poignant when music—and the music of the Grateful Dead in particular—becomes the only stimulus that allows *recovery* of the self. Sacks's comments about the access to both memory and affect are sprinkled throughout the article, but especially in its closing paragraphs: "With music, for whatever reasons . . . learning for Greg is neither slow nor inefficient, but swift, automatic, and enjoyable. Moreover, music does not consist of sparse propositions (like 'rays softened asphalt') but is rich with emotion, association, and meaning. Songs, quicker than anything, can evoke a character, an epoch, a world—what Thomas Mann, in *The Magic Mountain,* calls 'the world behind the music'" (p. 62).

III Desire

The first epigraph is from the opening of "The Boys of Summer," words and music by Don Henley and Mike Campbell. The second is from the opening of "The Muʿāllaqa" by Labid, translated by Michael Sells in *Desert Tracings*.

Works Cited

ʿArabī, Ibn. Forthcoming. *Risalah Ruh al-Quds (Epistle on the Holy Spirit)*. Trans. ʿAbd al-Wahhab Boase and Farid Shanoun. Unpublished manuscript, courtesy of the author.

Abu-Lughod, Janet. 1989. *Before European Hegemony: The World System, 1250–1350*. New York: Oxford University Press.

Abulafia, David. 1988. *Frederick II: A Medieval Emperor*. London: Penguin.

Adonis. 1990. *An Introduction to Arab Poetics*. Trans. Catherine Cobham. Austin: University of Texas Press.

———. Forthcoming. *Mihyar of Damascus, His Songs*. Trans. Michael Beard and Adnan Haydar. Unpublished manuscript, courtesy of the translators.

Affifi, A. E. 1939. *The Mystical Philosophy of Muhyid din-Ibnul ʿArabī*. Cambridge: Cambridge University Press.

Ajami, Fouad. 1992. "The Other 1492." *New Republic*, April 6, pp. 22–25.

Alonso, Dámaso. 1960. *Estudios y Ensayos Gongorinos*. Madrid: Gredos.

Andrews, Walter. Forthcoming. "Singing the Alienated 'I': Historicity of the Subject in Ottoman Verse." *Yale Journal of Criticism*.

Arié, Rachel. 1973. *L'Espagne musulmane au temps des nasrides (1232–1492)*. Paris: Éditions de Boccard.

Armistead, Samuel G. 1986–87. "*Encore les cantilènes!*: Professor Roger Wright's *Proto-Romances*." *La Corónica* 15:52–66.

———. 1987. "A Brief History of *Kharja* Studies." *Hispania* 70:8–15.

———. 1987. "From Epic to Chronicle: An Individualist Appraisal." *Romance Philology* 40: 338–59.

Ascoli, Albert Russell. 1989. "The Vowels of Authority (Dante's *Convivio* IV.vi.3–4)." In *Discourses of Authority in Medieval and Renaissance Literature*, ed. Kevin Brownlee and Walter Stephens: 23–46. Hanover, N.H.: University Press of New England.

———. 1990. " 'Neminem ante nos.' Historicity and Authority in the *De vulgari eloquentia*." *Annali d'Italianistica* 8: 186–231.

———. 1991. "Petrarch's Middle Age: Memory, Imagination, History and the 'Ascent of Mount Ventoux.' " *Stanford Italian Review* 10: 5–43.

———. Forthcoming. "Boccaccio's Auerbach: Holding the Mirror Up to *Mimesis*." *Studi sul Boccaccio.*

———. Forthcoming. "History's Truth: Review of María Rosa Menocal, *Writing in Dante's Cult of Truth from Borges to Boccaccio.*" *Envoi.*

Ashtor, Eliyahu. 1979. *The Jews of Moslem Spain.* Philadelphia: Jewish Publication Society.

Asín Palacios, Miguel. 1931. *El Islam cristianizado, estudio del sufismo a través de las obras de Abenarabi de Murcia.* Madrid: Estanislao Maestre.

Attar, Farid ud-Din. 1984. *The Conference of the Birds.* Trans. Dick Davis. London: Penguin Books.

Auerbach, Erich. (1946) 1957. *Mimesis: The Representation of Reality in Western Literature.* Trans. Willard Trask. Garden City, N.Y.: Doubleday.

———. (1948) 1961. *Introduction to Romance Languages and Literature.* Trans. Guy Daniels. New York: Capricorn Books.

———. 1949. *Introduction aux études de philologie romane.* Frankfurt: Vittorio Klostermann.

———. (1959) 1984. *Scenes from the Drama of European Literature.* Minneapolis: University of Minnesota Press.

Azmeh, Aziz al. 1981. *Ibn Khaldun in Modern Scholarship.* London: Third World Centre for Research and Publishing.

———. 1982. *Ibn Khaldun: An Essay in Reinterpretation.* London: Frank Cass.

———. 1986. *Arabic Thought and Islamic Societies.* London: Croom Helm.

Baer, A. Kristina, and Daisy E. Shenholm. 1991. *Leo Spitzer on Language and Literature: A Descriptive Bibliography.* New York: Modern Language Association.

Baer, Yitzhak. (1961) 1971. *A History of the Jews in Christian Spain.* Philadelphia: Jewish Publication Society of America.

Baldick, Julian. 1989. *Mystical Islam: An Introduction to Sufism.* London: Tauris.

Barbi, Michele. (1933) 1954. *Life of Dante.* Trans. Paul G. Ruggiers. Berkeley: University of California Press.

Beard, Michael, and Adnan Haydar. 1989. "Making Mihyar: The Familiarization of Adunis's Knight of Strange Words." In *Critical Pilgrimages: Studies in the Arabic Literary Tradition,* ed. Fedwa Malti-Douglas: Austin: University of Texas Press.

Benítez-Rojo, Antonio. 1992. *The Repeating Island.* Trans. James Maraniss. Durham, N.C.: Duke University Press.

Benjamin, Walter. 1969. "The Task of the Translator." In *Illumination,* ed. Hannah Arendt: 69–82. New York: Schocken Books.

Bernardo, Aldo, trans. 1985. *Petrarch: Letters on Familiar Matters.* Baltimore: Johns Hopkins University Press.

Beverley, John. 1983. "Can Hispanism Be a Radical Practice?" *Ideologies and Literature* 16: 9–22.

Bloch, Howard. 1989. "The First Document and the Birth of Medieval Studies." In *A New History of French Literature*, ed. Denis Hollier: 7–13. Cambridge, Mass.: Harvard University Press.

Bloom, Harold. 1975. *Kabbalah and Criticism*. New York: Seabury Press.

———, ed. 1988. *The Song of Songs*. New York: Chelsea House.

Boase, Roger. 1990. "The Morisco Expulsion and Diaspora: An Example of Racial and Religious Intolerance." In *Cultures in Contact in Medieval Spain: Historical and Literary Essays Presented to L. P. Harvey*, ed. David Hook and Barry Taylor: 9–28. London: King's College, London Medieval Studies.

Boitani, Piero. *The Tragic and the Sublime in Medieval Literature*. Cambridge: Cambridge University Press.

Bonner, Anthony. 1990. "Ramon Llull and the Dominicans." *Catalan Review* 4: 377–92.

Boorstin, Daniel. 1983. *The Discoverers: A History of Man's Search to Know His World and Himself*. New York: Random House.

Boswell, John. 1980. *Christianity, Social Tolerance, and Homosexuality*. Chicago: University of Chicago Press.

———. 1992. "An Unhappy Family." Unpublished manuscript, courtesy of the author.

Brann, Ross. 1987. "The 'Dissembling Poet' in Medieval Hebrew Literature: The Dimensions of a Literary Topos." *Journal of the American Oriental Society* 107: 39–54.

———. 1987. "Judah Halevi: the Compunctious Poet." *Prooftexts* 7: 123–43.

———. 1990. "Of Rhetoric, Revelry, and Rabbis." *Association for Jewish Studies Review* 15: 119–32.

———. 1990. "Rosen-Moked's *The Hebrew Girdle Poem*." *Jewish Quarterly Review* 80: 380–83.

———. 1991. *The Compunctious Poet: Cultural Ambiguity and Hebrew Poetry in Muslim Spain*. Baltimore: Johns Hopkins University Press.

Bregman, Dvora. 1991. "The Emergence of the Hebrew Sonnet." *Prooftexts* 11: 231–39.

Bresnick, Martin. "Authentic Music Is Synthetic Music." Unpublished manuscript, courtesy of the author.

Brownlee, Marina, Kevin Brownlee, and Stephen Nichols, eds. 1991. *The New Medievalism*. Baltimore: Johns Hopkins University Press.

Burke, Peter. 1990. *The French Historical Revolution: The Annales School, 1924–89*. Stanford, Calif.: Stanford University Press.

Burns, Robert I. 1989. "The Significance of the Frontier in the Middle Ages." In *Medieval Frontier Societies*, ed. Robert Bartlett and Angus MacKay: 307–30. Oxford: Clarendon Press.

Cachey, Theodore J., Jr. 1991. "Petrarch, Boccaccio, and the New World Encounter." *Stanford Italian Review* 10: 45–59.

Cardillac, Louis. 1977. *Morisques et chrétiens: Un affrontement polémique (1492–1640)*. Paris: Klincksieck.

Carmi, T., ed. 1981. *The Penguin Book of Hebrew Verse*. New York: Viking Press.

Carruthers, Mary J. 1990. *The Book of Memory*. Cambridge: Cambridge University Press.

Castro, Américo. 1971. *The Spaniards: An Introduction to Their History*. Trans. Willard F. King and Selma Margaretten. Berkeley: Universary of California Press.

Cerquiglini, Bernard. 1989. *Eloge de la variante: Histoire critique de la philologie*. Paris: Seuil.

Chazan, Robert. 1988. "Representation of Events in the Middle Ages." *History and Theory* 27: 40–55.

Clapton, Eric (Derek and the Dominos) (1970) 1990. "Layla." *Layla and Other Assorted Love Songs*. PolyGram: 847 090-2.

———. 1978. *Eric Clapton Deluxe*. Chappell.

Clapton, Eric, and Nizami (Derek and the Dominos) (1970) 1990. "I Am Yours." *Layla and Other Assorted Love Songs*. PolyGram: 847 090-2.

Clifford, James. 1988. *The Predicament of Culture: Twentieth-Century Ethnography, Literature, and Art*. Cambridge, Mass.: Harvard University Press.

Corbin, Henry. (1958) 1969. *Creative Imagination in the Sufism of Ibn ʿArabī*. Trans. Ralph Manheim. Princeton, N.J.: Princeton University Press.

———. 1960. *Avicenna and the Visionary Recital*. Trans. Willard Trask. Princeton, N.J.: Princeton University Press.

Curtius, Ernst Robert. (1948) 1973. *European Literature and the Latin Middle Ages*. Trans. Willard Trask. Princeton, N.J.: Princeton University Press.

Dante. 1970, 1973, 1975. *The Divine Comedy*. Trans. and ed. Charles Singleton. Princeton, N.J.: Princeton University Press.

———. 1973. *Vita nuova-Rime*. Ed. Fredi Chiappelli. Milan: Mursia.

———. 1979. *Convivio*. Ed. Cesare Vasoli and Domenico de Robertis. Milan-Naples: Ricciardi.

———. 1990. *De Vulgari Eloquentia: Dante's Book of Exile*. Trans. and ed. Marianne Shapiro. Lincoln: University of Nebraska Press.

De Campos, Augusto, ed. 1988. *Verso reverso controverso*. São Paulo: Perspectiva.

DeCurtis, Anthony, ed. 1992. *Present Tense: Rock & Roll and Culture*. Durham, N.C.: Duke University Press.

DeJean, Joan. 1992. "The Death of the Author: Chartier Versus Foucault." Unpublished manuscript, courtesy of the author.

Deleuze, Giles, and Félix Guattari. 1986. *Kafka: Toward a Minor Literature*. Minneapolis: University of Minnesota Press.

de Man, Paul. (1971) 1983. *Blindness and Insight*. Minneapolis: University of Minnesota Press.

de Rougemont, Denis. (1940) 1956. *Love in the Western World*. New York: Harper and Row.

Dodds, Jerrilynn D. 1990. *Architecture and Ideology in Early Medieval Spain*. University Park: Pennsylvania State University Press.

———. 1992. "Mudejar Tradition and the Synagogues of Medieval Spain: Cultural Identity and Cultural Hegemony." In *Convivencia: Jews, Muslims, and Christians in Medieval Spain*, ed. Vivian Mann, Thomas Glick, and Jerrilynn Dodds: 113–31. New York: George Braziller and the Jewish Museum.

Duggan, Joseph. 1989. *The Cantar de Mio Cid: Poetic Creation in Its Economic and Social Contexts*. Cambridge: Cambridge University Press.

Durán, Manuel. 1990. "Ramon Llull: An Introduction." *Catalan Review* 4: 11–18.

Duri, A. A. (1960) 1983. *The Rise of Historical Writing Among the Arabs*. Trans. Lawrence I. Conrad. Princeton, N.J.: Princeton University Press.

Durling, Robert M., and Ronald L. Martinez. 1990. *Time and the Crystal: Studies in Dante's Rime Petrose*. Berkeley: University of California Press.

Einbeinder, Susan. 1989. "The Current Debate on the Muwashshaḥ." *Prooftexts* 9: 161–77.

Faulhaber, Charles, and Jerry Craddock. 1991. "Preface." *Romance Philology* 45: 1–5.

Fernández, James. 1992. "Escenas de un patrimonio: Cervantes and the New World." Unpublished paper, courtesy of the author.

Fernández-Armesto, Felipe. 1992. *Columbus*. Oxford: Oxford University Press.

Filoramo, Giovanni. 1990. *A History of Gnosticism*. Trans. Anthony Alcock. Oxford: Blackwell.

Finnegan, Ruth. 1977. *Oral Poetry: Its Nature, Significance and Social Context*. Cambridge: Cambridge University Press.

Fleischman, Suzanne. 1991. "Philology, Linguistics, and the Discourse of the Medieval Text." *Speculum* 65: 19–37.

Foley, John Miles. 1987. "Reading the Oral Traditional Text: Aesthetics of

Creation and Response." In *Comparative Research on Oral Traditions: A Memorial for Milman Parry,* ed. John Miles Foley: 185–212. Columbus, Ohio: Slavica.

———. 1988. *The Theory of Oral Composition: History and Methodology.* Bloomington: Indiana University Press.

Forcione, Alban, Herbert Lindenberger and Madeline Sutherland, eds. 1988. *Leo Spitzer: Representative Essays.* Stanford, Calif.: Stanford University Press.

Friedrich, Otto. 1989. *Glenn Gould: A Life and Variations.* New York: Random House.

Fuson, Robert H. 1987. *The Log of Christopher Columbus.* Camden, Me.: International Marine.

García Gómez, Emilio. 1991. *El escándalo de las jarchas en Oxford.* Madrid: Industrias Graficas Artegraf.

García Márquez, Gabriel. 1983. "The Solitude of Latin America." *New York Times,* February 6, sec. 4, p. 17.

Gerber, Jane S. 1992. *The Jews of Spain: A History of the Sephardic Experience.* New York: Free Press.

Giamatti, A. Bartlett, ed. 1983. *Dante in America: The First Two Centuries.* Binghamton, N.Y.: Medieval and Renaissance Texts and Studies.

Gibson, Charles. 1977. "Reconquista and Conquista." In *Homage to Irving A. Leonard: Essays on Hispanic Art, History and Literature,* ed. Raquel Chang-Rodriguez and Donald A. Yates: Ann Arbor: Michigan State University, Latin American Studies Center.

Giddens, Anthony. 1990. *The Consequences of Modernity.* Oxford: Polity.

Gil, Juan. 1977. "Colón y la Casa Santa." *Historiografía y Bibliografía Americanistas* 21: 125–35.

Gilman, Stephen. 1972. *The Spain of Fernando de Rojas: The Intellectual and Social Landscape of La Celestina.* Princeton, N.J.: Princeton University Press.

Goitein, S. D. 1988. *A Mediterranean Society: The Jewish Communities of the Arab World as Portrayed in the Documents of the Cairo Geniza.* Berkeley: University of California Press.

Goldman, Albert. 1968. "The Emergence of Rock." *New American Review,* pp. 118–39.

González Casanovas, Roberto. 1990. "Llull's Blanquerna and the Art of Preaching: The Evolution Towards the Novel-Sermon." *Catalan Review* 4: 233–62.

González Echevarría, Roberto. (1977) 1990. *The Pilgrim at Home: Alejo Carpentier.* Austin: University of Texas Press.

———. 1983. *Isla a su Vuelo Fugitiva.* Madrid: José Porrúa Turanzas.

———. 1985. "La literatura desde el Barrio de Cocosolo." Unpublished paper, courtesy of the author.

———. 1986. "Emir and the Canon: An Obituary Note." *Latin American Literary Review* 28: 7–10.

———. 1987. "Guillén as Baroque: Meaning in *Motivos de son*." *Callaloo* 10: 302–17.

———. 1987. *La Ruta de Severo Sarduy.* Hanover, N.H.: Ediciones del Norte.

———. 1987. "Narrative and Prophecy in the Post-Modern Novel: Sarduy's *Maitreya*." *World Affairs* 150: 147–62.

———. 1988. "Love in the Golden Years." *Yale Review* 78: 472–78.

———. 1990. *Myth and Archive: A Theory of Latin American Narrative.* Cambridge: Cambridge University Press.

Goytisolo, Juan. 1992. "Fortress or Common Land?" *Yale Review* 80: 23–27.

———. 1992. "On the Path to Modernity." *Times Literary Supplement,* February 28, p. 18.

Graff, Gerald. 1987. *Professing Literature: An Institutional History.* Chicago: University of Chicago Press.

Graff, Gerald, and Michael Warner, eds. 1989. *The Origins of Literary Study in America: A Documentary Anthology.* New York: Routledge.

Green, Arthur. (1987) 1988. "The Song of Songs in Early Jewish Mysticism." In *The Song of Songs,* ed. Harold Bloom: New York: Chelsea House.

Green, D. H. 1990. "Orality and Reading: The State of Research in Medieval Studies." *Speculum* 65: 267–80.

Green, Geoffrey. 1982. *Literary Criticism and the Structures of History: Erich Auerbach and Leo Spitzer.* Lincoln: University of Nebraska Press.

Greene, Jody. 1991. "New Historicism and Its New World Discoveries." *Yale Journal of Criticism* 4: 163–98.

Greene, Roland. 1991. *Post-Petrarchism: Origins and Innovations of the Western Lyric Sequence.* Princeton, N.J.: Princeton University Press.

Greene, Thomas. 1982. *The Light in Troy.* New Haven, Conn.: Yale University Press.

Grunebaum, Von. 1944. "The Concept of Plagiarism in Arabic Poetry." *Journal of Near Eastern Studies* 3: 234–53.

Gumbrecht, Hans Ulrich. 1984. "History of Literature—Fragment of a Vanished Totality?" *New Literary History* 16: 467–79.

———. 1986. "'Un Souffle d'Allemagne ayant passé': Friedrich Diez, Gaston Paris and the Genesis of National Philologies." *Romance Philology* 40: 1–37.

———. 1991. "Historiografía de la literatura española ¿Un romance hispano-germano?" In *Homenaje a Don Rafael Lapesa Melgar*, ed. Buenos Aires: Ministerio de cultura y educación.

———. 1992. *Making Sense in Life and Literature*. Minneapolis: University of Minnesota Press.

Hamdani, Abbas. 1979. "Columbus and the Recovery of Jerusalem." *Journal of the American Oriental Society* 99: 39–48.

———. 1981. "Ottoman Response to the Discovery of America and the New Route to India." *Journal of the American Oriental Society* 101: 323–30.

Hamori, Andras. 1974. *On the Art of Medieval Arabic Literature*. Princeton, N.J.: Princeton University Press.

———. 1985. "Lights in the Heart of the Sea: Some Images of Judah Halevi's." *Journal of Semitic Studies* 30: 75–83.

Harris, William. *Ancient Literacy*. Cambridge, Mass.: Harvard University Press.

Harrison, Robert Pogue. 1986. "The Ambiguities of Philology." *Diacritics*, Summer, pp. 14–20.

Hart, Mickey. 1990. *Drumming at the Edge of Magic: A Journey into the Spirit of Percussion*. New York: Harper.

Harvey, L. Patrick. 1990. *Muslim Spain, 1250–1500*. Chicago: University of Chicago Press.

Harvey, Ruth. 1963. "Minnesang and the 'Sweet Lyric.'" *German Life and Letters* 17: 14–26.

Haskins, Charles Homer. 1927. *The Renaissance of the Twelfth Century*. Cambridge, Mass.: Harvard University Press.

Hitchcock, Richard. 1977. *The Kharjas: A Critical Bibliography*. London: Grant and Cutler.

Hollier, Denis, ed. 1989. *A New History of French Literature*. Cambridge, Mass.: Harvard University Press.

Idel, Moshe. 1988. *Kabbalah: New Perspectives*. New Haven, Conn.: Yale University Press.

———. 1988. *Studies in Ecstatic Kabbalah*. Albany: State University of New York Press.

———. 1989. *Language, Torah, and Hermeneutics in Abraham Abulafia*. Albany: State University of New York Press.

Jay, Martin. 1988. *Fin-de-siècle Socialism and Other Essays*. New York: Routledge.

Jayyusi, Salma Khadra, ed. 1992. *The Legacy of Muslim Spain*. Leiden: E. J. Brill.

Jones, Alan. 1988. *Romance 'Kharjas' in Andalusian Arabic Muwaššaḥ Poetry: A Paleographical Analysis*. London: Ithaca Press.

Kelley, Mary Jane. 1991. "Virgins Misconceived: Poetic Voice in the Mozarabic *Kharjas*." *La Corónica* 19: 1–23.

Kemp, Anthony. 1991. *The Estrangement of the Past: A Study in the Origins of Modern Historical Consciousness.* New York: Oxford University Press.

Kutzinski, Vera. 1990. "Unseasonal Flowers: Nature and History in Plácido and Jean Toomer." *Yale Journal of Criticism* 3: 153–79.

Lenowitz, Harris. 1986. "Text and Context in Halevi's 'Hesiqatni Teshuqati Le'el Hai.'" In *Methodology in the Academic Teaching of Judaism,* ed. Z. Garber: 135–44. New York: University Press of America.

Lewis, Archibald. 1990. "The Islamic World and the Latin West, 1350–1500." *Speculum* 65: 833–44.

Lezama Lima, José. 1972. "Imagen de América Latina." In *América Latina en su Literatura,* ed. César Fernández Moreno: Paris: UNESCO.

Lisciandro, Frank. 1989. "Jim Morrison: an American poet and an American rock lyricist." Unpublished paper, courtesy of the author.

Liu, Benjamin M., and James T. Monroe. 1989. *Ten Hispano-Arabic Strophic Songs in the Modern Oral Tradition.* Berkeley: University of California Press.

Llull, Ramon. 1946. *The Book of the Lover and the Beloved.* Trans. E. Allison Peers. New York: Paulist Press.

———. 1950. *Libre d'Amic e Amat, Libro de Amigo y Amado.* Barcelona: Juan Flors.

———. 1985. *Libro de amigo y amado.* Ed. and Intro. Lola Badia. Trans. Martín de Riquer. Barcelona: Planeta.

López Baralt, Luce. 1985. *Huellas del Islam en la literatura española: De Juan Ruiz a Juan Goytisolo.* Madrid: Ediciones Hiperión.

———. 1985. *San Juan de la Cruz y el Islam.* Mexico City: Colegio de México.

———. 1988. "In Memoriam: Stephen Gilman." *La Torre* 2: 241–43.

———. 1992. *Islam in Spanish Literature from the Middle Ages to the Present.* Trans. Andrew Hurley. Leiden: Brill.

López Morillas, Consuelo. 1982. *The Qur'ān in Sixteenth-Century Spain: Six Morisco Versions of Sūra 79.* London: Tamesis.

Lord, Albert B. (1960) 1971. *The Singer of Tales.* New York: Atheneum.

Madariaga, Salvador de. (1940) 1991. *La vida del muy magnífico señor Don Cristóbal Colón.* Buenos Aires: Editorial Sudamericana.

Malkiel, Yakov. 1956. "Ernst Curtius." (necrology) *Romance Philology* 10: 92.

———. 1957. "Erich Auerbach" (necrology) *Romance Philology* 11: 162.

———. 1961. "Leo Spitzer." (necrology) *Romance Philology* 14: 362–64.

———. 1975. "Scholar, Philologist, Critic, Analyst, Essayist." *Romance Philology* 29: 38–39.

———. 1976. "Friedrich Diez and the Birth Pangs of Romance Linguistics." *Romance Philology* 30, special supp.: 1–15.

Matter, E. Ann. 1990. *The Voice of My Beloved: The Song of Songs in Western Medieval Christianity.* Philadelphia: University of Pennsylvania Press.

Mazzotta, Giuseppe. 1978. "The *Canzoniere* and the Language of the Self." *Studies in Philology* 75: 271–96.

———. 1979. *Dante, Poet of the Desert.* Princeton, N.J.: Princeton University Press.

———. 1986. "Petrarch's Song 126." In *Textual Analysis: Some Readers Reading,* ed. Mary Ann Caws: 121–31. New York: Modern Language Association.

———. 1988. "Antiquity and the New Arts in Petrarch." *Romanic Review* 79: 22–41.

———. 1988. "Humanism and Monastic Spirituality in Petrarch." *Stanford Literature Review* 5: 57–74.

———, ed. 1991. *Critical Essays on Dante.* Boston: G. K. Hall.

———. 1991. "Petrarch's Thought." In *Mimesis in Contemporary Culture. Volume 2: Mimesis, Semiosis and Power,* ed. Ronald Bogue: 27–43. Philadelphia: John Benjamins.

———. 1993. *Dante and the Circle of Knowledge.* Princeton, N.J.: Princeton University Press.

———. 1993. "The Life of Dante." In *Cambridge Companion to Dante,* ed. Rachel Jacoff: 1–13. Cambridge: Cambridge University Press.

———. 1993. *The Worlds of Petrarch.* Durham, N.C.: Duke University Press.

Meisami, Julie. 1987. *Medieval Persian Court Poetry.* Princeton, N.J.: Princeton University Press.

Menéndez Pidal, Ramón. (1938) 1969. *Flor nueva de romances viejos.* Madrid: Espasa Calpe.

———. 1953. *Romancero hispánico.* Madrid: Espasa Calpe.

———. 1968. *La lengua de Cristóbal Colón.* Madrid: Espasa Calpe.

Menocal, María Rosa. 1987. *The Arabic Role in Medieval Literary History: A Forgotten Heritage.* Philadelphia: University of Pennsylvania Press.

———. 1988. " 'We Can't Dance Together.' " *Profession 88*: 53–58.

———. 1988. "Bottom of the Ninth, Bases Loaded." *La Corónica* 17: 32–40.

———. 1991. "Review of *Leo Spitzer, Representative Essays.*" *Hispanic Review* 59: 207–9.

———. 1991. *Writing in Dante's Cult of Truth: From Borges to Boccaccio.* Durham, N.C.: Duke University Press.

———. Forthcoming. "The *Questione della lingua* as an Impediment to the Understanding of Language History." *Canadian Journal of Italian Studies.*

Metcalf, Barbara. 1990. "An Islamic Ironist." *Times Literary Supplement,* June 1–7, pp. 580, 585.

Milani, Virgil. 1973. *The Written Language of Christopher Columbus*. Buffalo: State University of New York at Buffalo.

Miura, Isshu, and Ruth Fuller Sasaki. 1965. *The Zen Koan: Its History and Use in Rinzai Zen*. New York: Harcourt, Brace, Jovanovich.

Monroe, James. 1970. *Islam and the Arabs in Spanish Scholarship (Sixteenth Century to the Present)*. Leyden: Brill.

———. 1974. *Hispano-Arabic Poetry: A Student Anthology*. Berkeley: University of California Press.

———. 1986. "Poetic Quotation in the Muwaššaḥa and Its Implications: Andalusian Strophic Poetry as Song." *La Corónica* 14: 230–50.

———. 1988. "Ibn Quzman on Iʿrāb: A *zéjel de juglaría* in Arab Spain?" In *Hispanic Studies in Honor of Joseph H. Silverman*, ed. Joseph Ricapito: 45–56. Newark, Del.: Juan de la Cuesta.

Morison, Samuel Eliot. 1942. *Admiral of the Ocean Sea: A Life of Christopher Columbus*. Boston: Little, Brown.

Morony, Michael. 1988. " 'Isolating Andalus.' " *Journal of the American Oriental Society* 108: 445–48.

Morrison, James Douglas [Jim]. 1988. *Wilderness: The Lost Writings of Jim Morrison*. New York: Villard Books.

———. 1990. *The American Night: The Writings of Jim Morrison*. New York: Villard Books.

Morrison, Karl F. 1990. *History as a Visual Art in the Twelfth-Century Renaissance*. Princeton, N.J.: Princeton University Press.

Nasr, Seyyed Hossein. 1969. *Three Muslim Sages*. Cambridge, Mass.: Harvard University Press.

Nelson, Lowry, Jr. 1961. *Baroque Lyric Poetry*. New Haven, Conn.: Yale University Press.

———. 1980. "Erich Auerbach: Memoir of a Scholar." *Yale Review* 69: 312–20.

———. 1992. *Poetic Configurations*. University Park: Pennsylvania State University Press.

———, ed. 1986. *The Poetry of Guido Cavalcanti*. New York: Garland Press.

Nichols, Stephen G. 1989. "The Old Provençal Lyric." In *A New History of French Literature*, ed. Denis Hollier: 30–36. Cambridge, Mass.: Harvard University Press.

———. 1990. "Introduction: Philology in a Manuscript Culture." *Speculum* 65: 1–10.

Nieto, José. 1988. *San Juan de la Cruz, poeta del amor profano*. Madrid: Swan.

Nizami. 1966. *The Story of Layla and Majnun*. Trans. R. Gelpke. London: Bruno Cassirer.

Norton, Charles Eliot. (1859). "*The New Life* of Dante." In *Dante in America*, ed. A. Bartlett Giamatti: 52–68. Binghamton, N.Y.: Medieval and Renaissance Texts and Studies.

Oppenheimer, Paul. 1989. *The Birth of the Modern Mind: Self, Consciousness, and the Invention of the Sonnet.* Oxford: Oxford University Press.

Parker, Alexander A. 1984. *The Philosophy of Love in Spanish Literature.* Edinburgh: Edinburgh University Press.

Patterson, Lee. 1990. "On the Margin: Postmodernism, Ironic History, and Medieval Studies." *Speculum* 65: 87–108.

Pattison, Robert. 1987. *The Triumph of Vulgarity: Rock Music in the Mirror of Romanticism.* Oxford: Oxford University Press.

Paz, Octavio. 1974. *Children of the Mire.* Cambridge, Mass.: Harvard University Press.

———. 1988. *Sor Juana or, The Traps of Faith.* Trans. Margaret Sayers Peden. Cambridge, Mass.: Harvard University Press.

Pederson, Johannes. 1946. *The Arabic Book.* Trans. Geoffrey French. Princeton, N.J.: Princeton University Press.

Pérès, Henri. (1937) 1983. *Esplendor de al-Andalus.* Trans. Mercedes García-Arenal. Madrid: Hiperión.

Pérez Firmat, Gustavo. 1986. *Literature and Liminality.* Durham, N.C.: Duke University Press.

———. 1989. *The Cuban Condition.* Cambridge: Cambridge University Press.

———, ed. 1990. *Do the Americas Have a Common Literature?* Durham, N.C.: Duke University Press.

———. 1990. "The Strut of the Centipede: José Lezama Lima and New World Exceptionalism." In *Do the Americas Have a Common Literature?*, ed. Pérez Firmat: 316–32. Durham, N.C.: Duke University Press.

———. 1992. "Christopher Reborn." *Washington Post Book World*, October 13, 1992, pp. 1, 14.

Pound, Ezra. (1910) 1952. *The Spirit of Romance.* Norfolk, Conn.: New Directions.

Rainey, Laurence. 1991. *Ezra Pound and the Monument of Culture.* Chicago: University of Chicago Press.

Reill, Peter Hanns. 1976. "Philology, Culture and Politics in Early Nineteenth-Century Germany." *Romance Philology* 30, special supp.: 18–29.

Riding, Alan. 1992. "500 Years After Expulsion, Spain Reaches Out to Jews." *New York Times*, April 1, p. A14.

Rorty, Richard. 1989. *Contingency, Irony, and Solidarity.* Cambridge: Cambridge University Press.

———. 1989. "Is Derrida a Transcendental Philosopher?" *Yale Journal of Criticism* 2: 207–17.

———. 1991. "Just One More Species Doing Its Best." *London Review of Books*, July 25: 3–7.

Ross, Andrew. 1989. *No Respect: Intellectuals and Popular Culture*. New York: Routledge.

Roth, Michael. 1990. "Review Essay: Rorty, Contingency, Irony, and Solidarity." *History and Theory* 29: 337–57.

Rushdie, Salman. 1991. "Christopher Columbus and Queen Isabella of Spain Consummate Their Relationship, Santa Fé, January 1492." *New Yorker*, June 17, pp. 32–34.

———. 1991. *Imaginary Homelands*. London: Granta.

Sacks, Oliver. 1992. "The Last Hippie." *New York Review of Books*, March 26, pp. 53–62.

Said, Edward. 1978. *Orientalism*. New York: Pantheon.

———. 1983. *The World, the Text and the Critic*. Cambridge, Mass.: Harvard University Press.

Sale, Kirkpatrick. 1990. *The Conquest of Paradise*. New York: Knopf.

Salusinszky, Imre, ed. 1987. *Criticism in Society*. New York: Methuen.

Saperstein, Marc. 1981. "Halevi's West Wind." *Prooftexts* 1: 306–11.

Scheindlin, Raymond. 1976. "Rabbi Moshe Ibn Ezra on the Legitimacy of Poetry." *Medievalia et Humanistica* 7: 101–15.

———. 1986. *Wine, Women, and Death: Medieval Hebrew Poems on the Good Life*. Philadelphia: Jewish Publication Society.

———. 1991. *The Gazelle: Medieval Hebrew Poetry on God, Israel, and the Soul*. Philadelphia: Jewish Publication Society.

———. 1992. "Judah Abravanel to His Son." *Judaism* 41: 190–99.

———. Forthcoming. "Ibn Gabirol's Poem and the Fountain of the Court of Lions." *Cuadernos de la Alhambra*.

———. Forthcoming. "Ibn Gabirol's Religious Poetry and Sufi Poetry." Unpublished manuscript, courtesy of the author.

Scholem, Gershom. (1941) 1961. *Major Trends in Jewish Mysticism*. Jerusalem: Schocken.

———. (1962) 1987. *Origins of the Kaballah*. Trans. Allan Arkush. Princeton, N.J.: Jewish Publication Society/Princeton University Press.

———. 1965. *On the Kabbalah and Its Symbolism*. New York: Schocken Books.

Sells, Michael. 1984. "Ibn ʿArabī's Garden Among the Flames: A Reevaluation." *History of Religions* 23: 287–315.

———. 1989. *Desert Tracings: Six Classic Arabian Odes.* Middletown, Conn.: Wesleyan University Press.

———. Forthcoming. *Beyond the Name.* Chicago: University of Chicago Press.

———. Forthcoming. "Ibn al-ʿArabi's 'Gentle Now Doves of the Thornberry and Moringa Thicket,' Introduction and Translation." *Journal of the Ibn Arabi Society.* (Unpublished manuscript, courtesy of the author and translator.)

Sennett, Richard. 1991. "Fragments Against the Ruin." *Times Literary Supplement*, February 8, p. 6.

Shapiro, Marianne. 1990. *De Vulgari Eloquentia: Dante's Book of Exile.* Lincoln: University of Nebraska Press.

Shumway, David R. 1992. "Rock and Roll as a Cultural Practice." In *Present Tense: Rock & Roll and Culture,* ed. Anthony DeCurtis: 117–33. Durham, N.C.: Duke University Press.

Shusterman, Richard. 1989. "Postmodernism and the Aesthetic Turn." *Poetics Today* 10: 605–22.

Six, Abigail Lee. *Juan Goytisolo: The Case for Chaos.* New Haven, Conn.: Yale University Press.

Smith, Barbara Herrnstein. 1988. *Contingencies of Value: Alternative Perspectives for Critical Theory.* Cambridge, Mass.: Harvard University Press.

Smith, Nathaniel. 1982. "Ramon Llull, *trobador exalçat.*" *Hispanófila* 26: 1–7.

Speer, Mary B. 1991. "Editing Old French Texts in the Eighties: Theory and Practice." *Romance Philology* 45: 7–43.

Spitzer, Leo. 1949. *A Method of Interpreting Literature.* Northhampton, Mass.: Smith College.

———. 1959. *Romanische Literaturstudien, 1936–56.* Tübingen: Niemeyer.

———. 1962. *Linguistics and Literary History.* New York: Russell.

Stern, Samuel Miklos. 1974. *Hispano-Arabic Strophic Poetry: Studies.* Oxford: Clarendon Press.

Surtz, Ronald, Jaime Ferrán, and Daniel Testa, eds. 1988. *Américo Castro: The Impact of His Thought.* Madison, Wis.: Hispanic Seminary of Medieval Studies.

Todorov, Tzvetan. 1984. *The Conquest of America.* Trans. Richard Howard. New York: Harper and Row.

Urvoy, Dominique. 1990. "La place de Ramon Llull dans la pensée arabe." *Catalan Review* 4: 201–20.

Valesio, Paolo. 1984. "Foreword." In *Scenes from the Drama of European Literature.* vii–xxviii. Minneapolis: University of Minnesota Press.

Vickers, Nancy. 1988. "Vital Signs: Petrarch and Popular Culture." *Romanic Review* 79: 184–95.

Weckmann, Luis. 1951. "The Middle Ages in the Conquest of America." *Speculum* 26: 130–39.

———. 1984. *La herencia medieval de México.* Mexico City: Colegio de México.

Wilson, Sheila R. 1978. "The Form of Discovery: The Columbus Letter Announcing the Finding of America." *RCEH* 2: 154–68.

Wolfe, Bernard. 1972. "The Real-Life Death of Jim Morrison." *Esquire,* June, pp. 109 ff.

Yates, Frances. 1954. "The Art of Ramon Llull: An Approach to It Through Llull's Theory of the Elements." *Journal of the Warburg and Courtauld Institutes* 17: 115–73.

———. 1960. "Ramon Llull and John Scotus Erigena." *Journal of the Warburg and Courtauld Institutes* 23: 1–44.

———. 1982. *Llull and Bruno: Collected Essays.* London: Routledge.

Zamora, Margarita. 1988. *Language, Authority and Indigenous History in the "Comentarios reales de los incas."* Cambridge: Cambridge University Press.

Index

María Rosa Menocal received her Ph.D. in Romance philology at the University of Pennsylvania and has written on a broad range of medieval topics, including two previous books, *The Arabic Role in Medieval Literary History: A Forgotten Heritage* and *Writing in Dante's Cult of Truth: From Borges to Boccaccio*, also published by Duke University Press. She was a Mellon Fellow in Comparative Literature at Bryn Mawr College and also taught at the University of Pennsylvania. Currently she is R. Selden Rose Professor of Spanish and Portuguese at Yale University.

Library of Congress Cataloging-in-Publication Data

Menocal, María Rosa.
Shards of love : exile and the origins of the lyric / María Rosa Menocal.
p. cm.
Includes bibliographical references and index.
ISBN 0-8223-1405-3. — ISBN 0-8223-1419-3 (pbk.)
1. Literature, Medieval—History and criticism.
2. Romance philology. 3. Civilization, Medieval—Historiography. 4. Renaissance. I. Title.
PN671.M45 1993
809'.02—dc20 93-26530 CIP